ROBERT
ADAM

ROBERT ADAM

by

DOREEN YARWOOD

CHARLES SCRIBNER'S SONS, NEW YORK

Library of Congress Catalog Card Number 73-108198

PRINTED IN GREAT BRITAIN

CONTENTS

ILLUSTRATIONS

Photographs

ILLUSTRATIONS

Drawings

GLOSSARY

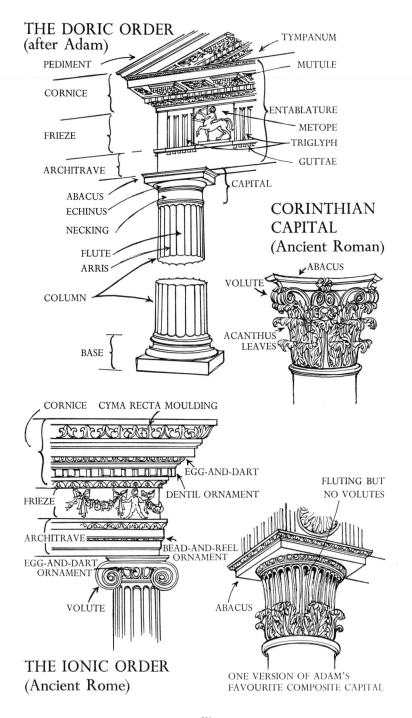

THE DORIC ORDER (after Adam)

PEDIMENT

CORNICE

FRIEZE

ARCHITRAVE

ABACUS
ECHINUS
NECKING

FLUTE
ARRIS

COLUMN

BASE

TYMPANUM

MUTULE

ENTABLATURE
METOPE
TRIGLYPH
GUTTAE

CAPITAL

CORINTHIAN CAPITAL (Ancient Roman)

ABACUS
VOLUTE

ACANTHUS
LEAVES

CORNICE CYMA RECTA MOULDING

EGG-AND-DART

DENTIL ORNAMENT

FRIEZE

ARCHITRAVE

EGG-AND-DART
ORNAMENT

BEAD-AND-REEL
ORNAMENT

VOLUTE

FLUTING BUT
NO VOLUTES

ABACUS

THE IONIC ORDER (Ancient Rome)

ONE VERSION OF ADAM'S
FAVOURITE COMPOSITE CAPITAL

SPHINX

ANTHEMION

KEY or FRET PATTERN

PATERA

GRIFFIN AND ARABESQUE (scroll) BORDER

EGG-AND-DART

LEAF-AND-DART

BEAD-AND-REEL

ACANTHUS

COFFERED CEILING

CONSOLE

ANTHEMION BORDER

HALF PUTTI AND SCROLL DECORATION

OVAL PATERA

SCROLL

ADAM'S RAINCEAU
(arabesques and griffins)

FAN AND ARABESQUE

Astylar: a classical façade without columns or pilasters.

Caryatids: sculptured female figures in the form of supports or columns. Used especially in fireplace design.

Chiaroscuro: treatment of light and shade in a painting. Sometimes applied to a work in monochrome.

Crypto-porticus: a partly enclosed or hidden portico or entrance.

Exedra (pl. -*ae*): in secular buildings, a semicircular or rectangular recess with a bench seat.

Girandole: a branched candle-holder.

Grisaille: grey monochromatic painting illustrating figures and detail in relief.

Oculus: a circular or oval opening.

Ormolu: a metal used for decoration. A gold-coloured alloy of copper, zinc and tin.

Piano nobile: an Italian Renaissance term meaning literally 'the noble floor'. In classical building it is the first and principal floor of a house.

Rustication: a treatment of masonry with sunk joints and roughened surfaces.

Scagliola: an imitation stone material made from plaster and glue. It is then often treated with marble fragments, coloured and polished to imitate genuine marble.

INTRODUCTION

Cᴙɪᴛɪᴄᴀʟ appreciation of all great artists fluctuates in the years after their deaths. First comes adulation, over-praise. This is followed, after five or ten years, by adverse assessment. The pendulum swings and the artist's standing falls. Later, sometimes over seventy years later, a steadier, more accurate assessment emerges and another reputation takes its balanced place among all the rest. Changes of fashion, thought and way of life alter such assessments, even after a hundred years, but the genuinely original artist, who has contributed something which touches a need in every human spirit, lives for ever in the work he has left behind.

Such an artist was Robert Adam. Much of what he did is nearly two hundred years old, and it has taken a great part of that time for the balanced assessment of Adam to evolve. The fluctuations of critical opinion have been extreme and long lasting. For much of the nineteenth century, during both Nash's Regency and Scott's Gothic Revival, Adam's name was reviled or ignored. He was mistakenly believed to have based his ideas only on his studies of the Palace of the Emperor Diocletian at Split (a late period of Roman art, thought by the Victorians to be decadent). He was also erroneously credited by them with the inferior work of many of his imitators. In a violent reversal of taste the *fin de siècle* rediscovered him. Everything was then by Adam, all the work of his contemporaries and successors. In the 1920s he was thought to be a firm of decorators, referred to as 'Adams', and there was confusion: was there one Adam or several?

Today the name Adam is a household word. Everyone interested in the arts, interior decoration and furnishing has heard of him. The paradox is that very few of such people know anything about him or what he really did. We all know that Wren designed St Paul's Cathedral, but if you ask someone 'what did Robert Adam do?', the reply will be 'he designed those fireplaces which rich Americans buy for six thousand pounds each', or, 'he made furniture', 'he painted ceilings', 'he made those elegant brass fire-irons or door-knobs'.

Who was Robert Adam? What did he do? How has the reputation of one of England's greatest architects become inextricably interwoven with doorknobs and fireplaces? What sort of a man was he? Did he really merit both the adulatory praise and the vituperation showered upon him during his lifetime and since? The purpose this book is to try to answer these questions, simply and chronologically.

There have been several biographers of Adam since 1900 when interest in him rekindled. Until 1950 they were all handicapped by the paucity of material available to show what type of a man he was. There is no difficulty in judging his work (though assessment has varied according to fashion and the books published before 1930 tend to over-praise and to attribute all 'Adam style' buildings to him, though many were by Wyatt, Leverton or Holland). We are fortunate in possessing many of his buildings, mostly town and country houses, and these are nearly all in good or superb condition and in the hands of the original family for whom they were designed. It is a tribute to Adam's popularity and importance that his services were sought by the richest and most important people in the land. Such families have so far, in the main, survived the vicissitudes of world wars and penal taxation in death duties, and the Adam rooms are still in their possession. The only concession to the times, and one for which we are grateful, is that such owners of 'stately homes' compete for our entrance fees, though no owner of an Adam mansion need offer 'extra-mural' entertainments. Robert Adam is enough. It is a sobering thought that he designed or decorated all these buildings – some thirty-seven of them – plus the ones which have been demolished, in only thirty years. Robert's tremendous capacity for concentrated work is equalled only by his invariably high level of artistry.

We are now able also to ascertain something of what kind of a

person he was. We have known for a long time that he came from a
large family in Scotland, that there were four brothers all partici-
pating in the architectural profession and following the example of
their father, who was an important Scottish architect. Also that the
family was a devoted one, its members remaining close in affection,
work and home, all their lives; that most of them never married and
that Robert and James went on the Grand Tour before starting up
practice in London. But there has always been a lack of contact with
Robert's thoughts and ideas, because so few of his letters or verbal
comments seemed to have survived or have been recorded. As the
eighteenth century was the great age of letter-writing, and since
Robert was a friend and contemporary of such men as Sir Joshua
Reynolds, David Garrick, David Hume, William Robertson and
many other famous men, this lack has surprised as well as disappointed. The discovery about 1950 of the letters written from the
Continent (averaging one per week to his family) from 1754 to 1758
amongst the Clerk family papers has given us an understanding of
what he was like, his ambitions, thoughts, tastes in food, entertainment, ladies and a thousand other things. Once he returned to
England and set up his practice in London he was so successful and
so busy that he had, apparently, little time or inclination for writing
letters apart from necessary business ones to clients. For our
knowledge of him, in the thirty-four years of his hectic, creative life
after the age of thirty, we have to rely upon letters from the rest of
the family and comments recorded by his friends and enemies.

In addition to the actual buildings and the letters, there is the
great collection of drawings which Robert made; further testimony
to his industry and to the infinite care which he gave to every project
and commission. Over nine thousand of these are in the Soane
Museum in London. They include his working drawings and
original designs for commissioned buildings and speculative schemes,
showing colour directives, measurements and detail. There are also
many of his pen-and-ink, pencil or wash sketches and finished
drawings which range from imaginative landscapes to those done on
the Continent of the ruins of ancient Rome and masterpieces of
Renaissance Italy and France. At Blair-Adam, the family estate in
Kinross-shire, Captain Adam possesses some beautiful drawings,
some of which date from 1783 to 1787, a time when Robert was

3

vastly overworked, constantly commuting by post-chaise from London to Scotland, engaged on a variety of large projects; yet he found energy and desire for drawing delicate, romantic, idealized landscapes of the sort which had appealed to him since he was a young man. Some remind one of the Italian Apennines, others of his native Scotland. All have mountains, streams, bridges and a castle or ruin perched high upon the crags. A retreat or compensation perhaps for the bureaucratic frustrations of this period of his life?

Lastly, we have published books of drawings which maintain a superb standard of engraving and presentation, produced by Italian and French craftsmen and carefully supervised by Adam himself. Unlike so many of his contemporaries, he took infinite pains over this and never permitted his work to go to press before he was fully satisfied with the quality of the production. The books also contain his ideas and comments on what he was trying to do. The two famous publications are *Ruins of the Palace of the Emperor Diocletian at Spalatro in Dalmatia*, based on his work at Split in 1757 and published in 1764, and the *Works in Architecture of Robert and James Adam*, published in three volumes from 1773 onwards. These contain drawings of what Robert felt was his best work. They vary from complete exteriors and interior perspective views to details of furniture and furnishings.

There have been only two basic styles of architecture in pre-twentieth-century England: Medieval, or more commonly Gothic, and Classical. Since the Norman Conquest these two forms of building have been used for roughly equal periods of time; the former until the Renaissance and again in its nineteenth-century revival, and the latter from Elizabethan England until modern architecture was fully established after 1945. Classical design in building, in its various guises, enjoyed a monopoly during the seventeenth and eighteenth centuries and competed as an alternative during the nineteenth and twentieth. Because human beings welcome change, and talented artists and architects of initiative are always seeking new means of expression, the classical form during this four-hundred-year epic run was not static or unalterable. Different interpretations evolved one after another to suit current needs and as influenced by the outside world, in the English case by Flanders, Italy and France. These interpretations are described by such terms as Jacobean,

Renaissance, Baroque, Rococo, Greek Revival and many more.

At bottom they all stem from the original source which was ancient Greece and, in particular, Hellenic Greece of the years of the sixth to second centuries B.C. This type of architecture is a trabeated one or, as it is often called, post and lintel construction. It derives from the Greek temples, stoas and other public buildings which were created for a southern Mediterranean climate. Vertical members (the posts) support horizontal ones (the lintels), and the concept was extended into colonnaded structures which were roofed and, inside, had walled compartments and subdivisions. The colonnade provided shade from the sun and cover from rain and did not exclude the air. The Greeks evolved a system of orders for this architectural theme, of which they had three: Doric, Ionic, Corinthian. Each order had a number of constituent parts which, with the passing of time and experience in design, acquired certain proportions relative to one another and specific features of ornament which appeared to give the best aesthetic result. The finest era is generally regarded now as the fifth century B.C. and it was then that these proportions and ornamentation became most satisfactory to the human eye.

Greek orders are not ornate; sometimes, especially in the favourite – the Doric – they are severely plain. Their beauty lies in the subtle relationships of line and form and of one part to another. The Greeks spent years in perfecting their designs and evolving a system of refinements. It is these which make all the difference between a beautiful classical building and an ordinary one. The refinements used by the Greeks in their hey-day are so subtle as to be barely visible to the casual glance. That is their purpose: to make the building appear correctly delineated and not curved and also to give it vitality and plasticity. The true horizontal or vertical line, especially when silhouetted against a brilliantly blue sky, appears to be concave and, to offset this illusion, the Greeks created a convex line and form so subtly and meticulously calculated that it would appear to be a straight vertical or horizontal. The Parthenon in Athens is the superb instance of this. All its lines and planes are curved, not straight, but so restrainedly that the curve is visible only on close inspection. All surfaces are so treated: columns, bases, lintels, pediments.

Each of the three orders consists of a column (sometimes with a base beneath) with a capital above to support the weight of its horizontal lintel member, called the entablature. This is made up of three divisions, the lower one the architrave, then the frieze and, at the top, the cornice which projects partly to give shade and partly to throw the rain water forward and free of the building. The Doric order, most often used by the Greeks, has no base, a sturdy fluted column and a capital consisting of a square block at the top (the abacus) and below this a curved echinus moulding. The entablature, usually about a quarter of the height of the whole order, has a plain architrave. The frieze is distinctive, being divided into triglyphs and metopes. The former are carved with vertical channels and are placed one over each column and one between, while the latter represent the remaining spaces. These, as in the Parthenon, are enriched by sculptured groups. The cornice projects boldly, and under it, set over each triglyph, is a flat block called a mutule which has eighteen round projections (guttae) underneath. These are both decorative and obviously functional.

The Ionic order has a slenderer column, fluted and with a moulded base. Its capital has a scrolled volute at each side like a shell or rams' horns. Below is an ornamental echinus moulding and necking. The entablature is less deep than the Doric; its architrave is set forward in a three-plane triple fascia, and the frieze has no triglyphs or metopes but often a continuous band of ornament or sculpture. It is an elegant, refined order as opposed to the strength and power of the Doric.

The Corinthian is much like the Ionic, but has a distinctive capital. This is shaped like a bell and decorated with two rows of acanthus leaves which rise to four corner volutes supporting a four-faced curved abacus.

There are many variations on these basic themes, but the Greek pattern is nearly always of high-quality design and beautifully enriched. The Greek ornamental scheme was generally based on floral or geometrical motifs, immortalized in such carved mouldings as egg and dart (life and death) bead and reel, anthemion (honey-suckle), guilloche (like a plait) and many more. The illustrated glossary on pages viii–ix shows these designs. Generally classical mouldings received specific enrichments, as it had been discovered

that they looked at their best in this way, but the rules governing
the use of certain mouldings with decoration were never considered
infallible or immutable on Greek work and they varied from large-
to small-scale buildings. It was the Renaissance interpretations that
gave them such rigidity, and one of Adam's contentions was his
refusal to submit to those shibboleths.

The subsequent Roman civilization took much from ancient
Greece, which in 146 B.C. became one of its provinces. The Romans
too used a system of orders, creating five from the original three,
adding a Tuscan which was like the Doric and the Composite which
had a capital, mixing the features of Ionic and Corinthian. Whereas
the Greeks preferred the stark Doric order, the Romans liked the
richer Corinthian and, in general, their classical architecture is
more ornate. The overall contribution of ancient Rome was in their
engineering skills, which led to their wide-scale use of the vault and
the arch. This arcuated system they formed into an amalgam with
the Greek trabeated one and provided buildings like the Colosseum,
where the orders became decorative (not structural) and the construction was based on the arch and vault. The vast Roman Thermae,
such as the Baths of Caracalla in Rome and those at Pompeii, were
engineering feats. They were made possible by the use of Roman
concrete, which derived its durability and strength from *pozzolana*.
This was a volcanic ash found between Naples and Rome which,
when mixed with lime from the local stone, produced an extremely
hard concrete. Fragments of brick and travertine were incorporated
to provide a solid core for vaulting.

There are far more examples of Roman building extant than of
Greek, and a much greater variety in form and function of structure.
This led to Adam's contention that classical buildings designed in the
eighteenth century for use in England should be based on Roman
domestic work, not on temples, which were unsuited for the
purpose and which had been the prime classical model for the whole
Renaissance.

The western half of the Roman Empire collapsed in the fifth
century A.D., and, after several centuries, there emerged in Western
Europe a different form of building which, in the Middle Ages,
became Gothic architecture. It was the Renaissance that brought
back classical form, and this was first rediscovered, in the natural

way of things, in Italy, the country which had last used it. The first genuinely classical buildings of the Renaissance are by Brunelleschi in Florence, and they antedate any Renaissance work in England based on true classical principles by nearly two hundred years. It was Inigo Jones who, having studied in Italy, brought the correct Roman/Italian Renaissance architecture to Britain, and the first example can still be seen in his Banqueting Hall in Whitehall. He was followed by other architects, of whom Sir Christopher Wren was the most outstanding and the most famous.

Classical architecture in its rediscovered form was therefore based on that of ancient Rome, not of Greece. Though study of the Greek literature and theatre had been made, it was a widely held view in the sixteenth and seventeenth centuries that ancient Rome was the fountain of classical art and, since the Italians had made the early discoveries and studies, this was a natural development. From the early works of Brunelleschi in the fifteenth century, the style evolved through Renaissance to Mannerism and into Baroque; Italy always in the lead until the end of the seventeenth century, when France became paramount and Rococo was the dominant theme. The differences between these forms of classicism are plain to see but less easy to define. In general, Renaissance work was patterned as closely as possible on the ancient Roman temple and palace building, and Bramante's circular Tempietto in S. Pietro in Montorio in Rome is regarded as the most perfect interpretation of this. But after seventy or eighty years architects wanted something new. They toyed with Mannerism, which broke many of the classical rules; it put decoration where it was not usually placed, or set columns which bore no load. It was the Roman Baroque which finally broke away from the rigid precepts of what was thought to be the work of ancient Rome, and the mainspring of this was a movement and plasticity often created by convex and concave forms. Borromini and Bernini were two of its principal exponents. Some of Borromini's churches in particular almost seem to move as one watches the undulating walls flow from convexity to concavity: S. Ivo alla Sapienza or S. Carlo alle Quattro Fontane in Rome, for instance. Bernini's famous version of this style was the colonnade in front of St Peter's in Rome. Adam, whose overriding precept in architecture was 'movement', quotes this as the supreme example, commenting on the convexity of the dome (Michelangelo) in relation to the concavity of the piazza colonnade.

English architecture of the first half of the eighteenth century saw a brief flowering of the Baroque under Vanbrugh, with Blenheim Palace as the *pièce de résistance*. This is a Baroque which has little in common with the Roman version or indeed with that of other countries like Germany or Switzerland. England never really took to Baroque. It was too rich, too ostentatious, too sensuous. Vanbrugh's and Hawksmoor's Baroque is immense in scale; it certainly has 'movement', but it lacks the curves and the sensuality. It was a foreign implant, duly anglicized. It died a rapid death. In the 1720s its place was taken by something much more English: Palladianism. The basis of this movement was equally foreign as its prophet was Andrea Palladio, a Venetian architect of the sixteenth century, but it was made into something acceptable which was far from the concepts of the originator. The Palladian school in England, which held sway over architecture from 1720 to 1760, was really a three-pronged movement with Palladio as the spear-head. Palladio had tried for much of his life to pattern his work on what he believed to be the genuine Roman manner. He made hundreds of drawings of Roman remains and used as his guide Vitruvius's books on architecture.[1] He published his own works, '*I Quattro Libri dell'Architettura*' and '*L'Antichità di Roma*', which were translated into many languages, including English. The third inspiration, apart from Palladio and Vitruvius, was Inigo Jones, who had also based his ideas on those of the other two and also tried to re-create the genuine Roman classicism.

English Palladianism was not quite the same as any of these. It was more rigid and prescribed. Many architects designed in this way, and the work of William Kent, for example, includes some of the finest of English houses such as Holkham Hall in Norfolk. The exteriors of such houses were severe. The larger examples were in stone, correctly classical, having 'movement' in the skyline and projecting side pavilions, but appearing foursquare, solid and indisputably English. What made them into masterpieces, on the exterior, was the site and surroundings which acted as a foil to the architecture.

The upper classes in the eighteenth century were superb patrons.

They were cultured, had travelled on the Continent and knew what they wanted. They were not, like their nineteenth-century successors, haunted by the passion to make yet more money. They were prepared to plough it back into the estate. The Industrial Revolution had yet to get under way. The English aristocracy was not as biassed or limited as a monarchical one such as that of France. It had greater freedom and individuality. There were not only the great nobles, but also the squires, the wealthier clergy and an established middle class. All were patrons according to their purse and needs. In the eighteenth century sites were more carefully chosen, and the Palladian house was set on rising ground, at the foot of a vista, or by a stream or lake. The particularly English garden or park was then laid out around it with sweeping lawns, great spreading trees and a natural landscape. Lancelot (Capability) Brown became famous as the chief exponent of this type of landscaping. He engineered serpentine lakes out of streams, moved whole hillsides and strategically planted great cedars and oaks to set off the rectangular stone house. Amidst the trees and hills he incorporated sham classical ruins (according to eighteenth-century fashion), and the picture was complete. When we visit such houses as Holkham, Harewood, Audley End or Kedleston today we see the mature results of such landscaping, now at their best. This is something indigenous, very different from French or Italian gardens based on the geometrical formalities of Versailles. It was envied and copied later by other European nations. Catherine the Great of Russia was one of the most enthusiastic *aficionados* of such parks and had some created for her near St Petersburg.

A new spirit was abroad in the 1740s and 1750s, which resulted in a reversal of thought on the origins of classical art and later overthrew Palladianism completely. An urgent desire for travel to study 'on the spot' arose in all the countries of Western Europe, especially among Englishmen, Frenchmen and Germans. People travelled distances according to their means. The nobility undertook the Grand Tour of France and Italy, lasting perhaps two or three years, and stayed part of the time as guests with friends or relatives and partly in inns and rented lodgings. They collected antique and Renaissance sculpture, paintings, coins and ceramics, and brought them back to decorate their homes. Often it became necessary to build new galleries and libraries to house these treasures. Such travel by the nobility and also by architects and artists led to increased knowledge. Interest was aroused in Greece, Dalmatia and even in lands as far away as Syria. In England the Dilettanti Society was formed in the 1730s to encourage such original research. It published a number of papers and commissioned and financially supported expeditions by certain members. Among these was Robert Wood who, accompanied by Bouverie and Dawkins, went to Palmyra (in modern Syria). In 1753 he published the result of their studies and drawings made there in *The Ruins of Palmyra*. This was followed by his second expedition, the results of which were published in *The Ruins of Baalbec* (1757). James Stuart and Nicholas Revett followed, also under the society's aegis. They went to Pula (now Yugoslavia), then to Greece, where they studied at Corinth and Athens. They returned in 1755 and in 1762 published their *Antiquities of Athens*.

Other expeditions and other publications came from different countries. The most notable were de Caylus's *Recueil d'Antiquités Egyptiennes, Etrusques, Grecques et Romaines* (1752), Le Roy's *Ruines des plus beaux Monuments de la Grèce* (1758), Winckelmann's *History of Ancient Art* (1763) and Dumont's *Temples of Paestum* (1764). This widening of the field for classical research made clear to both patron and architect in Western Europe that Greece, not Rome, was the originator of the classical form, and that in many instances the Greek was purer and more beautiful. The Greek/Roman controversy raged hotly, and protagonists in the 'battle of the styles' took up indefatigable positions on one side or the other. In retrospect, it appears to have been much ado about nothing. Both architectural forms were classical, with one derived from, then developed further than, the other. Why not use the better examples from both? This of course is what the great architects in Western Europe did, and Robert Adam was one of them. They left the argument to those of lesser perception and more rigid, circumscribed thought.

One factor which excited interest and controversy was the discovery of what the Greek Doric order was like. Ever since Brunelleschi in the fifteenth century, the Roman Doric or Tuscan [2] had been the model, based on Vitruvius and the ruins of Roman buildings, then reiterated in succeeding publications through the sixteenth and seventeenth centuries. This has a much slenderer column than the Greek version, and also a moulded base. The Doric type is fluted, the Tuscan plain. The drawings, now seen in the books published by those who had studied on the spot, showed the Doric order of the Parthenon, without base, fluted, with a more subtle echinus moulding to the capital than the Roman (which has a semicircular section) and, most notable, a sturdier column and deeper entablature, giving different proportions of height and width to the order. This Greek Doric version horrified the Palladians, and they were even more shocked when they saw drawings of the archaic period temples of Paestum and Sicily, which pre-date the Parthenon by a hundred years or more. For these earlier temples have even shorter, stockier columns and very large capitals supporting a weighty entablature. They are the most powerful-looking Doric buildings in Western Europe. The English adherents to the Roman style in the second half of the eighteenth century, led by Sir William Chambers, thought this work primitive and barbaric.

The pro-Greek designers tended to go too far the other way, feeling that everything Greek was better than anything Roman – an equally prejudiced view. But even they did not value, as we do today, the great period of Greek sculpture and decoration. We consider this to be the fifth century B.C., rating high the Parthenon sculptures and also the earlier archaic work from Olympia and other sites. The Greek enthusiasts of the eighteenth century were more impressed by the later Greek work of the second or first century BC. In decorative fields they used designs from Greek vases, usually fifth- or fourth-century, and, mistakenly thinking them to be Etruscan, incorporated their motifs into interior decoration and detail. Wedgwood used such sources, so did Adam. Indeed the new pottery manufactory established by Wedgwood was named by him 'Etruria', and Adam proudly refers to his new 'Etruscan' motifs and colours, which are red and yellow earths with black.

One European country did not cede Greek originality for some time. This, naturally enough, was Italy. As publication after publication appeared, piling up the weight of evidence, the Italians found their champion in Gianbattista Piranesi, a Venetian artist who became famous for his drawings of classical ruins. In 1748 he published his drawings of views of Rome under the title *Le Antichità di Roma*. In 1761 he fired his famous broadside, the book *Della*

Magnificenza ed Architettura de' Romani. In this he attempts the defence of Roman architecture against the Greek, asserting that the latter was much more ornate and decadent. As a treatise intended to evaluate the achievements of two civilizations, this had something in common with the equally unscholarly, prejudiced *Contrasts*, published by Pugin in nineteenth-century England. Pugin extolled the virtues of Gothic architecture as against the sinful expression of Renaissance classicism. Piranesi was making a last-ditch, hopeless stand. We cannot agree with his contentions, but we appreciate his sincerity and admire his drawings which accurately portray ruined Roman buildings dramatically lit against a romantic landscape backcloth. Robert, who became friendly with him in Italy, admired his drawings and was honoured when Piranesi dedicated to him one of his publications.

Robert Adam entered this architectural world as a creator in 1759. From then, until he died in 1792, he poured out a tremendous number of very personal designs. He was an eclectic, using many classical sources, fusing them into a quality entirely Adam. His concept of 'movement' came from the Baroque features of Borromini and Bernini. He absorbed Kent's, Gibbs', Vanbrugh's plastic, three-dimensional massing of blocks and columns. His early ceiling designs, especially, were rococo. From the beginning, even before he set out on his Grand Tour, he knew himself to be (as indeed he was) an innovator, not a copyist. His sense of the romantic, his feeling for elegance were instinctive. They led him to gauge unerringly what the aristocratic owners of houses in England would want in the 1760s, and he used this personal intuition to combine the architectural themes with motifs from his own archaeological studies in Italy and Dalmatia. He added to these the experience of other men, favouring especially Wood's drawings of Palmyra.

The second half of the eighteenth century was the last creative era of architecture in England and Europe until the advent of modern design. There followed only revival and regurgitation. Adam came in for the last act. After Robert's death only Sir John Soane, and perhaps John Nash, had anything personal and original to express.

Adam's formal education ended at eighteen and he spent a number of years working with the family firm under his father's direction, then with his brothers, until he set off on the Grand Tour in 1754. After three and a quarter years he returned to Britain, set up practice in London and, within an incredibly short space of time, became the fashionable architect of the day. By 1762–3 his services were in great demand, and in the 1760s he created the 'Adam style' in his finest masterpieces. Partly due to his success and partly to his temperament, which was self-confident, sometimes impatient, always wanting to tackle something new and on the grand scale, the 1770s were less fortunate for him. His phenomenal success had brought him many imitators, none of whom possessed his fertility of imagination and quality of originality. Submerged under quantities of work, he tried mass production schemes which lowered his own standards, particularly in stucco ornamentation. Financial problems arose from his impatience to get on with the work allied to inadequate business judgment, as at the Adelphi. This, combined with what was taken to be his patronizing attitude in his preface to the *Works in Architecture*, published in 1773, acquired for him enemies as well as envious colleagues; little is more infuriating than patronage from someone who is almost invariably right. The last decade of his working life sees him designing more and larger commissioned projects, many of them doomed to sterility as they foundered on financial inadequacy or bureaucratic opposition.

Robert's great ambitions were to create a new personal style, which he did, and to design and complete at least one great public building. This opportunity was denied to him. Like Inigo Jones, who suffered similarly, he evolved scheme after scheme, all manifesting careful thought, professional presentation and a superb standard of individual solution – Edinburgh University, Cambridge University, the New Town in Edinburgh and many more – but none was fully carried out. For this he was not to blame, nor indeed was anyone else. He died at the age of sixty-three while engaged on a number of such projects. Had he lived longer he might have realized his dream.

What is the 'Adam style'? Anyone who has visited Syon House, Osterley, Kenwood or Kedleston has found many different interpretations of classical design. Adam is always different, always searching for something new and suitable for a given commission or environment. Like Sir Christopher Wren, he found new solutions to differing problems, but, also like Wren, his work, though variable, is instantly recognizable as his own. He created a new form of classical architecture, of worldwide influence, but particularly suitable for English houses, as English as Capability Brown's land-scaped parks. He went back to first principles in classical archi-tecture, to ancient Rome and, particularly, to domestic Rome, which he found in palace remains, Herculaneum and the Thermae. He was alive to the stylistic battle of the time, but would not waste himself in argument.

He was convinced, by his research in Italy, as also was Piranesi, that the Romans had never abided by rigid rules like those the Palladians followed, but had adapted their classical orders to need and scale. Adam did this too. He would take an order, re-create its proportions and decoration, alter the accepted rulings, and the result would have more of the essence of the original than anything seen in England in the first half of the eighteenth century.

It is widely known that Adam designed everything in a house down to the smallest detail in order to achieve homogeneity of atmosphere, so much so that we tend to remember the detail rather than the scheme. His interiors varied from delicate stucco ara-besques, covering walls and ceilings, incorporating painted panels, to the Roman grandeur of the columned hall at Kedleston or the palatial richness of the ante-room at Syon. Many of his interiors in later years have been debased by the owners' redecoration which 'picks out' the ornament in colour or gilt. Adam did not intend this. He used pastel shades for ceilings and walls because he thought the white, in general use until then, was too glaring. He used colour on a number of his designs, many of them in the Soane Museum, and these show a mass grading of light colours with, perhaps, white stucco ornament. Gilt is used for antique figures or special features.

What Adam admired most in building was 'movement'. He achieved his interpretation of this by lightness, an ethereal, aerial quality, especially in his interiors. The fact that there are fewer exteriors by him was not because of his preference, but because he was so often asked to alter, enlarge or redecorate an existing building. In most cases his interior work is his best, but at Bowood, the Admiralty Screen, Fitzroy Square and in Edinburgh he showed himself equally an exterior architect.

To express and sum up his work in a phrase or with a label is not easy; the nearest and most appropriate is 'romantic classicism'.

NOTES

1 Marcus Vitruvius Pollio dedicated ten books of his *de Architectura* to the Emperor Augustus in 25 B.C. He was a Roman engineer, and his work contains measured details and proportions of the Roman orders and ornament of his day. It does not therefore include the architecture of Imperial Rome.

2 There is no illustration of the Tuscan order in Vitruvius, and little exists from ancient Rome. It was revived, and became fashionable, in the Italian Renaissance.

PREFACE

THE last full account of the life and work of Robert Adam was published in 1948. Since then light has been shed upon his character and personality by the letters deposited at H.M. Register House by Sir John Clerk, and further improvements, alterations and even demolition have overtaken the architect's surviving work. In view of the current interest in Adam's achievements, it is perhaps time to bring the information up to date and combine such data with an account of his life.

In six chapters in this book I have tried to tell his story simply and chronologically, using all the information which is available to show what Robert Adam was like and what he did. For those readers who are not already conversant with the characteristics of classical architecture and its evolution a brief account is given in the introduction, together with an illustrated glossary of terms.

At the end of the book are factual notes on the Adam work which exists. The information includes data on ownership and the condition of properties pertaining in 1969. Buildings are open to the public view only in the instances where specifically stated.

I wish to express my deep appreciation to the individuals and organizations who have given me invaluable help in research for this book. In particular I wish to thank Captain C. K. Adam, D.S.O., R.N. (Ret.), of Blair-Adam, for his kind reception of me and for his permission to reproduce three of the Adam family portraits. These works are in Captain Adam's possession at the family estate but were photographed by the Scottish National Portrait Gallery, who kindly supplied prints for this book. I am grateful to the Laing Art Gallery of Newcastle-on-Tyne for the print of the portrait of James Adam, now in their possession.

Sir John Clerk, Bt, D.L., of Penicuik, has kindly permitted me to draw freely, in quotation, on his Adam letters held in the Register House in Edinburgh. Mr Drummond Moray has given me similar generous permission with regard to Adam's letter to Lord Kames. I would like also to express my appreciation of the kindness and efficiency of the staff of H.M. General Register House (Historical Records Department) in Edinburgh, who produced endless letters and documents immediately on request during many days of study. I am grateful for the assistance given to me by the Research Division of the Library of the House of Commons, from Sir John Summerson and Miss Dorothy Stroud of the Sir John Soane Museum, the City Librarian and his staff of the Central Public Library in Edinburgh and the Curator and Librarian of the Public Library of High Wycombe.

I recently revisited the extant Adam buildings, and am most grateful for the unfailing courtesy of the many owners of these properties who permitted me to study and take photographs at my convenience. I would like to express my appreciation to the Marquess of Lansdowne for Bowood, Wiltshire; the Rev. J. K. Byrom, M.A., Warden at Brasted Place College; Mr R. N. Thompson of the Royal Society of Medicine for Chandos House, London; the Headmistress of St Joseph's Residential Special School for Croome Court, Worcestershire; the National Trust for Scotland for Culzean Castle, Ayrshire; the Ministry of Public Building and Works for Duff House, Banff; the Marquess of Bute for Dumfries House, Ayrshire; the Earl of Wemyss and March, K.T., LL.D., for Gosford House, East Lothian; the Earl of Harewood for Harewood House, Yorkshire; Major Hargreaves and the National Trust for Hatchlands, Surrey; the Marquess of Linlithgow for Hopetoun House, South Queensferry; Viscount Scarsdale for Kedleston House, Derbyshire; Mr John Jacob, Curator and the Greater London Council for Kenwood, Hampstead; Mr C. H. Lewis, M.B.E., M.A., J.P., Headmaster of Kimbolton School, Huntingdonshire; the Earl of Haddington for Mellerstain House, Berwickshire; Lord Brabourne and Miss Davies of the Caldecott Community for Mersham-le-Hatch, Kent; Mr Macpherson of the Moor Park Golf Club and Mr and Mrs Gray for Moor Park and the Tea House respectively; Major E. R. F. Compton, D.L., J.P., for Newby Hall, Yorkshire; Major R. T. A. Hog for

Newliston, West Lothian; Mr G. M. V. Winn and the National Trust for Nostell Priory, Yorkshire; the National Trust, the Ministry of Works and the Victoria and Albert Museum for Osterley Park, Middlesex; the Director of the Courtauld Institute of Art, University of London, for No. 20 Portman Square, London; William Willett Ltd, and the Landstone Investments Ltd. for Shardeloes, Buckinghamshire; the Chairman of the Directors of the Distillers' Company for No. 20 St James's Square, London; the Earl of Morley and the National Trust for Saltram, Devonshire; the Duke of Northumberland for Syon House, Middlesex; and Mr R. Maxwell Young, Factorial Secretary of the University of Edinburgh.

My thanks are also due to Mr A. F. Kersting, A.I.I.P., F.R.P.S. for permission to reproduce four of the photographs.

Finally, I wish to express my gratitude to my husband, Mr John Yarwood, for accompanying me to all these properties and for taking photographs which form the great majority of those shown in this book. This has enabled me to produce not only new photographs but ones specifically aimed at illustrating the varied facets of Adam's achievement.

1. SCOTTISH PRELUDE

THE tide is out. Sandy beaches
stretch in a level plain round the wide, low harbour. The land rises
towards a slight promontory at each arm of the bay where stand,
silhouetted and intrusive, grouped blocks of glass and concrete.
Traffic notices in the town direct the way: 'To the Industrial
Estates'. Dotted off the coast are islets and wooden islands. Pulled
up on the shore is a boat or two, but activity there is spasmodic. A
main road fringes the sea; behind it are desolate wastes of demolished
buildings and temporary car parks. Turning inland, at right angles to
the sea, up a narrow road, one comes to the old High Street.
Parallel to the sea, it still follows the line of the 'lang toun of
Kirkcaldy', when the town consisted only of this mile-and-a-half-
long coastal development. The High Street has one or two interesting older buildings, but behind it, up the hillside, are nineteenth-
century grey stone houses, terrace after terrace, crossed here and
there by a rarely used railway line. The garden area, where are set
the library and museum, is attractively landscaped; an oasis in a
town dragging itself out of its nineteenth-century industrial drab-
ness into its modern equivalent. It is not now a mining town, but
makes vinyl flooring and has electronics and optics industries. Its
population has risen in the last hundred years from ten thousand to
fifty-three thousand and many new boxes are springing up to house
the newcomers.

This picture of Kirkcaldy on the Fifeshire coast, the northern
shore of the Firth of Forth, is very different from what the young
Robert saw as he ran and played here in his first eleven years of life.
Then the harbour was the town, its livelihood and the centre of its
existence. It was the reason why settlers came there even before the

Middle Ages and established one of Scotland's most ancient burghs. The southward-facing harbour, its sandy beaches, abundant fresh-water streams and rolling, wooded countryside with fertile soil attracted early settlement. The seventeenth-century harbour was an important one: over a hundred ships traded here and, though it silted up and needed dredging from time to time, it remained important into the eighteenth century.

On 3rd July 1728 William and Mary Adam welcomed the arrival of their second son in their home, Gladney House, which stood in its own grounds facing the sea, in the Links district, on the east side of Bute Wynd (the word Bute is apparently a corruption of 'Boot', from a nearby boot factory). The baby, their fifth child, was baptized in the local parish church of Abbotshall on the 24th of the same month. The registration reads: 'Robert, lawful son of William Adam and Mary Robertson was baptised before the Congregation'. When he was old enough he attended the Burgh School, an unimpressive building, still standing in Hill Street. He was a schoolfellow, though five years younger, of Kirkcaldy's most famous son, Adam Smith the economist. Later in life they became close friends.

Robert's branch of the Adam family stemmed from John Adam, a stone-mason, who came to Fife from Angus soon after 1680. He married Helen Cranstoun and the couple lived in Linktown of Abbotshall near Kirkcaldy. Their son William [1] (Robert's father), a survivor of the many children of this family who died in infancy or childbirth, was first trained by his father, then sent to work with Sir William Bruce, the chief Scottish architect of the time, who introduced the Renaissance to Scotland and is best known for his work on the Palace of Holyrood House. After Bruce's death in 1710 William went into partnership with William Robertson of Gladney. These two men both had initiative and were keen business men. They worked diligently, lived thriftily and rose to prosperity from very modest beginnings; so much so that in 1733 William Adam was able to purchase the Kinross-shire estate, then called Blair Crambeth, consisting of 640 Scottish acres of lonely, uncultivated moorland. He built his home here, tamed the land, laid out an estate and, re-naming it Blair-Adam, proudly became its first laird. Captain Charles K. Adam, R.N.(Ret.), directly descended from William, is the present laird. He is also Lord Lieutenant of the County of Kinross.

Before this the two Williams, Adam and Robertson, had founded the Links pottery for making bricks and tiles, and had also acquired holdings and interests in the main industries of Kirkcaldy: the coal mines, the timber mills, the breweries and, above all, the salt pans. These last had been established in the seventeenth century, and by 1670 there were twenty salt pans in the town. But the workers – salt-workers and miners as well as iron-workers and maltmen – were little more than slaves, even in 1700; they were bought and sold with the businesses.

In 1716 William Adam married into the Robertson family, choosing for his wife Mary Robertson. They settled in at Gladney House and brought up their family of four sons and six daughters. It is thought that William himself may have designed the house. From its appearance this is possible, but doubtful. It was a stone house with flanking towers capped by Flemish curved gables. In the centre of the façade was a pedimented feature with Ionic pilasters at each side. There was a classical entrance doorway and fenestration. The whole building was well constructed but provincial in design, as might have been expected of a house of that size and date in a country district of Scotland. Gladney House existed until the twentieth century: it fell on bad times, ended as a lodging-house for the poor, and was finally demolished in 1931.

Robert spent his early childhood there, living a carefree but disciplined life with his elder brother John, his sisters and his younger brother James, born, as far as we know, two years after him. He was brought up in a Christian home, Presbyterian, but not of the bigoted, dogmatic type so redolent of Scotland in the 1730s. His parents were good-living people, honest and hard-working; they kept open house for their friends and acquaintances who were, especially for the Scotland of that time, cultured men of art and letters. Robert was taught to be kind, thoughtful of others, but also to think for himself, to argue and discuss, not merely to accept what he was told. His fertile genius expanded and flowered in this ideal climate.

He was fortunate to spend his early years in a small country town. He was not a strong child, and the fresh air and freedom helped him.

For some reason genius and weakness of physique are thought to go hand in hand. This has sometimes been the case but, in contrast, there have also been such figures as Michelangelo, Bernini and Titian, all of them fit, strong men who lived into their eighties and nineties. For Robert there were walks, horses to ride, boats to sail and a pleasant countryside to enjoy, but the Scotland of his early years was poor, backward and had immense problems.

The Act of Union between Scotland and England had been signed in 1707. This ended the separate existence of Scotland as a nation, and Scottish Members of Parliament, from then onwards, sat at Westminster. Kirkcaldy sent its first M.P. to London in 1722, and Robert Adam, in his turn, sat for Kinross-shire. This did not eliminate the Scottish mistrust of the English. Since the Middle Ages Scotland had allied herself with France against England. Neither James I and VI's accession to the joint throne in 1603 nor the Act of Union in 1707 could abolish overnight the distrust of centuries. But Scotland had to sign the Act of Union. Her poverty and problems forced her to do so; then the improvement, agriculturally and industrially, made the deed well worth while. Fundamentally the Union meant that Scotland had exchanged her parliamentary independence for a full partnership in England's markets and colonies. The benefits took a little time to establish themselves, but, by 1740, amelioration was noticeable, especially in agriculture.

In 1707 land was rarely enclosed, and cattle had to be tethered or shut up at night. There were few hedges, walls or trees. The housing conditions of the peasants were like those of medieval England – a one-roomed cottage with central hearth, a louvre in the roof above in lieu of chimneys, and all shared with the livestock. There was no furniture, an earth floor and no glass or windows. Due to out-of-date farming techniques, there were few potatoes or other root crops. Staple crops were beans and barley, and the cattle had to be killed each autumn for lack of winter feed – a medieval English custom. It did not help that roads and communications were almost non-existent. Even routes connecting Edinburgh and Glasgow with London were impassable. Little could get through: mail, newspapers passengers or travelling business men. Alexander ('Jupiter') Carlyle reports in his *Autobiography* (1800) that in Scotland, even in

1758, to see a post-chaise was rare. Only two-wheeled traffic was practicable, and four-wheelers were unknown as the roads made progress impossible.

Things had begun to improve by 1735–40. Agriculture began to be based on the English enclosed system; varied crops were sown in rotation; and cattle could be fed during the winter. Timber was planted and roads were improved. The city industries also got under way, especially in Glasgow where the port flourished. Edinburgh suffered a temporary setback as a result, but gradually re-established itself.

One of the most noticeable features of the post-1740 Scotland was the revival of arts, letters and learning. Robert Adam came of a generation of exceptionally gifted young men who took part in this revival. In his father's day, Scotland was justifiably regarded as provincial in architecture, painting, literature and all the arts and sciences. Robert's generation was intellectually a rich and lively one which took advantage of the upsurge of Scottish culture, though many of them made their names and reputations south of the border. They killed for ever the gibes that had been levelled at Scottish 'rural intellect'. The young Scots of this time included such outstanding men as Adam Smith, the economist; David Hume, historian and philosopher; William Robertson, academic and historian; Allan Ramsay, painter to George III; James Boswell, diarist; Dr Alexander Carlyle, minister; Adam Ferguson, professor of natural philosophy; and John Home, playwright. Robert Adam was not the least of these.

In 1739 William left Kirkcaldy and set up a household in Edinburgh, where the children went to school. It is difficult to find out where he lived and worked. Blair-Adam was the family estate of course, and all the children spent their free time in the Lowland countryside bordering Kinross-shire and Fife, which is now similar to the fields and softly rounded, wooded hills of Kent and Surrey. In 1739 there would have been fewer trees. Afforestation schemes were only beginning, and this part of Scotland had been treeless for a long time. William, presumably, had some sort of office and work-centre in the city, but, despite his importance as Scotland's leading architect until his death in 1748, and that his practice was continued by his eldest son John without interruption until he died in 1792, no evidence of the site of such a centre has come to light. Apart from the lack of official records on rating of houses and businesses at this date, Edinburgh in 1739 was such a small city that any 'Adam office' would have been rebuilt in the far-seeing expansion begun in the 1780s.

William Adam was born on 30th October 1689. He was educated locally, near Kirkcaldy, and, as mentioned earlier, grew up to be an energetic man of wide interests, especially in business. He worked extraordinarily hard, both in his business ventures and in the profession of architecture, at which he made himself proficient and, later, almost indispensable in Scotland. His zeal, initiative and self-confidence were all qualities which reappeared so noticeably in his second son. He was level-headed and firm in his business dealings, noted for his honesty and straightforwardness, but, also, for a ruthless persistence when necessary (Plate 2).

As a result of his efforts he became the best-known architect in Scotland, employed on many commissions. Most of the nobility and gentry went to him for new houses and alterations to existing ones. He was appointed Master Mason in North Britain to the Board of Ordnance, and it was in this capacity that he carried out so much work under government contract, building forts in the Highlands. He also became storekeeper under His Majesty's Master of Works in Scotland and a Burgess and Guild Brother of Edinburgh.

His large practice made him well-to-do. He invested in property in Edinburgh and bought the Blair Crambeth land, renaming it Blair-Adam, as described earlier. This land formed the nucleus of a much larger estate. This financial stability enabled his sons to start their architectural lives on a fairly independent basis. While John continued the family business, Robert and James, one by one, were able to study, travel and employ draughtsmen on the Continent. This made it possible for them to amass the quantity of material as well as paintings, sculpture and casts which they brought home with them and, in turn, enabled them to establish a flourishing practice in an incredibly short space of time. It is true that Robert would not have become the famous, fashionable architect that he was in a few years had he not possessed his own special qualities of character and ability, but, equally, it would have been a much longer process without the financial security provided by his father.

William was respected in Edinburgh as a citizen of importance. He interested himself in all branches of the arts and their furtherance in his country. To this end he became a founder member, in 1737, of the Society for Improving Arts and Sciences.

The years from 1730 till his death in 1748 were William Adam's busiest. From all parts of Scotland came inquiries and commissions to build houses, churches and various civic schemes from hospitals to libraries. His work was not original in the way that Robert's was. It was competent and fundamentally good design, but it was derivative. His sources were mainly English, with a touch of Dutch influence too, which shows itself in his house designs. He admired the work of Vanbrugh and Gibbs and the Palladian School of Kent and Campbell. He went on a trip in 1727 with Sir John Clerk of Penicuik, his patron and friend. Together they studied Gibbs' church in the Strand and St Martin-in-the-Fields. They visited Greenwich, then toured the country to see some of Campbell's and Vanbrugh's houses – Wanstead and Blenheim in particular.

In the 1730s William Adam evolved his own approach to classical architecture. Set against the standard of such architects as William Kent, James Gibbs or Sir John Vanbrugh, it appears pedestrian and stolid, but it holds its own with men of the second rank in England. It should be remembered, though, that in Scotland there was, even by 1730, no real tradition of classical architecture such as had existed for a long time in England. Sir William Bruce had introduced it in his alterations to the Palace of Holyrood House and, more notably, at Hopetoun. William Adam continued in this vein and, adding his own feelings about power and weight, produced a Scottish version of Palladianism mixed (if this is not a contradiction in terms) with a stolid Baroque.

That he fully appreciated his position as Scotland's leading classical architect is shown by his publishing, in sections, *Vitruvius Scoticus*. It appeared in parts, and in a desultory fashion, between 1720 and 1740, but it enjoyed insufficent support and the project had to be dropped. It was presumably intended as a Scottish equivalent to Colin Campbell's *Vitruvius Britannicus*; but, whereas the latter contained drawings not only of Campbell's own work, but also of other contemporary architects, and was enriched by an explanatory text, *Vitruvius Scoticus* had no text and was a collection of drawings almost entirely selected from Adam's designs. It was eventually published in 1810, long after its author's death, simply as a collection of drawings entitled *Vitruvius Scoticus, being a collection of Plans, Elevations and Sections of Public Buildings, Noblemen's and Gentlemen's Houses in Scotland*. A prefatory note states: 'The following plans, drawn by the late William Adam Esq., Architect, were engraved at his expense by the most eminent artists of the time with a view to publication.' Leafing through the drawings, one's impression is of careful, thorough work, unoriginal and, in the main, stodgy and unimaginative. The drawings fail to do justice to his work, which, in actuality, has much more life and substance. Over the years, in fact, *Vitruvius Scoticus* has had the effect opposite to that intended by its author. The usual reaction has been gentle disparagement.

It is in his country houses that we can still study William Adam's work, and one or two are described here. His civic buildings, such as the Royal Infirmary and Orphans' Hospital in Edinburgh, the University Library and the Château of Chatelherault in Glasgow, the Robert Gordon Hospital in Aberdeen or the Town House at Dundee have, to a large extent, been destroyed or altered. A number of houses remain in a more or less original condition, except that a number of them have received redesigned or redecorated interior schemes from John and/or Robert, who continued their father's work for certain clients.

William's best and most typical work can be seen at Hopetoun House, the Drum and Duff House. Hopetoun is the best known and most extensive of these. Situated on rising ground, just outside South Queensferry, it gives magnificent views of the Firth estuary and the two bridges, the latter of which, on its opening by H.M. the Queen in 1964, replaced the eight-hundred-year-old Queen Margaret passage, as the ferry route was called. This route, named after the Scottish queen, must have been familiar to William and his sons in their comings and going between Edinburgh and Blair Adam. Hopetoun House was built by Sir William Bruce, with William Adam assisting while yet a young man. After Bruce's death (1710) Lord Hopetoun asked William to extend the building and bring it up to date in modern architectural idiom – that is, Palladian. The completed scheme was on the grand scale, particularly so for

Scotland, where it was a rarity at that time. The entrance elevation sweeps across 500 feet, and fronting the house are immense green lawns and wide gravel drives. The approach view offers an impressive pile-up of grey masonry; a great centre block, quadrant colonnades and terminal pavilions. A giant Corinthian order spans the *piano nobile* and second storey, taken up in Doric form in the pavilions. This is the Palladian manner, but the skyline and the sweeping convex and concave contrasting curves of bays and quadrants are Vanbrugh-inspired Baroque, as is the weightiness of the entire composition. Most of the exterior was finished in the 1740s. The quality interior work is by Robert.

William was engaged at the same time on Duff House, which he built in extensive grounds for the Earl of Fife just inland from the town of Banff. This is entirely Palladian. The uncompromising single large block, about a hundred feet by eighty on plan, cost over £70,000, mainly because of the ready-worked stone brought by sea from the Firth of Forth. There is a rusticated lower storey; a giant Corinthian order in pilasters spans the next two floors with attic and balustrade above. The building now belongs to the Ministry of Works, who are restoring it to its former condition. This will mean the expenditure of much time and money. For the last fifty years Duff House has been used first as a hospital, then by army units, and the interior has little to show of William's decorative schemes, though the structure is sound. The original staircase balustrade has disappeared, also all the furniture and nearly all the fireplaces. Outside the stone work is in quite good condition, apart from bomb damage to the balustrade of the approach staircase.

Dun House, near Montrose, was of similar design, but built a little earlier. Arniston dates from about 1735. It is near Baron Somerville's country seat in Midlothian. Built about 1725, and usually referred to as Drum House or 'the Drum', it is judged by Mr Bolton [2] to be William Adam's masterpiece. A smaller house than Hopetoun, it is also on the pattern of central block with wings, though only one of these was built. Of Palladian design with Dutch flavouring, there are no rumbustious curves here. A pale stone was used with stucco. The decoration was applied in an old-fashioned manner. For instance, rustication covers the main block façade and overweights the Ionic pilasters, also with rustication blocks. A dominant central Venetian window offsets this to some extent, and below is a curving staircase.

The interior ornamentation is typical of William Adam and contrasts clearly with Robert's approach in the next generation. A Netherlandish rococo, handled ornately and plastically, became monotonous and repetitive. The hall stucco is elaborate, displaying trophies of arms, plumes and flags, and the dining-room is vastly overdone. The ambitious upstairs saloon was designed with an impressive ceiling in great square panels, the centre one of which has a plaster high-relief picture of Juno and Jupiter in front of a background of trees and clouds and animals. A similar note was struck in the mantelpiece panel, where Neptune is driving his sea-horses with vigour. The overall white finish used here, so typical of the time, is what Robert used to call 'glaring', a harshness which he muted with his sophisticated pastel tones of the 1760s.

About 1725 also Adam began work at Mellerstain, near Kelso, There had been a house here which was pulled down, and William built wings on either side of the site, intending a central block here to join them. Nothing further was done for over forty years, when Robert was commissioned to finish the job.

Meanwhile the Adam children were growing up in the ancient city of Edinburgh. The choice of this site had been an obvious one. It was easily defensible with a natural precipitous rock for fortification. There was convenient access to the Forth estuary, only a couple of miles away, and so direct sea routes to the ports of Flanders and France. Ties with France had been strong from the beginning, and French influence was still clearly to be seen in the city's layout and customs in the 1740s. Like so many medieval French towns – Carcassonne, for instance – the city had grown up on a ridge and hill, sloping steeply and, in places precipitously, to the surrounding plain. It had been easy to construct walls where necessary, with fortified gates for entrance and exit, thus forming an admirable seat for a royal capital in the Middle Ages. The problem in the eighteenth century was that Edinburgh (again like a number of French towns) was still medieval. Because of its site it could not expand laterally without complex schemes of drainage and bridge building, and the country's recent poverty and backwardness had prevented the smallest improvement. It seems fairly certain that if

Scotland had not decided in 1707 to join forces with her old enemy south of the border, neither the money nor the skills with which Scotsmen finally created the new Edinburgh between 1750 and 1830 would have been forthcoming.

Edinburgh today is a beautiful city. One of its prime attractions is its natural scenery, and the builders of the new city used these to best advantage. In 1740 this same topography was the stumbling block to expansion. While English cities, especially London, had for centuries spread out laterally, Edinburgh had been forced to extend vertically, building the six-, ten- or even twelve-storey tenement blocks on crowded sites, many of which are still there and are so characteristic of the place.

When Robert came to Edinburgh the city was bounded by its fortified walls, built just after Flodden Field and extended only marginally in the seventeenth century. They started at the foot of Calton Hill, ran eastwards to the Palace of Holyrood House and back westwards to the castle. The northern confine of the city did not need walls. It was bordered by marsh and a lake, called the North-loch, which spread over what is now Princes Street. The watery area covered the present Waverley Station and Princes Street Gardens as far as the Castle Rock. It was noisome and pestilential, its shores made less salubrious by the tanneries and butchers' slaughter-houses which, by tradition, lined the edges.

It was a small confine for such a city, built entirely on a narrow ridge, sloping east–west and ascending all the way from Holyrood to the castle. At one end the royal residence, at the other the city defence. In between, one long, magnificent road (by medieval standards), now called the Royal Mile and made up of Canongate (the Canons' gait), High Street, Lawnmarket and Castle Hill. There was only one other street in the town, Cowgate, which ran parallel on fairly level ground on the southern shoulder of the ridge which, apart from this, dropped steeply both southwards and northwards towards the plain below. The whole of Edinburgh was packed into this strip, one mile long and about one-sixth of a mile wide. It comprised tall stone blocks squeezed together on the available land with narrow passages between called wynds, each on average about three to five feet wide, and running north–south off the two streets along the backbone ridge. These wynds are still there in the old town, with their steep steps and slopes and metal hand-rail up the centre, just like their Montmartre counterparts. Since there were no squares or spaces in the town, and so few public buildings, these two streets teemed at all times with market trading; there was nowhere else to do it.

The people who lived in these lofty tenements with their dark, dirty stairs and alleyways were not all poor, nor was the town just a slum. All classes of the population lived here. They had to; there was no other accommodation in the capital. A kind of social custom and distinction had been evolved so that in the eight or ten floors of a good-class tenement the aristocracy would live on the third floor, the gentry on the fourth, while shopkeepers would find it convenient to be at street level and innkeepers perhaps one floor up. At the top would be trades and professions – tailors, milliners, surgeons, artists.

Though it was possible in this way to maintain a social distinction, everyone had to use the single flights of narrow stairs which gave access to the wynd or close outside. Walking along these was like entering a dark, clammy tunnel, the dilapidated blocks towering, as in a canyon, on either side. The worst problem was that of sanitation, and Edinburgh's customs in this respect made her the laughing-stock of the English, so archaic did they seem to the Londoner. Close stools had to be used and were permitted to be emptied only once a day, in the evening. To walk the wynds at that time was hazardous. At any moment a shout from the windows above would reverberate along the alley: 'Gardy-loo!' (*Gardez l'eau!*). This was the custom at least of the more courteous of the tenants.[3] The passer-by, running hopefully for shelter, would answer 'Haud yer han!'. The streets were left till the morning's inadequate decontamination and, on Sundays, they were left uncleaned. Excrement lay where it had fallen.

The Scottish Sunday was another subject for English incomprehension. The Kirk in Scotland was the power in the land. The ordinary man, deprived of political representation, gave strong support to his parish church and made himself a part of it, feeling it to give him strength and succour. The building itself was unpretentious and there was barely anywhere to sit, but it was so crowded that part of the congregation had to take part in the service from outside. The religious system was stern, and the power of the Kirk extended to every detail of everyday life. It ruled Edinburgh, where each week the Kirk Court tried cases of stealing, slander, argument, witchcraft and many other offences, among which 'breach of the Sabbath' was high on the list of indictable crimes. On Sunday almost everything was forbidden: dancing, making music, loitering, prying, even reading (apart from Bible study). The harsh treatment meted out to sexual offenders, house-breakers and thieves almost eradicated those transgressions and, at least in this respect, Edinburgh was envied by the outside world.

Many attempts had been made since 1688 to solve Edinburgh's population problem. But until the North-loch was drained and bridges built linking the north side of the city, across the loch basin, with the Royal Mile, expansion on any scale was impossible, as was also the creation of public buildings, utilities or market-places. Efforts had to be confined to demolishing the worst tenement blocks and building new ones on the same sites. This made the city cleaner and provided a little more light and air for these wealthy enough to move into the few new buildings.

Such was life in the city when eleven-year-old Robert came to live there. It is not known where he lived in 1739, but a number of his letters from Italy are addressed to his mother at

> *Mistress Adam's House*
> *Foot of Niddry's Wynd*
> *Cowgate,*
> *Edinburgh.*

Niddry's (or Nidries) Wynd was one of the passages running northwards out of Cowgate, up the steep hill towards the High Street on the backbone of the ridge. It was quite close to South Bridge and ended near the High Street beside the Tron Church (Fig. 6). If the house had been at this end of the wynd it would certainly have been demolished in the 1780s when the South Bridge, designed by Robert himself, was constructed to span the Cowgate. Most of Robert's letters to his family from Italy were sent care of his sister, Mrs Clerk in London. Presumably this meant that they were more likely to arrive safely than if addressed to the Kinross-shire estate or even Edinburgh where, since each flat was termed a 'house' and no homes were numbered, delivery was difficult.

William Adam sent his sons to school and some of them (Robert, James and possibly William) to university. His daughters, of course, had no formal education, even in Scotland where the academic standards of the time were much in advance of England and where this type of study was considered important. The girls would stay at home, learning domestic arts, most efficiently, from their mother.

When the family arrived in Edinburgh Robert began to attend the local high school. In those days it was a gloomy place, packing about ninety or more boys into a Tudor building in Blackfriar's Wynd leading off the High Street. Later the Edinburgh High School [4] was built next door to the old one, in High Street Yards, near the university dating from 1778.

The pupils worked hard, about six hours a day, but on almost every day of the year with no vacations or Saturdays off. Robert was eleven when he began at the high school, about a year older than most of the children; but being a bright lad he caught up and, like them, left at fifteen. Classics were the prime study, and boys would often leave with a sound knowledge of Latin but unable to speak English properly. For in 1740 the people of Scotland did not find it easy to speak English. Even Scottish M.P.s at Westminster were laughed at for their speech and could barely be understood. It was Robert's generation in university who altered this reputation.

On 1st November 1743 Robert attended the university for the first time (the college, as it was then called) and his signature 'Rob. Adams' can still be seen in register of matriculation there, a few lines above 'Walter Scott', presumably the grandfather of the famous writer. The college had been founded in 1582 and had four faculties which had been awarding degrees since 1741. The academic year ran from November to June, and lectures included subjects like the history of Britain and of the world, the ancient Roman civilization, and newer topics embracing natural philosophy, astronomy and mathematics. These were taken by Professor Colin MacLaurin, a remarkable man, son of a minister. He had proved to be a young prodigy, entering Glasgow University at the age of eleven, taking his M.A. at fifteen, and had been appointed Professor of Mathematics at Aberdeen University at nineteen. In 1725, at the age of twenty-seven, he came to Edinburgh. Dr Alexander Carlyle, who began his studies there before Robert in 1735, says that MacLaurin was the favourite professor and the most agreeable lecturer he had ever heard. He also comments that the professor had been so successful in making mathematics a fashionable study that in the 'war of 1743' (presumably the Dettingen campaign) nine-tenths of the British army engineers were Scots officers.

Robert obviously agreed. He too enjoyed MacLaurin's lectures and also liked his anatomy studies, but he had, in addition, to work at Greek and metaphysics. He had a number of friends and colleagues in the university who, with him, became the bright young men of Scotland, finding their fame and fortune both north and south of the border. They included Dr William Robertson (1721–92), Robert's cousin, who in 1762 became principal of the university; he was largely responsible for insisting on the adoption of Robert's designs for the new buildings in the 1780s. His outstanding work was his *History of Charles V*. Others were John Home the author and David Hume the philosopher and historian. Hume died fairly young, in 1776, and was buried in Old Calton Hill Burial Ground [5] where Robert designed his mausoleum (erected 1778), based on that of Theodoric at Ravenna. It was such men, together with Adam Smith, Professor at Glasgow University, who helped to give Scotland her new intellectual pre-eminence and a more tolerant religious background.

Robert and his colleagues were very much favoured by circumstances. They had parents able to support them in their studies, which as often as not failed to culminate in graduation. But students in Scotland came from all classes, being not only the sons of nobles and lairds but also of farmers and peasants. Such lads found study hard, and only determination enabled them to persevere. They lived in poor lodgings in the town, maintaining life and energy on the sack of oatmeal hanging on the wall of their room. In the vacation they took it home empty for a refill at the farm before return.

James Boswell, in his *London Journal*, tells us about his days at Edinburgh University. He was there about ten years later than Robert and would have been a contemporary of James Adam, who matriculated in 1752.

England, at this same period, was vastly in arrears educationally. Dr Trevelyan tells us: [6] 'The slumbers of the English University were more scandalous than the lighter and more broken slumbers of the Church. There were practically no examinations held at Oxford and few at Cambridge. [There were still only the two universities to serve all England and Wales.] Lord Eldon, then plain John Scott, graduated at Oxford in 1770; he used to relate that he was asked only two questions by way of examination for his degree: "What is the Hebrew for the place of a skull?" and "Who founded University College?" By replying "Golgotha" and "King Alfred" he satisfied the examiners in Hebrew and History.'

In England, after 1688 and the subsequent Union of 1707, people settled down to Hanoverian rule. The Stuarts had gone, and although the present régime left much to be desired it was better to let matters rest. The Old Cavaliers became law-abiding Tories who, now and then, drank to the 'King-over-the-Water', but only nostalgically. They did not really intend doing anything about it.

In Scotland the situation was different. No Scottish family could stand apart. Many, like William Adam, felt like the English and wanted to get on with life and away from the futile struggles, but many others did not. A Scottish family could not avoid the issue. It had to stand up and be counted. Scottish Old Cavaliers mostly became Jacobites dedicated not to nostalgic toasts but to action: to restore the House of Stuart to the throne of Britain. In such a climate the Scottish rebellions of 1715 and 1745 inevitably collapsed for want of English support. In 1715 the rebel army marched as far south as Preston. In 1745 it reached Derby, but this is no true reflection of opinion. By 1745 England had enjoyed thirty years of peace under Robert Walpole, with spasmodic interruptions by French and Spanish scuffles. A new generation had grown up under the House of Hanover; it did not greatly admire George I and II or their courts, but it had come to accept them.

When Prince Charles Edward, the Young Pretender, landed in the Highlands he found, due to the Franco-British war which had started a few months earlier, a country denuded of troops. With only five thousand Highlanders armed with antique weapons he swept through to Derby. The English Government could not allow him to succeed. Its small but efficient modern army was instructed to return, and the prince found it impossible to persuade his Highlanders to march farther south. Returning north they suffered more.

To have continued to London would have been hazardous. To return was fatal. It all ended, for good, on Culloden Moor in 1746.

Each family in Edinburgh had to make its own decision. William Adam made his for the English Government and, as the better part of valour, retreated to Blair-Adam. Most of the intellectuals and youth of the city opted to defend it. Alexander Carlyle describes how he returned to Edinburgh on 13th September 1745 from a holiday trip to find that his companions were enlisting in the Corps of Volunteers, then being formed to defend the city against Prince Charles. William Robertson and John Home were among them and Carlyle joined too.

Professor MacLaurin of the university was put in charge of the defence of the walls of Edinburgh. Seventeen-year-old Robert rallied enthusiastically to his aid. MacLaurin told Carlyle that it would be possible to make the walls defensible, but he would need help, equipment and time. He did not get the first two, and time certainly had run out.

On 17th September Prince Charles arrived at Holyrood. He was greeted by a cheering crowd, estimated by an Edinburgh newspaper, *The Caledonian Mercury*, to be about twenty thousand. Having taken over the city His Royal Highness issued a proclamation stating that he would give three weeks' grace to those who had opposed him, including the Corps of Volunteers, and that, if they came to pay court to him at Holyrood Abbey during that time, they would receive a free pardon. Carlyle relates how he went there with his friends: 'I went down to the Abbey Court at about 12 o'clock, to wait till the Prince should come out of the Palace and mount his horse to ride to the east side of Arthur's Seat to visit his army. He was a good-looking man of about five feet ten inches, his hair was dark red, and his eyes black. His features were regular, his visage long, much sunburnt and freckled, and his countenance thoughtful and melancholy.'

Perhaps the melancholy was prophetic. The story of the succeeding months of hardship and suffering, ending with his romantic escape from the islands, has passed from history to legend.

For Scotland it was the end of an epoch. Things were never the same again. The English had decimated the Highlanders at Culloden with modern firepower, intelligently used. As at Crécy and Agincourt the newer, more powerful factor won. The English could not afford further scuffles; nor, least of all, could Scotland. Having committed herself to the Union of 1707 she had to make it work, or founder.

The English Government broke finally the power of the Highland clans and abolished feudalism for good. They established Lowland customs and farming methods farther north, but the Highlands could not support their population and in the 1750s the trek to the New World became a flood. Some returned, their fortunes won, and invested their money in the old country. More stayed to people the U.S.A. and Canada.

One brilliant scheme of the English, under Pitt, was to harness the fighting power and spirit of the Highlander by creating the Highland regiments. In war after war, for Scotland and Empire, they amassed fame and glory.

The 1750s brought peace to the glens, which were gradually being turned into sheep runs; but the English Government determined never again to be held at pistol-point by the Scots. They completed the building of a line of forts along the Caledonian Canal with its flanking lochs: Fort William at the southern end, under the screes of Ben Nevis; Fort Augustus (built earlier) in the centre; and, at the top, near Culloden and the Moray Firth, Fort George. As master mason of Scotland, this project was one of William Adam's chief tasks; it was completed by his sons John, Robert and James.

William Adam died on 24th June 1748 at the age of fifty-nine after spending a full, rich life as architect, family man and citizen. Though not the innovator that his second son was to become, he broke new ground in Scotland both in his architecture and in his pattern of life at home. These factors contributed to the richness of background which his sons received from him. Their father's architecture was their starting point, and it gave them, in the Scotland of their day, a head start over their colleagues. William's 'open house', his varied circle of friends – artists, poets, writers, historians, politicians, economists – joined him and his wife in stimulating discussion on topics of the day. The children learnt from this early in life, absorbing, questioning, listening and, as they grew up, taking part. They took for granted this background of intellectual vitality, which was not the general rule at that time and in such families.

William's gifts to Robert were important, but there is an immeasurable gap between an intellectually vigorous personality such as William possessed and the quality of genius which was his son's. This quality appears in some families, here and there, running as a thread but appearing seldom on the surface fabric of their history. There was nothing in William's work to compare with Robert's brilliance. There was even less in that of the other sons. With Robert's continuing stimulus, James could work well. When it was absent, as on his tour in Italy or after Robert died, James seemed unable to accomplish or complete anything. It seems virtually certain that without Robert there would have been no 'Adam brothers' in the architectural history books, and it is doubtful whether the work of John, James and William would have approached the standard of their father's. They worked well, they were competent, they made a good team under Robert's leadership. That is all.

William Adam was buried in Greyfriars Churchyard in Edinburgh. An inscription on his large mausoleum states that it was erected in 1750 by his son John who, with his wife Jean and his mother Mary, are also buried there. The mausoleum is of plain, solid classical design in stone; the Doric order used only in the entablature without architrave. Robert made a drawing of the scene in the churchyard showing this mausoleum in the foreground. There are no other monuments shown and behind the containing wall is indicated Heriot's hospital and the castle (Soane Museum). It is not certain whether the design was John's or Robert's or a joint affair. Next to it is another, to the Robertson family from whom Mrs Adam came. The monument is to Dr William Robertson (1721–93), Robert's cousin, who was at university with him and later became its renowned principal.

Mary Adam, Robert's mother, was about ten years younger than her husband and outlived him by many years. She died in 1761 when James was in Italy. Little is known about her except that she seems to have been a good wife and affectionate mother who brought up her children sensibly, taking a great interest in all their doings. The beautiful portrait of her at Blair Adam, painted by Allan Ramsay (son of Allan Ramsay the poet who was a close friend of her husband), shows her at about fifty years of age, a pleasant woman with a strong, firm character (Plate 3).

It is certain that she was bound by close ties of affection with all her children. The whole family were unusually devoted to one another, and this seems to have been especially so after William Adam's death in 1748. At that time John was twenty-seven and William ten, the other children ranging in between. John married, and so did two of his sisters: Susan (or Susannah) to John Clerk, author and artist and son of Sir John Clerk; Mary to John Drysdale. The others remained single and, even more surprisingly, lived mainly together. They all lived at home with Mrs Adam till Robert returned from Italy, at the age of thirty, and set up practice in London. Then, as ever after in their lives, when Robert moved the others went too; Margaret and Elizabeth to look after his household, James and William to join the firm. The other daughters and their mother stayed in Scotland, but paid frequent visits to London. For all of their lives the family stayed close to one another and, judging from their letters, were ever affectionate, close and uncritical, if joking, with one another.

Various contemporaries and friends commented on this unusual bond which held them all, but no one seems to have found a reason why so few of them broke away from this tightly knit circle to marry and start families of their own. It has been suggested that it was Mrs Adam's strong hold over them which kept them single and at her side. Reading Robert's and James's letters from Italy, this does not sound likely. They just seemed to prefer life together.

There was a strong physical resemblance, at least in the males of the family. No portraits exist of the daughters, but in those of William, their father, John, James (Plates 2, 5, 4, 1) and Robert this is clearly noticeable. Even discounting the effect of wearing a wig, which gives a similarity to the forehead and hides the ears, both nose and mouth are distinctive, and William's portrait, painted when he was about forty-five, and Robert's, at a year or so older, show remarkable similarity of features.

Confusion arises because the family sometimes spelt their surname 'Adam' and on other occasions 'Adams'. William did this, and so did his sons at first. After the age of about twenty-five Robert seems to have dropped the 's' and the others followed suit. At the end of the nineteenth century there was a vogue for calling him 'Robert Adams', but this died again after the First World War.

Once the Adam firm was established we hear much less of John that of the other brothers. He was considerably older, having been born in 1721, and he went to work with his father, with whom he was very close, while the others were at school and university. On his father's death he was appointed Master Mason to the Board of Ordnance in his place and, from 1750, spent a number of years in the construction and fortifying of Fort George on the Moray Firth. He carried on the family business in Edinburgh all his life. He was a partner in the firm of Adam Bros., but his name rarely appears in documents and records. Like his father, he was an astute business man and developed wide interests in Scottish undertakings such as, for example, the Carron Iron and Steel Company (Plate 5).

As the eldest son, John inherited the estate at Blair-Adam and became its laird. He married Jean Ramsay in 1750, raised a family and was devoted to them as well as to the estate, which now covered 3,922 Scots acres. It was his pride, and he spent much of his time laying out and developing it. By the 1780s it had four and a half acres of garden in lawns, paths and flower beds, terraces of shrubberies and fruit trees, five hundred acres of sheep pasture, and the rest in woods and arable land.[7] Strangely enough, the Adam family never seemed to get round to building an 'Adam style' house for themselves. Robert designed one in 1772 (rough plans and layout are in the Soane Museum), but it was never built.

In architecture John's work was rather like his father's, bearing in mind the changes in fashion in succeeding years to which he responded. He designed a number of schemes in Edinburgh, which include the Exchange (1753–60) and work on the original North Bridge (1772). The Exchange façade (High Street) is still there, but since the building has now been swallowed up in the larger City Chambers it is now the existing main elevation inside the courtyard, and flanking wings on a similar theme have been added.

It is not certain whether James, the third son, was born two or four years after Robert. He was a more light-hearted, gay personality. He is reported to have been pleasant, well-informed and cheerful as a young man. He had many ideas, was intelligent and lively, but lacked the application and determination which drove Robert. He became a neat, capable draughtsman and an ideal second-in-command of the family firm. Under Robert's guidance he was reliable and hard-working. When this was removed he became more dilettante, in both senses of the word. He found it hard to concentrate or to get things done on his own; time seemed to vanish or be frittered away, but he was certainly a genuine lover of the arts, of beautiful things, and had a wide and scholarly knowledge of their history and evolution (Plate 4).

We hear little of William Adam, junior. He was ten years younger than Robert and joined the family firm some time after Robert's establishment in London. Apparently he designed some buildings, but there exists little data about them. His main function seems to have been to act as business adviser and accountant. Many of the business dealings and patents are in his name.

The interruption to Robert's university career caused by the '45 was permanent. He never returned to the university and did not graduate. In the winter of 1745 he was taken ill, a malady of a feverish nature which lasted for some time. When he recovered, in the spring of 1746, his father requested his services and he followed John as his father's assistant. It was not at all unusual in the eighteenth century not to graduate. Education was regarded as a means not an end. It provided a background, a fertile soil in which the youngster would later implant the experiences of life. An ordinary bachelor's degree was not thought important, as it is now, despite the few students taking it. It was what a man accomplished in life – his architecture, his painting, his written work, his political achievement, his scientific discovery – which mattered, not a paper qualification showing that he had reached an adequate standard in absorbing study given to him.

We know little at first hand of the Robert of 1746. Those who met him at home thought him charming, friendly, deferential to his elders and particularly intelligent in his reactions. He does not seem to have shown any special interest in architecture. He liked to draw in pencil and pen and wash. His compositions were romantic landscapes with dramatic lighting, rivers and lakes, ruined castles and dark trees. The medieval seemed to fascinate him much more than the classical.

After his father's death he lived at home with the family, all eleven of them – his mother, his brothers John, James, William, his sisters Jenny, Elizabeth, Margaret, Mary, Susan and Nell. He made a number of friends in this family circle, all Scots, and all of whom proved to be lifelong attachments.

His generation was a gifted one, and his friends were an illustration of this. They included Dr Alexander Carlyle, the minister at Inveresk, whose autobiography gives us much interesting background of the Adam family and their period. Carlyle was a moderate and, as such, in opposition to the Kirk of his day. His broad-mindedness caused difficulties for him, but he surmounted them and was well beloved by his parishioners and friends. There was William Robertson, Robert's cousin, also a son of the manse, who became Principal of Edinburgh University. A scholarly man, he established an international reputation for his publications, especially his *History of Scotland* and his *History of Charles V*. David Hume, philosopher, historian and political economist, was another of the group. He suffered ill-health, but had a volatile personality which made light of it. He affected atheism, for he hated the hypocrisy and cant of the contemporary, Puritan Scottish Kirk. He was certainly a sceptic and a man of honest thought and feeling, but he did not try to impose his views on his friends and colleagues. He published his theories in the *Treatise of Human Nature* and the later *History of England*. Latterly he became obsessed with the conviction that there was an English conspiracy to destroy everything Scottish. His *History of England* reflects this attitude, but its value is undeniable. Adam Ferguson, philosopher and historian, became Professor of Natural Philosophy at Edinburgh University. He was an intellectual, a Scottish Nationalist, a man of balanced, worldly opinions. Some of his ideas are unusual, most were original, and he led a number of groups of theorists. He published several treatises on society, both contemporary and that of ancient Rome. John Home was a charmer, elegant, good-looking, and a cultivated, highly intelligent man. He wrote plays, one of which – *Douglas* – later became popular despite the general antipathy to Scots. For some time he was Lord Bute's private secretary, and before this he was tutor to the Prince of Wales (later George III).

William Adam when he died left most of his wealth and his estate to John. To Robert he gave Dowhill Castle, former seat of the earls of Crawford. The castle had two circular turrets in a ruinous state, and its site measured about 78 feet by 27 feet. The estimated value was not great, but Robert soon acquired some further assets. He joined John at Fort George where the government contracts brought fair profits. He worked there in the summers from 1750 to 1754, and at the same time was able to continue the architectural studies in which he had become interested. He also learnt the fundamentals of building and construction. The work at Fort George was in masonry on a difficult subsoil. It was excellent training for him.

Robert took at least one trip south in those years. He briefly visited London with John Home and thence travelled on horseback in various parts of England. Few of his drawings from this journey exist, but they show his special interest in things medieval (at Winchester, for example) and his feeling for landscape, settings and fundamental construction. Gothic buildings of Decorated and Perpendicular style barely existed in Scotland, and this was exciting new ground. He also visited Palladian houses like Inigo Jones' Wilton, and the Baroque appealed to him. He found it too heavy, but was stimulated by its power and plasticity.

Robert's letters home, sent weekly from Fort George, are gossipy, family letters, well written but not of special interest after two hundred years. James joined him, and the two brothers forged close links. They were very different personalities, the one serious, the other gay, but they complemented one another and they were of an age. John, so much older, married, with a family, seemed worlds apart from a couple of twenty- to twenty-five-year-olds. Robert's closeness to James, established here, never faltered or wavered during the remainder of their lives.

It was also in the years 1750–4 that Robert, with John and James, began work in earnest on architectural commissions, and it is interesting to compare those designs with what he produced on his return from Italy. At this time Robert had very little experience. It was based entirely on what he had learnt from his father, what he had seen in a short tour in England and what he had read. It resembles William Adam's work, but is more advanced and much more lively and sophisticated.

At Hopetoun House the brothers were asked to decorate the state rooms. The designs were Robert's and the two drawing-rooms here have been little altered. Called the yellow and red drawing-rooms respectively, after the predominating colour in each case of the wall hangings, they typify his deep desire to get away from Palladian interior decoration, but also show how he was hampered by his limited knowledge and experience of anything else.

Both rooms are large and well proportioned. The general colour scheme, apart from the red and yellow material, is white with a restrained use of gilt on the enrichments. Quality materials have been used and there is a great deal of fine, classical wood-carving in the doorcases and doors, skirting and window-frames. All of these are also white with gilt enrichment. Robert's later preference for polished mahogany doors had not yet shown itself. The ceilings are deeply coved and richly ornamented in high-relief stucco, rococo in form. Below, there is a frieze and heavy cornice. The mantelpieces are entirely in white marble; a simple one in the yellow drawing-room, but the other has a more elaborate design with supporting caryatid figures at the sides, by Michael Rysbrack (Plate 9). The furniture is chiefly good, solid, mid-Georgian mahogany with floral-pattern silk-covered upholstery to match the walls. There are also a number of gilded, carved pieces, especially lamp standards.

The total impression is of two homogeneously designed rooms of good quality workmanship in all media and of the beginnings of a break away from Gibbs and Kent.

Dumfries House in Ayrshire was built by Adam in 1754 for the Earl of Dumfries. Now one of the seats of his descendant the Marquess of Bute, it still presents a characteristic picture of Robert's work at this time. The exterior and the state rooms have been scarcely touched. It is a simple house outside, and a little dull. There is the traditional three-storeyed central block and two side pavilions connected by lower ranges to the centre. An unoriginal Palladian layout in good taste.

Inside there are three main rooms, two drawing-rooms and a dining-room, which show more of Roman grandeur than Hopetoun. They are more serious and classical in the cornices, door-frames, window-frames and picture-frames, which are all of a piece in one scheme. The ceiling stucco is in high relief and, here, rococo has

broken through Roman gravity. Swags of fruit and flowers pre-
dominate. The ceilings are flat except the one in the dining-room,
which is deeply coved. The whole scheme is all white, even more
than Hopetoun: ceilings, walls, doorcases and window-frames. Gilt
has been used a little, especially in the dining-room, but very
sparingly. The furniture was not designed by Adam, but he ordered
it specially and most of it is Chippendale. It includes sofas and chairs
in mahogany with silk flowered upholstery covering and beautiful
mirrors with gilded, carved frames.

To step into these rooms is like entering a past age, so little has
anything been changed. Fundamentally it is Palladian, with a dash of
rococo and also of Robert.

Later in the summer of 1754 Robert heard from the Hon. Charles
Hope that he definitely planned to make the Grand Tour, starting
that autumn, and that Lord Hopetoun, his elder brother, had
suggested that Robert should accompany him, paying his own
expenses. Robert had been hoping for this and was prepared. It
would help him socially to travel with the aristocracy and it would
also assist in his travelling costs. His five thousand pounds[8] was put by
ready for this, and he was prepared to spend every penny on this
investment for his future.

NOTES

1 It will be seen how the Adam family repeats the use of John and
William as Christian names. This is because of the Scottish custom
of calling the eldest son after his grandfather.

2 Arthur T. Bolton, 'The Architecture of Robert and James Adam',
Country Life, 1922.

3 G. M. Trevelyan, *Illustrated English Social History*, vol. III, *The
Eighteenth Century*, p. 138, Longmans, Green and Co., 1952.

4 Not to be confused with the Royal High School, a Greek Revival
building situated on the A.1 road on the slopes of Calton Hill.

5 Next to St Andrew's House in Regent Road (Fig. 6).

6 G. M. Trevelyan, *History of England*, pp. 521–2, Longmans, Green
and Co., 1948.

7 Sadly, the passage of time has not been kind to Blair Adam. John's descendant, the present laird, owns a much smaller estate which, despite his protests, is now being bisected by the motorway from the Forth road bridge to Perth. The road runs within 200 feet of the house itself.

8 See page 75.

2. CHANCE OF A LIFETIME

THE coach was on its way to Dover. Robert was at last starting out on that journey for which he had been working and saving ever since he had begun to assist in his father's office. From that time stemmed the dreams and the ambitions. They had slowly grown, culminating in the determination to go and see for himself. He had become more and more certain that, if only he could study the 'real thing', the buildings of the ancient classical civilization *in situ*, he might prove what he had begun to suspect, namely that the modern classical framework was too rigid and too limited; that the ancient work was richer, full of exciting possibilities for using it and adapting it to buildings of the second half of the eighteenth century in England. He was sure that if he could study for some time at this fount of classicism he could produce something new, something personally Robert Adam.

Whilst the heavy vehicle rumbled its slow way along in the autumn sunshine, Robert's thoughts ran ahead to what the next few weeks might bring. They were lucky that it had not rained for a few days. After all, October can be a wet month. When it rained heavily the pot-holes filled with water and the mud churned up by the coaches could let the wheels sink up to their axle hubs. In those conditions vehicles could easily overturn. Robert was not nervous of danger or mishap for its own sake. He was a fit young man and did not easily frighten. But impatience and excitement bubbled within him. Beneath his grave, controlled exterior he was a romantic, sensitive, mercurial, full of life. He wanted to get there, to reach the Channel, to cross the sea to Calais, to France, to the continent of Europe.

As a young man of twenty-six, intelligent, well read and of a prosperous middle-class family, with hardly any experience of life outside Scotland – even England was largely foreign to him – he was now going for three and a half years to live on the Continent. He had read so much about these countries he was going to see that they seemed real to him.

He had plenty of time to dream as the journey progressed. Getting about was a slow business in 1754, even if one travelled in the more gentlemanly style by post-chaise. Roads had been improving since the early eighteenth century, at which time they were a disgrace and no one who could avoid it travelled at all. Each parish was supposed to maintain its own roads, and for years nothing had been done. The Turnpike Acts slowly altered the situation. Turnpike Trusts were formed which were empowered to levy tolls on roads built and maintained. By 1750 usable roads linked larger towns, and the London–Dover route was one of these. There was still no proper surfacing by modern standards (John Macadam was yet in the future), but the road was maintained. October was, of course, a difficult time and could mean that a wheeled vehicle became stuck – and a sitting target for the ubiquitous highwayman.

Stagecoaches were now running on main routes between fixed stops, which were generally inns. If one had the money one could hire a post-chaise. Both vehicles would go the full distance, but changed horses every few miles. The stagecoach, pulled by two or four horses, was a ponderous vehicle, bumping up and down incessantly. It had seats for six passengers inside but none outside, though those who could not afford interior seating were allowed, at their own risk, to cling to the roof luggage. An armed guard was a necessary precaution, for stagecoaches at this time were still slow vehicles. The post-chaise was lighter and faster. It held two people, or possibly three. Since you had hired the vehicle, you travelled with the person of your choice and did not pick up passengers *en route*. You were also able to choose your own inns for overnight stops, providing of course that the vehicle did not meet with an accident or breakdown, which it often did.

The journey from London to Dover therefore was a long one, but Robert was happy, his thoughts full of seeing Florence and Rome, and visiting Paris. Perhaps, if only he had enough money and the opportunity came, he could get to Athens, then the Mecca for serious classical travellers. Perhaps he might follow in Stuart and Revett's footsteps, studying the Parthenon and Erechtheion on the Acropolis hill. He might even go, like Robert Wood, to Palmyra or Baalbec. He turned to James beside him, younger and even more excited, and they planned together.

James was not going on the Grand Tour, not yet, but he had come with Robert from Scotland and was intending to take the opportunity on the Continent to spend a short while studying in Belgium and Holland. Then he would return home to carry on the family business with John while Robert was away.

They had left Edinburgh on 3rd October with their manservant Donald, and arrived in London on the 10th. This was a long time to be on the road, but it was an improvement upon thirty years earlier, when even a post-chaise would take three weeks to do the four-hundred-mile journey. On the other hand, James Boswell [1] tells us that in 1762 he did the trip in under five days, spending the nights at Berwick, Durham, Doncaster and Biggleswade. He averaged nearly a hundred miles a day and the cost was eleven pounds.

Reaching London, Robert and James met some Scottish friends at the Exchange and went to eat at a chop-house. These were places where one would go for a quick meal, good quality but no frills. If wanting fuller service or to linger over a meal one would go to a tavern and could have a private room. According to Dr Johnson, taverns varied in standard from the ultra-respectable 'Mitre' in Fleet Street, where a gentleman and his lady must both dress correctly, to less particular ones where 'the waiters are in league with the wenches'.

But Robert and James had no time to spare that day. They had to find somewhere to stay, for they wanted to spend a week or so in London, and hotels were few and costly. Visitors usually stayed with friends or relations, or found lodgings in a private house. The Adam brothers had a little difficulty, but they finally got fixed up with a bedroom and sitting-room each near the Strand.

Indefatigable tourists, they crammed full the hours they spent in the city. They went to St Paul's, duly 'whispered' in the gallery, toured the city churches, saw the Mansion House (still not quite complete) and the Horse Guards (also not yet quite finished) and took in Westminster Abbey. They were both enchanted and thrilled.

They had never seen a city so large, so bustling and so clean, with so many great buildings. Wren's work in the rebuilding of London after the Great Fire stimulated them. They enjoyed a trip to Windsor, they met some of their friends and spent evenings over a meal and some wine. They visited coffee-houses, discussing the topics of the day and reading the newspapers. It was all new and cosmopolitan. As young men out in town on their first proper visit, they were intrigued also by the clothes fashionable people wore. They visited the tailors for themselves to make sure that they, too, were up to date before representing Britain on the Continent.

Robert and James crossed to Calais by packet boat on 28th October. It was a stormy time of year and, dependent on wind and weather, the length of the passage was more variable than now. James, in a letter to his sister Nelly from Rotterdam on 19th November, is replying to her fears that the two brothers, far from home and enjoying themselves, would get bored with reading her dull, domestic news. He explains how both he and Bob long to hear from home and asks if she imagined that they had left all their affection in Britain or 'that in my passage betwixt Dover and Calais I had thrown up my feelings along with my Breakfast'. In the same letter James is discussing his expected return route and says that he will cross from Hellvoetsluys (Hellevoetsluis) to Harwich 'as 'tis impossible for me to think of going by Calais at this season when the Roads are so deep besides that I apprehended no danger from the passage here as there is no instance of a packet Boats' being lost and, 'tis but 16 hours passage'. The present crossing, now from the Hook to Harwich, is a seven-hour trip.

The brothers visited Dunkirk and Ostend, travelled by boat up the canals to Bruges and thence to Brussels, where they were by 4th November when Robert wrote home: 'On Saturday at 6 at Night Jamie and I and our Two Valets arrived at the famous City of Brussels, where we found Mr Hope [the Hon. Charles Hope] who had been here for seven days before us. But as he had many acquaintances, Prince Charles of Lorrain's Court and other amusements, he had not wearied. But was extreamly glad to see us safely arrived.'

Robert and James stayed a few days in Brussels. They had a gay, fully occupied time. They were accepted by the aristocracy as Charles Hope's friends and made to feel welcome. They went to dances (masquerades), dinner parties, breakfast parties and met a number of people. Robert only bewails that his friend Stevenson's warnings had been timely. 'Much discourse passed during our repast, without our understanding one word that was said,' and, again; 'We went to the play last night and had the pleasure to see extreme fine action, But the grief not to know one word of a Million.'

Despite these drawbacks, two charming young men found means of communication and enjoyed their visit enormously. Robert's serious approach to what he had come for shows through in all his letters, as does also his careful assessment of his finances. He managed, though, to keep a balance between these thoughts and living gaily and to the full each joyous hour. For example, 'Every moment of spare time is employ'd in seeing the Churches, Paintings, Palaces and Curiosities of this City, among which the Tapestrys are remarkable.' 'Jamie and I have each bought a Suit of Ruffles of the Lace here, mine cost £6 and Jamie's £4.' Carried away by the beauty of the lacework he buys presents for his sisters too, then stops, characteristically, when he finds it a costly business. 'You can't buy anything for a Lady under £10 or £12.' He promises to buy more things later in the 'Expedition' when he sees how the money lasts. He visits a local sculptor's studio where he sees 'many models of Figures and Bas-Reliefs in Clay that I should like to buy if they cou'd be convey'd home'. A perennial problem to Robert for the next three and a half years. So much beautiful work. Could he afford it? and could he get it home? He achieved a great deal in this direction.

They continued their way to Tournay (Tournai), with more gaiety and hospitality, and then to Lille, where James left Robert and Charles Hope to make his own way back through Holland. Robert explained: 'He [James] is also to see Antwerp which I find I can't see till my return from Italy, affairs forbid it, as you will see by looking at the map of the Country, where you will find it is going fifteen or 16 leagues back and to return here again, which our present time won't allow of.' He also reassured his mother, who had been worrying about crossing the Alpine range: 'It is now past the season of going over the Alps so . . . we must go to Antibes from that to Genoa by water. But we have not in all above 24 or 25 hours sailing, and that all along the Coast of the Mediterranean.'

By 12th November Robert and Charles Hope had arrived in Paris, where they stayed for the rest of the month. Even the conscientious Robert could not resist the fashions of the French capital. Both young men bought complete outfits of velvet and satin in pastel shades and vivid hues, their Brussels lace foaming at neck and wrists and powder on their wigs. Lowland Puritan Scotland had gone overboard at last.

They were disappointed in the French. After their friendly welcome in Belgium they could not understand the coldness which they met with in France from the formal aristocracy of the Court of Louis Quinze. Many another Britisher in latter-day France has felt the same. Robert made a few successful contacts. He was introduced to Mr Collins, painter to the king, whom he describes as a 'prodigious Conoisseur in painting'. This led to a further introduction to M. Portail, King's Painter at Versailles, and access to some fine collections of paintings.

Meanwhile James had regretfully left the other two and set off homewards. He travelled to Antwerp via Menin and Courtray (Courtrai) and stayed to study churches and paintings. He was very moved by Rubens' 'Descent from the Cross' and fervently wished that Johnie or Bob were there to share the experience with him. He travelled on to Rotterdam via Delft, Leyden and Haarlem to Amsterdam. From there he proposed to set out for the coast for a boat home.

After a few weeks of 'doing the town', visiting restaurants, opera, theatre and seeing the churches and palaces and other works of art, the other two set out on their journey to Italy. As Robert had already told his mother, in winter the Alps were impassable to wheeled traffic and the route was down the Rhône valley (almost exactly the line of the present-day Route Nationale 7), then by boat to Genoa.

En route they called at Dijon, Lyons, Montpelier, Nîmes, Aix-en-Provence, Marseilles, Toulon and Nice, from where they embarked for Italy. Some of these places were little trips, which they made off the direct run mainly because Robert was so keen to see the great Roman engineering remains. One of the high spots for Robert was Lyons, which he thought a beautiful town both for its setting and for its buildings. He writes on 5th December to his sister Elizabeth:

'Lyons is one of the most Romantick Citys I ever beheld situated on a neck of land between two Rivers the Soane [Saône] and the Roane [Rhône] which join here and proceed down to the Mediterranean.' He then gives a little instruction in geography to his sisters on the courses of French rivers and exhorts them (as he often does) to study their maps so that they will know what he is doing. He continues: 'High hills, which form the suburbs of the Town are covered with Convents, Churches and Houses to the very top. The many publick and Spacious Buildings, Gothick and Modern, its romantick Rocks, Trees, Bridges and Spires form a scene which would delight and even charm one that has no taste for Landscape.'

As in Brussels and Paris, Robert once again falls victim to the beautiful fabrics and elegant clothes. This time it is the silks which he covets. Encouraged by Hope, he has a spending spree. 'I have bought here a Gold Stuff Vest [2] which I verily believe in London would cost 16 or 18 pounds but here does not amount to above 1/3^d of that sum. I am also getting one of the Genteelest and richest embroider'd Vests that I ever saw which will cost me at least £14 or 15 Sterling. But there was no help for it as Hope thought I could not do without them and he had shown me an example by taking 3 of much the same kinds with mine. His embroidery is in Silver, narrow, mine in Gold and Broad. Both upon rich, rich, vast rich thick silks of a Red colour.' Robert continues his glowing descriptions of these beautiful vests, then endeavours to justify his lapse of carefulness: 'At Genoa we both propose taking Black Velvet Suits with which we can wear all our waistcoats by turns, and we will probably take for common forenoon, uncutt velvet suits, quite plain.'

Then a cry from the heart: 'My Teeth water'd after some of the prettyest things for Ladys which I saw in Shops in this Town. Head caps, Breasts for covering the Stays [3] of Gold and Silver, and Mon Dieu, magnifique, and of the best Taste imaginable. But I could find no way of transporting them.'

Tearing themselves away from the shops, they visited 'a Roman Acqueduct which convey'd the water to the Town from above 8 Leagues. In many places it was so entire that I number'd a Hundred Arches all in a straight line'. Robert was most impressed. He described the construction as 'magnificent' and 'stupendous'. They moved south on 9th December and, travelling via St Vallier, Montélimar, Pont St Esprit and Remoulins, they arrived at Nîmes on the 12th. While there they took a trip to Montpelier and also to the Pont du Gard. Robert's interest in these places, as well as in Nîmes itself, was for the remains of Roman architecture, and he was especially impressed, as are present-day visitors, by the great engineering structures of aqueducts and amphitheatres.

They had also a gay time at Nîmes, being introduced to the Duke of Richelieu and other members of the aristocracy with whom they dined and danced. Robert seems to have been more courageous or, perhaps, rash than his companion. 'No sooner were we enter'd the Ballroom but I found Hope had been press'd to dance, but would not. I was immediately sett on and immediately comply'd. I had Madam herself for a partner with whom I tript my Minuet. I was desired by her to take out The Intendant's Lady who is one of the greatest in the Town, with her I danc'd my Second, was much press'd to dance a Country Dance, but I found them so difficult that I wish not consent'd.'

Robert found the preoccupation of the French aristocracy with gaming rather boring (though the English were much the same at this time) and says that it went on till four or five in the morning, but that he and Hope retired about twelve; they had enjoyed themselves, but had had enough.

From Nîmes they started on the route to Aix via Arles. It was a secondary road and very bad and their horses were also poor, so they had to turn back and retreat as far as Remoulins, cross the river to Avignon, where they spent a few hours, and then go on to Aix-en-Provence, which they reached on 21st December. Robert commented happily that the weather was as warm as a May day in Scotland and said how thrilled he was by the fertility and interest of the countryside (so different from his native land), planted with acres of olive trees and bordered by evergreen oaks and clumps of cypresses. The hills were covered, he says, 'with Boxwood, Junipers, Rosemary and Vineyards here and there up to the very tops of them. The verdure on the ground was as fine as on Barefoots parks in the Spring, and the wheat was so strong and thick that they were cutting it in many places to give to their cattle to prevent it growing too hard. Thus did we travel 2–3 hundred miles in this

1   *Robert Adam, artist unknown, c. 1770.*

National Portrait Gallery, London

Above, left to right

2   *William Adam* (senior). *Blair-Adam*

3   *Mary Adam by Allan Ramsay, 1748–50, Blair-Adam*

4   *James Adam by Allan Ramsay, 1754*

5   *John Adam by Francis Cotes. Blair-Adam*

Opposite

6   *Robert Adam. Plaque by James Tassie, c. 1792*

7   *Robert Adam by Laurent Pêcheux. On ivory. Blair-Adam*

8   *The Admiralty Screen, Whitehall, London*

Opposite

9   *Fireplace (Michael Rysbrack), Red Drawing-room,*
Hopetoun House

10   *Plate from Adam's book on the Palace of Diocletian at Split, showing the town and harbour from the south-west*

11   *Chimneypiece, drawing-room, Hatchlands, Surrey*

12   *Ante-room, Syon House, Middlesex*

paradisical land whose chief Beauty is in this Season, as Summer scorches it up and makes everything Brown. We have eat Grapes the whole way and are now in the land of Almonds, Olives and Figues which we have for our desert at every Male.'

His womenfolk are obviously getting anxious again about the dangers of the proposed Mediterranean sea trip. Robert reassures his sister: 'We go in water so shallow that no pirate can come within reach of us. Besides that every body assures us they never come within 200 miles of where we sail. If the least blast of wind comes we can land in a few minutes at any place on the shoar and at any rate we go ashore and sleep all night in a publick house.' After further assurance Robert tells his family that they are bound to be all right because General Paterson commands the galleys at Nice and will be sure to give them one to take them to Genoa.

They travelled on to Marseilles, Toulon, Fréjus, Antibes and Nice, enjoying further hospitality as they went. On 3rd January 1755 they arranged their transport to Genoa. In his letter to his mother, written from Nice on that day, Robert says: 'We have engaged our Felucca or Vessel . . . which rows with twelve men and we propose leaving this on Sunday morning to have the prayers of the Godly. It is at present charming weather and if it continues we shall have a very pleasant saill, and are assured we will not be above 24 hours on the water and consequently but one night ashore, by the way. We have provided ourselves with some charming wine, some cold roasted fowls and some Bread for Eatables and drinkables. And in case our Bedding should not be good that night we sleep ashore I bought a pair of excellent sheets at Lyons and have just now purchas'd a pair of charming Blankets, while with the assistance of my Furr Coat, Furr Boots etc. will bid defiance to the coldest air.' Robert was obviously covering all contingencies for the Italian winter and the Mediterranean Sea. He goes on to assure his family that the dangers are negligible, and it would appear that he is suffering some apprehension over the idea of this trip.

They reached Genoa safely by 9th January, but the weather was bad, very cold and rainy. They had to stay in the city, storm-bound, till the 18th when they set sail again south-eastwards. The sea was now flat calm with a mist hanging low, so that the felucca had to be rowed all day long, and the only place that they could discern on the nearby Mediterranean coast was Sestri. Charles Hope was relieved at the lack of wind, for he had been very sea-sick on the first leg of their trip. Robert commented rather unkindly that he thought fear was at the bottom of this. However, they met no pirates or other hazards; they hugged the shore all the way and arrived safely at Lerici on the 19th. The following morning they were off in their chaise, hugging themselves against the bitter cold, but enjoying the beautiful countryside. They passed Viareggio and went on to Pisa on 21st January.

Robert's impressions of the city were distinctly overcast by the extremely cold weather which froze the Arno, and all the vegetation on both banks stood up spiky and steel hard. He says that he was never so bitterly and diabolically cold in Scotland as he was in Pisa. Perhaps this also impaired his judgment of the great Piazza dei Miracoli, for his summing-up of Pisa architecturally was 'there is nothing remarkable except the famous Tower which is a Horrible but a most astonishing object. It leans over so much that you can't help thinking it is to tumble down every moment, and gives you a sensation not at all pleasing'. He admits, though, that he returned for a more minute study on several occasions and found that it grew on him.

They go on to Leghorn (Livorno) and arrive on 30th January in Florence, where they propose to spend a few weeks. Here they resume their gay social life and Robert only regrets his inability to converse in Italian. His attempts to do so, mixed with broken French and English, cause amusement to the Italians, and Robert remarks that he does not mind being laughed at so long as it is his linguistic powers and not himself which arouse the mirth.

The mountains are snow covered; the River Arno is still frozen hard from bank to bank and they go skating, when they meet the English sculptor Joseph Wilton and become friendly with him.

Robert and Charles Hope often go to the opera and are very intrigued to see one evening 'a very pretty Girl dress'd in Masquerade'. The girl seems to know everyone and, when she pulls her mask from her face, Robert notes, 'the agreable Features to any I have seen whilst, and prodigious delicate shape and thorough bred manner made us cock our Ears, and make enquiry about her'. They discover that she is a member of the Medici family named Maria and now married to Signor Gianni, a customs officer. They are duly impressed, and they meet her on a number of occasions, but Robert is most frustrated while the lady speaks rapid Italian and Hope converses ably with her. Robert says sadly: 'I cou'd say nothing. Think how I curs'd Italian and all foreign languages.' He does his best in broken French, eventually finds an interpreter at the opera and then gets on like a house on fire.

There are a number of occasions during Robert's three-year stay in Italy when he describes such elegant, beautiful women who have attracted him, but they all seem to be *Signore*, never *Signorine*. Invariably he appears to behave in a courtly, gentlemanly manner. The affair goes no further, at least as far as his letters to his family suggest.

Apart from meeting Wilton and one or two other interesting contacts, it was in Florence that Robert made Clérisseau's acquaintance, which proved to be an important happening in his life. In Robert's words: 'I have also got acquainted with one Clérisseau who draws in Architecture delightfully in the free manner I wanted. I hope to reap some Instruction from him. Chambers, whom Jamie knows of, owes all his Hints and Notions to this Man with whom he has differ'd and to whom he has behaved ingratefully.' This was William (later Sir William) Chambers (1723–96), Adam's contemporary and lifelong rival.

Charles-Louis Clérisseau, a Frenchman, was born in 1721 or 1722 and lived to be nearly one hundred years old. He had studied architecture at the Académie in Paris under Blondel and had lived in Rome for some years after winning the Prix de Rome in 1746. He studied there under Pannini and was one of his outstanding students. Clérisseau was a difficult personality to get on with, prickly, resentful of authority, not always scrupulously honest in academic affairs and of strongly individual temperament. He was taken up by Chambers and other artists, but when his scholarship ended in 1754 he went to Florence and there met Robert. The meeting was as important to Clérisseau as it was to Robert. His work by then had diverged from Pannini's teaching, though still owing much to it, and Clérisseau had branched out into a freer, more individual style of portraying archaeological remains, which appealed so much to Robert. Certainly Clérisseau had the grounding necessary to teach

Robert architectural draughtsmanship, but he also possessed an artistic feeling in water-colour and pen-and-ink media, rather as Piranesi did of depicting the remains of ancient Rome correctly (in the archaeological sense) and dramatically. He interpreted rather than merely recorded and in so doing expressed the essence of the work. It was this quality that Robert was after and wanted to learn.

In his letter to his sister Elizabeth on 13th February, Robert describes the Carnival Festival which has raged in Florence for many days. He says that it started quietly with the opera, a play or two and a ball, but worked up to a giddy climax, till everything in the city was involved and no one did any work at all. Both he and Hope joined in and seem to have thoroughly enjoyed and exhausted themselves. People were singing and dancing all night in the streets, then started again at ten o'clock next morning, with market stalls mingled with strolling, chatting people and gay songs everywhere. Robert says that the balls did not finish at their usual hour of eleven or twelve, but went on till four o'clock in the morning or sometimes till seven. He and Hope had danced two hundred minuets and three hundred country dances. He writes: 'You may perhaps be anxious to know who I could get to dance so many with and of what kind they were. To which I can give you no other answer than, that I danced with all the Greatest Quality and with some of the greatest Whores and with the Handsomest of both kinds whenever I could get at them.'

After the carnival Robert got down to work again in earnest. He started to survey the paintings and sculpture which he might buy, considering that they would be more usefully drawn and copied than work to be found in England, since they were more closely based on the antique. His enthusiasm grew and he became passionately interested and absorbed in his studies, his discussions with Wilton and Clérisseau, his perusal of portfolios of drawings, and his viewing of Renaissance masterpieces.

On 19th February he writes to James and, as always, these letters to his younger brother contain his thoughts, ideas and schemes for his career and his projects and studies. He assumes, probably correctly, that his sisters will be less appreciative of these subjects, and would rather hear about the country and the people and what he has been doing. He writes meticulously to each member of the family in turn, never missing anyone out, and presuming that they will all read each letter. He tells James that he is leaving for Rome the next day and discusses his impressions and future plans.

He explains the arrangement which he has made with Clérisseau, that he will pay for the Frenchman's board and expenses, that they will live in the same house and that Clérisseau will teach Robert the science of perspective drawing, knowledge of the antique, the craft of water-colour, and serve him as an antiquarian. Robert says of Clérisseau: 'There is the utmost knowledge of Architecture and Perspective and of Designing and Colouring that I ever saw, or had any Conception of. He rais'd my Ideas, he created emulation and fire in my Breast, I wish'd above all things to learn his manner and to have him with me at Rome, to study close with him and to purchase of his Works.'

Robert also speaks warmly of the sculptor Wilton and of his sincere, warm-hearted friendship and help. He mentions Cipriani,[4] whom he describes as 'the Best natur'd lad in the world who draws in the Most Delightful Manner imaginable, in the stiles of all the Great Masters, ingraves charmingly and is exceptionally modest'. Robert buys some of Cipriani's work and also purchases a wide selection of drawings by outstanding Italian artists. He rightly assumes that, though these might cost him a fair sum of money at the time, being originals, they would appreciate. Since his collection includes works from his favourite masters – Michelangelo, Raphael, Veronese, Correggio – it is clear that he knows what he is doing. He also buys a set of architectural detail drawings by Pietro da Cortona, which would appreciate and would prove valuable to him later when in practice. Robert proudly says that he acquired the whole collection for under £100; an achievement indeed.

He then goes on to explain a situation which has become a problem to him. He has, until now, been enjoying the gay social life to which he has been given the entrée because he was accompanying Charles Hope who had this as of right, being the brother of Lord Hopetoun. It is not only in the operas, dinners, balls and conversation that Robert has taken pleasure, but also in the knowledge that they represent the world of wealthy, aristocratic potential patrons; a world with which he knows he must be *au fait* and which he must impress if he is to establish himself as a fashionable architect. Hope has promised to introduce him to a number of such suitable people in Rome, like Cardinal Albani, the wealthy art collector, and Robert wishes to take advantage of this offer while he and Hope are still together. On the other hand, both Clérisseau and Wilton have impressed upon him that if he wishes to become *au fait* with the professional side of his work, and get the most out of his studies in Rome, he must follow in the path of all the other great classical architects since Brunelleschi and Inigo Jones and spend most of his time drawing, measuring and giving detailed study to the remains of antique buildings and ornament, as well as drawing Renaissance monuments.

One would imagine that it was not too difficult to do both these things and that a compromise would be possible. In the eighteenth century, however, especially in Italy and France, this was not so. Professional men, artists, architects, doctors and so on were inferior beings socially and not to be received on equal terms with the aristocracy who governed this social system. There was little difference in eighteenth-century eyes between an architect who designed the Palace of Schönbrunn or the Panthéon and a capable artisan who decorated a ceiling. Such people were important and necessary, and the ruling classes enjoyed employing them, but they did not entertain them in their drawing-rooms. Robert knew that 'if I am known in Rome to be an Architect, if I am seen drawing or with a pencil in my hand, I cannot enter into genteel company, who will not admitt an Artist, or if they do admitt him, will very probably rub affronts on him, in order to prevent his appearing at their Card playing, Balls or Concerts'.

What should he do? Robert was very much at the crossroads of decision. If he did as Wilton and Clérisseau advised he would lose Hope's entrée into society. If he took up Hope's offer he would lose time and Clérisseau's teaching. Eventually he decided to follow Wilton's advice. Robert writes: 'Mr Wilton, who interests himself much in my affairs . . . says that he would advise me to give up thoughts of the Great Ones entirely, as there are not one of a Hundred that in Rome that ever see them.' Wilton had then gone on to suggest to Robert that a certain compromise might be possible, and that he should take up the offer of introductions to Cardinal Albani and a few others, then leave the city for a week or so to visit

Naples or somewhere else useful to him and return incognito and start studying while living privately and inconspicuously. Thus he would probably get the best of both worlds. That is very much what Robert did.

A last plea comes in this letter to James: 'You will always take care to avoid putting the word Architect on the back of my letters. You shou'd either Direct "For Rob' Adam. Esqr. or "A Mon^r, Robert Adam, Gentil'homme Anglois".'

The travellers arrived in Rome on 24th February. As Robert wrote to his mother on 1st March, the weather was wet for some days and he was suffering from migraine. Having tried various remedies, from stomach powders to blood-letting, he recovered his normal good health and sallied forth to see the city, which had been his goal for so long.

His first impressions he gives to his mother: 'We are situated upon the Banks of the Tybur. From our window we have a most enchanting prospect of St. Peters, the Castle of St. Angelo, and of the Hills, fields and woods in the Country. . . . Where we live at present was during the time of the Antient Romans without the City and occupy'd in places for Games, exercises and other places for shows and amusements. Now it is the fashionable end of the town, and the Old Rome and its Ruins are inhabited only by people who love retirement, cheap palaces and study. Here Ramsay [5] has retired.' This gives a picture of mid-eighteenth-century Rome, which was a small, half-empty city, the Forum – then aptly called the Campo Vaccino – and adjacent antique sites used as cow and sheep pastures. Naples was the bustling centre of life and population in this part of Italy.

Robert continues: 'What pleased me most of all was the pantheon, of which the Greatness, and Simplicity of parts, fills the mind with extensive thoughts, stamps upon you the Solemn, the Grave and the Majestick, and seems to prevent all those ideas of Gaity or Frolick which our Modern buildings admitt and inspire. St. Peters is a very noble building, and is not admired without justice. The proportions are so well afix'd to particular parts of the whole, that though a monstrous building, it has the very opposite air, neither being heavy nor huge to appearance.' By 'monstrous' he is referring to its size, not its quality.

Robert's enthusiasm and preference for the antique over the

Italian Renaissance and Baroque was still in its early stages, but during his months in Rome it grew and became dominant in him. He never disdained what he thought of as 'modern interpretation' of the classical theme, but to him the original was vastly superior as inspiration for his own ideas.

On the domestic front, he settled in to his accommodation, his 'French friend Clérisseau lodged in the next room to mine', and began to meet and be introduced to the other British residents of the city, as well as to French and Italians. Charles Hope was still with him and he became very friendly with the Abbé Grant, Allan Ramsay and Robert Wood, author of the *Ruins of Palmyra* (page 11). He began a serious study of the Italian language, realizing that it would have been much more useful to have done so before he came, and he lamented the waste of time and opportunities in not being able to converse freely with people. He set out with determination to put this right. His French was improving and soon became fluent, due to living in the same house with Clérisseau and being friendly with the French painter Pêcheux. He sent home presents to his family and friends in Scotland. These included rounds of Parmesan cheese which cost him £3 each,[6] and he suggested to James that they should be divided up as they were too large for one person and would go bad.

Robert stayed in Rome till early April, getting used to the city, the life, his new friends and his work. Having been in constant company with Charles Hope since they met in Brussels the previous November, the two young men began to get on one another's nerves. They had little in common; Hope was a typical young aristocrat, paying lip service to classical study, but really more intent of making the best of his opportunities for a good time on the Continent before settling down in Scotland. He and Robert got bored with each other, bickered endlessly and, eventually, agreed to part company and go their separate ways. They kept in touch and were both astonished to find how well they got on and how much they liked each other when they seldom met or wrote letters.

Robert was looking out for suitable apartments in which to settle down more permanently in Rome. He needed accommodation for himself, domestic staff and Clérisseau. In his own words: 'I wanted to secure myself a good house and a convenient one which shou'd be cooll in the summer and contain the following Chambers, a good Bedchamber for myself and a little one for my friend Clérisseau, a Hall in which to have 2 or 3 Tables for draughtsmen and other myrmidons of Art whom we employ, a good Dining Room and a chamber for Donald and a kitchen.' He acquired such accommodation from its owner, Sir Charles Hotham, whom he met at the Duke of Bridgewater's. He was very pleased with it since it was on a hill, with a fine view of Rome.

After a week or so of visiting the chief architectural monuments and sites, and discussing his future plans with Clérisseau, Abbé Grant and Robert Wood, he becomes passionately interested in Rome and its antique heritage and of the possibilities it offers for his future career. He realizes how little he knows, how low was the standard in Scotland, how high in Italy. He gets down to hard study, doing everything that Clérisseau advises, beginning at the beginning as if he were a novice student instead of a man of twenty-seven. He is modest but self-confident, and very determined to get the utmost out of his opportunity and to be a success. He refers to Chambers who, a few years older than himself, has been some time in the city, and recognizes, even now, that here is his most dangerous future rival. He writes: 'Chambers who has been here Six Years is superior to me at present, for greatness of thought and nobility of Invention, Drawing and in ornamenting. But damn my Blood, but I will have a fair tryal for it, and expect to do as much in Six months as he has done in as many Years. But then it will require Study and attention with application.'

Robert goes on to say that he is 'getting moulds made of all the Antique ornaments, of Freezes, Cornishes, Vases etc.', in plaster and he will send these to Scotland. He employs draughtsmen and painters to record sculpture, fountains, building detail, and he purchases useful books of Architecture, which also illustrate designs for altars, chapels and churches. He collects drawings by Piranesi and others. He contemplates making a collection of original antique marble fragments of capitals, cornices, ornament, bases, columns, etc., for, as he says, 'here they lye like knocking stones up and down through all the streets of the town'. The problem is the question of transport to Britain, for marble is a good deal heavier, and therefore more costly to move than plaster.

Robert, like so many men of outstanding ability, never wastes his time in doing something the long or painstaking way if there is a good short cut. He uses all the methods available to bring home to Britain material in these different forms so that he will have it in his office, when he begins practice, as source-material for his future designs. Sir John Summerson [7] notes that Robert's surviving Italian sketches do not include measured studies of Classical or Renaissance buildings, and that he only used the scholastic approach when studying something like the Palace of Diocletian at Split, where there was hardly any published material available.

His drawings done in Italy are usually in pen and ink and wash. They are artists' impressions, with an emphasis on light and shade, composition, romanticism and perspective. Nevertheless the essence of the building and the classical features are there. A number of drawings, like Clérisseau's, are in full colour. In his later work he did many drawings of interiors, including a number of Renaissance and Baroque buildings. He seemed especially interested in vaulting design. In contrast, when drawing for information, as in portraying ornament or decorative schemes, his drawings are extremely detailed. This applies to a number of ceiling designs which he drew in Renaissance palaces and villas.

It is certain that were Robert Adam alive today he would use all modern methods of cutting short the tedium of recording, from photography to photo-copying, in order to save his energies for the work of original design which so few can do.

After his few weeks' preliminary survey Robert says: 'In short I am antique Mad, or what they would call in Scotland an Antick. Rome is the most glorious place in the Universal World, a grandeur and tranquillity reigns in it. Every where noble and striking remains of Antiquity appear in it, which are so many that one who has spent a Dozen Years in seeing is still surprised with something new.'

Robert went with Clérisseau and some other friends to spend the month of April in Naples. He travelled by chaise and took five days to cover the 150-odd miles from Rome. They had a merry trip despite the uncomfortable lodgings en route. The lively air of the people and the bustling excitement of the city surprised him. He wrote to his sister Peggy on 8th April: 'I never was more pleased and surprised with anything than the appearance of People upon approaching Naples Sunday night. The suburbs contained above 3 Thousand people who danc'd along the Road to Musick of all different kinds in the most antique or Baccanalian Manner I ever saw, whilst others were assembled in Gardens, at the Doors of their Houses, in Drinking, Eating and Gaming. These Multitudes of Men, women and children, their Gay Dresses and active spirit form'd a most delightful scene.'

They visited many places while in Naples, and were excited and absorbed by it all. They went to Puteoli (Pozzuoli) and saw the sacred lake, the grotto, and the temples; also Baia with its ruined temples and palaces. They spent a great deal of time at Herculaneum, which had been the scene of excavation since 1738. The buildings were explored by means of tunnels at a great depth. None of these is visible except the theatre (referred to by Robert), the orchestra of which is eighty-five feet below the surface. Pompeii has proved in modern times an easier site to excavate. It is more open and accessible, the modern town being next door to it; but Robert would have seen little or nothing of the excavations here, as they had only begun in 1748 and were not undertaken systematically till 1763.

He was most impressed by Herculaneum, by its sculptures, frescoes and architectural remains, as well as by domestic utensils and food uncovered by the excavations. He crawled through underground passages lit by torches, and studied mosaic pavings, amphitheatre remains, temples and ornament. He was especially fascinated by the palaces and houses, for remnants of domestic classical architecture were rare, and especially interested him even at this early stage. He said in his letter: 'I soon perceiv'd that the vulgar notion of its being swallowed up by an earthquake was false. But it was still worse. It was quite overrun with a flood of liquid stone from Mount Vesuvius, which runs out upon an eruption, is called Lava, and when cooll is as hard as our Whinstone. Of this you find a solid Body, of 50 to 60 foot high in many places.' He went on to describe vividly the horror of that night in A.D. 79. He was moved and horrified by it, as are modern visitors today.

There is a timelessness about the fearful attraction of the crater of Vesuvius which still beckons tourists every summer. The Adam party also submitted doubtfully to this magnetism, and Robert's description to his mother in his letter of 19th April could, apart from the eighteenth-century phraseology, have been written by a modern traveller. 'I have been at Mount Vesuvius which is a most surprizing Mountain, and though I had conceiv'd a very horrible Notion of it, I assure you I was much disappointed to the better, as that great mouth which is immensely deep and which sends out a pillar of Flame and sulphurious Smoak of an immense volume, exceeded much my conception, and from the Growing Thunder (which every 2 or 3 Minutes seem'd to rise from the foundations of the Hill surrounding the volcano) your ideas were converted into the most Hellish Solemnity, whilst the view of nothing but Sulphur, Burnt Rocks, and Ashes all around augmented the savage and fiery Prospect. For a quarter of a mile we walked over great lakes of sulphur which were spew'd out by an Eruption, in many places Smoaking and flaming like a Bogg burning for Ashes. The Ground was so hot that our shoes were consumed and render'd useless, whilst such sulphurious Steams issued from the cracks of that sulphur we walk'd over, that we thought to have been choak'd many a time in crossing them.'

Comments and hints are dropped from time to time by John and Mrs Adam that Robert should practise some financial economies. Equally, from time to time, Robert (who does not intend to do any such thing, being convinced that the money is spent wisely for future investment) makes some attempts to placate these family warnings. In this same letter to his mother he writes, referring to news of the prosperity of the family business, sent to him from home: 'I am glad last year has been a good one for worldly affairs as Realy it is impossible to Live and Travel at a moderate Rate. When I return to Rome I shall be as frugal as possible and intend to keep house with Clérisseau. We shall have a Cook, who's honesty my companion has proved these Six years, who will buy what we need and Dress our victuals. We shall have our Valet Donald for Shaving and Dressing our Hairs. We shall have our Coach which in the summer time costs about 4 shillings, for the whole Day, Coachman and all, and we shall have our valet de place, or servant, for going Errands and behind the Coach, whom we will pay at the Rate of a Shilling a Day, for which he feeds, Cloaths and provides himself in everything. In short I imagine for 12 shillings for one Day with another, we shall defray our whole expenses of Eating, Drinking and Equipage which Lord knows is not dear.' It may not have been dear, but it certainly seemed to provide for a reasonable standard of living.

Robert returns to Rome at the end of April and settles down to a programme of concentrated personal study. He is introduced to Cardinal Albani, from whom he obtains permission to make drawings and take plaster and wax models of ornament in palaces and churches. He makes many friends, English, French and Italian, and goes to a few dinners, concerts and operas. His Italian is now improving immensely and he practises most evenings with his Italian friends. He writes to his sister Nelly on 24th May of his daily programme: 'The forenoon I devote to Study and Drawing, every after Dinner [8] I ride out to see places and draw on the Spot and after returning I pay some English visits till 9 o'clock and from that go among my Italians where I stay till 11 or 12 and then I go home and to bed.' He is amused and gratified at the difference between spending Sunday in a Latin, Catholic country and in Scotland. He says: 'The Sunday evening in other Countreys, so dull and dowed, is here the great rejoicing as the Conversations are fuller and always a Concert or Dance.' He adds proudly: 'The ladys are so partial as to think me amongst the best minuet dancers of any English man they ever saw in Italy.'

Though he seems to keep fit and well, Robert suffers from the heat in his first summer in Italy after being used to the climate of Edinburgh and Inverness. At Naples in April he was complaining of exhaustion, and by 18th June in Rome he sighs: 'It was so sultry hot that it absolutely made me incapable either to think or scrawl so I saunter'd about the house or threw myself on the bed, slept and yawn'd, sweat and broil'd, till I had not the strength of a Louse.' However, then as now, Rome always cools in the evening in the hottest heat-wave as the winds blow up the Tiber valley from the sea, and so he goes for a long walk with the Ramsay family, Abbé Grant and some other friends. They 'walk'd through a great part of antient Rome, amongst Ruins and remains of the Temples, then along the Borders of the Tiber all with moonlight. Our Ramble ended in the Venetian Coffee house where we refresh'd ourselves with extream good ice'd Cream, ice'd strawberries etc.'.

A reminder that life in Rome in 1755, as in England, was quite different from 1970, despite the timelessness of the classical ruins, comes in a letter written on the 21st. 'To show you that Death neither spares great nor small in any Countrey we have a Cardinal just now Stinking in State, but is to be buried Privately as the pope is in the Countrey. Their is onother man just hanging and quartering for Robbery but luckily the Castle of St. Angelo prevents my seeing anything of the Cerimony from my windows.'

By this time Robert had met Piranesi [9] and they became friendly. They went on sketching expeditions together with Clérisseau and Pêcheux, both in Rome, in the Forum Romanum and the Baths of Caracalla, and out in the Campagna, drawing aqueducts and temples. Robert writes on 21st June: 'Piranesi who is I think the most extraordinary fellow I ever saw is become immensely intimate with me and as he imagined at first sight that I was like the other Englishes who had love for Antiques without knowledge, upon seeing some of my Sketches and Drawings, was so highly delighted that he almost ran quite distracted and says that I have more genius for the true noble architecture than any Englishman ever was in Italy.' Piranesi had a typically Italian temperament, volatile, generous, impulsive. He and Robert were contrasts and, as such, enjoyed each other's company and ideas immensely for a while, but later the differences became too marked and they fell out. Robert learnt a lot from Piranesi and his work. He admired it greatly and was thrilled when Piranesi dedicated one of his works to him.

The total absorption in his own affairs and the single-mindedness of purpose with which he pursued his chosen course was apparent in Robert at this stage. These were characteristics which, later in life, earned him enmity and disapproval, for he tended to be judged in some quarters as self-centred and patronizing. Neither was true. It was simply that when Robert was engaged on a project it took his whole mind and being, and anything outside did not exist for him at that time. It is this type of concentration which all great works of art demand, and it is a quality found especially in such artists as Michelangelo and Bernini.

Something of this absorption is shown in Robert's letter to Jenny on 9th August, which refers to the impending war with France.[10] His concern here was solely with his career and the probable effect of the war on the safety of the materials which he was sending home. He says: 'If this War is in Earnest, their is nothing to be done at Home. The Architects may go to bed and sleep till peace is Made, or they may travel to divert themselves. But I suppose the Forts will be push'd on with more vigour than ever,[11] this will be no bad circumstance for the Travellour who had need of money to support his Extravagance. Lord knows how I shall get all my things sent home. If the French take any of them I'm undone. I believe I must send them by Leghorn till all warlike deeds are ceas'd. The only thing I regret is not getting to Paris for 2 months.'

Another instance comes in his later reference to the Lisbon earthquake of 1st November 1755. This was the greatest of all known earthquakes, which almost totally destroyed the city and whose shock waves set the waters in motion as far away as Loch Ness and Scandinavia. Robert writes on 13th December to his sister Nelly: 'The news of the earthquake of Lisbon is very terrible and I dare say both Scottish and English have lost many friends in that distruction. However I can't help thinking it better in that place of the World than either in our Island or in Italy as I should be sorry any harm befell the Antiquitys of this place till I have made all the life of them I intend as well as any of my Friends who want to make progress in Architecture.'

Between 24th September and 12th October Robert and Clérisseau made an extensive journey in their coach across the Apennines via Spoleto to the Adriatic coast, where they visited Ancona, Fano and Ravenna. This was an ambitious journey on the mountain roads of the day, especially as they both made a large number of drawings of bridges, triumphal arches, churches and temples. As Robert said, they drove on from one town to another, stopping only for half a day at a time to work and then on to the next place. This is a tiring enough occupation in a modern car on present-day roads. It must have been an exhausting three weeks for them.

Among the many spectacles which Rome had to offer, Robert described one at St Peter's, where he saw a religious procession progressing round the adjacent streets and the piazza, which were all decorated for the occasion. He referred to the displaying in the open air of the tapestries for which Raphael had designed the Cartoons which were then at Hampton Court Palace. Robert thought the actual tapestries inferior to the Cartoons, which he refers to as 'originals'. The tapestries are now in the Vatican Museum Picture Gallery. Since 1865 the Cartoons have been on display in the Victoria and Albert Museum in London.

An amusing sidelight is thrown on the differing customs in Latin countries from those in the Anglo-Saxon in a letter to his mother written in August. She has told him that Mrs Clerk (presumably his sister Susan) is, unfortunately, pregnant again – apparently an all too frequent occurrence in this case. Robert's comment is that: 'If she had lived in Italy she never would have been subject to these Disasters, and in France after a certain number of children, much inferior to the number she has whelp'd, the man and wife never lye together more; a very effective method to prevent racking agony – the Husband takes a Mistress, and the Wife fends for herself.'

In several letters written during 1755 Robert refers to two portraits being painted of him. The first was by Allan Ramsay, but unfortunately there is no trace of this. The second was by Pêcheux, the French painter who so often accompanied Robert and Clérisseau on their sketching expeditions. Robert is very enthusiastic about this one, saying that it is much better than Ramsay's. On 2nd January 1756 he writes to Betty: 'My portrait now quite finish'd by Pêcheux and nothing can be a better likeness as he has made me smiling and in good humour. Ramsay's picture is quite a Sciocco as the Italians say.'

The painting at Blair-Adam is by Pêcheux (Pêchaux), but as this is on ivory and measures four and a half inches by three and a half, it is presumably not the one described by Robert as difficult to roll up for sending to Scotland (Plate 7).

Robert stays in Rome for the whole of 1756. He had originally planned to leave in the spring and go north to Venice and thence home. His departure is postponed several times. He is working extremely hard, recording on paper and with moulds everything of note in ancient and Renaissance Rome, as well as visiting villas, temples and aqueducts within about a seventy-mile radius of the city. He knows he will not be able to repeat the trip, so he puts off the date of leaving again and again. In the end he stays until May 1757.

His letters of this period are interesting, portraying life in the city, his own activities and his personality and character. The tenor of his programme continues similarly to that of 1755.

He receives quiet admonitions from home on the importance of saving money and being more frugal and, from his mother, on leading a Christian life. In answer he says: 'It is certain I am rather Graceless. But as I am in constant resolution to amend my ways, and that I think their is plenty of time, I doubt not that I shall be enabl'd to keep the Commandments of God well at Last, as you may remember I spent no short time in the study of them. And if once I had got a little time to spare from these Worldly cares which at present too much employ my thoughts I will read Psalms and all manner of Holy Books. There are no Bibles to be got in this Place (as I fancy that is forbid by the Church). It is not my fault that I have not read a Chapter Morning and Evening.'

Robert evidently feels that he has time enough in which to make his peace with the Almighty. On 3rd July, though, he seems to be worried that time is running out for his career. He begins his letter to Nelly: 'Upon reflecting that this very day I enter into my 29th year, I became vastly melancholy, and thought for half an hour wambling within me the most green eyed Ideas. But upon considering seriously, I banish'd these useless Reverées, Thank'd God next July did not bring 40 in place of 30 years, hearten'd myself By thinking how many were older than me and every bit as unsettled and uncertain of their Situation and Success in Life.'

In this second summer in Rome Robert is getting used to the climate and enjoying it immensely. He finds it infinitely preferable to Scotland with its 'enshrouding fogs and damp cold'. He thinks that perhaps the Almighty might have arranged things a little more equally for mankind. In his letter to his mother of 19th June he says: 'What a blessed thing it would be for both Countreys I mean those of Italy and Scotland could they intermingle Climates, whilst you seek and pray for dry weather we are gasping for air and seeking but a shower to refresh the Earth which God does not see meet to send us. . . . Thus famine will ensue from quite an opposite cause. Surely their are good reasons to be given for Gods Burning the one half of his people and Drowning the other. Though I own my weak abilitys cou'd never fathom so deep judgements or dispensations.'

His description of life in Rome a fortnight later will awaken an echo in the memory of many a modern traveller to mid-Italy. 'Last week was so hot that I had it not in my power to write you so great was my Laziness. Though every body I saw was as much reduced as myself and owned they cou'd do nothing but sitt Blowing and Fanning themselves the whole day. I was for 8 days I did not do a single thing but slept and Drank and Eat a little and daudl'd about the House sweating Though Naked.'

In the first half of June Robert and Clérisseau left on one of their trips, returning on the 16th. They went south-east, about seventy miles towards Naples on the Monte Cassino road, in their four-wheeled chaise, then struck off north into the Apennines to visit some villages which have interesting Etruscan remains. They found it extremely hot and Robert recounted at length his adventures when the road became so rocky and precipitous that they had to get out and, with the aid of the local peasantry, 'push up our vehicle while we in an Ocean of Sweat walked 5 miles in the Unsufferable sunshine of Miday'. They finally got to Attina, where they were mystified at being entertained both by a local farmer and the aristocracy as if they were persons of immense importance. Embarrassed and puzzled, they discovered that their servant Donald had told the lads, while pushing the coach the day before, that they were English princes. To avoid staying longer under false pretences they tried to sneak off at three o'clock in the morning, but 'Such was the Curiosity of the village to see a foreign prince that we drove thro' a crowd of near 2 or 3 hundred people next morning all drawn up to inspect us'. Laughing, they continued on their way to Sora.

With Robert's encouragement two of his sisters are learning French, and he writes passages of his letters in that language in order to give them practice. He is now fluent at French and Italian, and is in great demand at parties for his singing of Italian songs to the ladies. His voice is soft and lacking in range and power, but he apparently puts it over with an elegant and suitably emotional Italian air which appeals to the company.

In a truly masculine way he refers to the proper state of things when writing to James on 11th September. 'Perhaps Bess thinks this Letter is intended for her. But she is mistaken, when one writes of things of importance it is well known the Ladys were never made to receive such Intelligence.' He goes on to suggest that it is suitable for her to study French; otherwise she should attend to running the house and looking after the meals.

The 'things of importance' to which he refers are of course to do with his future career in relation to those of his brothers. Many letters on the subject had been written in 1755 and 1756 to both James and John, and many received. Though everyone concerned remained friendly, conscious of one another's rights and deferring to their opinions, 1756 was a time of the struggle for power in the Adam family. This power was centred on financial matters.

When Robert left Scotland in October 1754 it was presumed that he would be away about two years and that John would follow him and, later, James. While John and James remained in Scotland, facing the same problems with architecture and clients that they had all known, Robert had entered and become part of a much wider world. By the summer of 1756 his ideas and horizons had broadened enormously. His ambitions were set higher, and he could see clearly the course he ought to take. He was always prepared to risk an unusual and daring step, but it was also a calculated risk. He never stepped into the unknown without a great deal of thought and care.

It was thus that a gulf of misunderstanding opened, becoming wider with the passage of time and experience, between Robert in Italy and his brothers in Scotland. Their only means of contact were letters which took some time to arrive, and several weeks elapsed before a reply could be received. It was due only to their great mutual respect and affection that the rift did not become permanent.

For several years now Robert had been the leader of the family, and he took this responsibility seriously. He was determined to have freedom to decide his own future but, at the same time, he felt responsible to the family and tried to foster the democratic approach of discussion. Though his brothers did not always agree with his ideas, they both procrastinated and would not make up their minds. This was a trying frustration for the decisive Robert.

There were two main points of difference. How long should Robert stay in Italy, and how much capital did he need to establish himself in London?

In Scotland one or two influential clients had expressed themselves interested in employing Robert on his return, notably Lord Hope-toun and the Duke of Bridgewater. By mid-1756 John feels that

Robert has had long enough and should come back at once, or he may lose these opportunities. He wants to express this firmly as befits the head of the family, but he clearly acknowledges Robert as the real leader and hesitates.

He writes to Jenny: 'I have wrote a long Letter to Bob tonight, still advising him to think of setting out as soon as he can, but at the same time advising him that I have ask'd of Mr. Hope, to write to Mr. Wood that he [Bob] was soon to leave Rome and turn his face homewards, so as to prevent the D. of Bridgewater from employing any other. This he is to do, and to let Mr. Wood know that if he does not arrive the end of this year, he will early the next. This may give him a month or two's respite so as not to hurry him absolutely; But I dare not say more.'

Robert comments, much later in the year and still in Rome: 'I am somewhat uneasy at Bridgewater's silence, But hope without cause, I doubt not but Mr. Wood will say Something soon in case the Duke does not. But if they shou'd all dance Reels on one another's Heads, I can't return to England this Season.'

He had realized by now that he must set up practice in England, not in Scotland, on his return. It was there where he could make his name and enjoy the opportunity for great commissions. In Scotland he would have no problem in establishing himself, but in England his situation would be different. There the standard would be much higher and, since he would have rivals of great merit and ability, he would have to present himself as superior not only in intellect but also in experience and talent. He knew that men like William Chambers would present real competition, having behind them skill, draughtsmanship, years of study in Italy and an aristocratic following with solid financial backing.

Robert believed that he would not succeed as leading architect (which he was determined to become) unless he could offer the aristocracy something new which they preferred to what they saw in other people's homes. He had no doubt of his abilities to do so, but he must have the ammunition which, in this case, was knowledge and experience of antique building. He could use this, make it into a new style, but he must take advantage of all that Rome had to offer. That would take time, and he would not leave before he had learnt all there was to learn and had collected enough material to take back. He was sure that he could outdo Chambers if he put his whole effort into the task.

The other bone of contention was the sum of money which he would need to establish himself in London. He had set out with £5,000, which came from what he had saved while working for the family firm in Scotland. Since the brothers were expected to plough back into the business much of what they earned, Robert did not regard this money as his to do with as he pleased. He and his brothers had agreed that his Italian experience would count as a contribution to the firm, in return for the money, which was treated as a loan to be repaid. He estimated that he was spending the £5,000 at a rate of £800 to £900 a year. He and John had agreed that he should use that sum while John and James continued working in Scotland. When Robert returned and started earning a similar arrangement could then be made for his brothers.

Robert wrote to James urging that he and John should not waste time, but that one of them should come at once to Italy while they could benefit from Clérisseau's tuition and Robert's presence and advice. John is the eldest and must have first chance if he wants to come. If they leave it too long they will get neither and will be too old to benefit. Robert is convinced by his own experience that if one waits too long one's mind becomes set and one has to unlearn too much before beginning to learn. One has acquired prejudices.

Robert knows that John is fully capable of handling the family business alone in Scotland. He thinks honestly that he has reached his ceiling and will not benefit by coming anyway, but does not wish to tell him so. James is young enough and bright enough to take advantage of such a tour as Robert is having, and Robert would like him as his aide-de-camp in London after he has made himself *au fait* with antique classicism on the Continent.

John keeps hovering and will not make up his mind to travel to Italy. He lacks confidence and feels safer earning in Scotland. By 24th July Robert is convinced that he will never take the plunge.

He is now asking John and James if they will agree to extend the time limit of his loan, and increase it until at least one year after his return to Britain, so that he can establish himself properly in London. He points out that in order to make an impression on the wealthy aristocracy, needed as suitable clients, one must not appear to be poor, but must show confidence and a fair standard of living and culture.

He suggests that he will need a house with a good address, staff to run it and would like two of his sisters to come to oversee this. He is worried about his mother [12] who, he knows, will not wish to leave Scotland at her age, but suggests that the other two sisters should stay in Scotland with her. They will all be near John and his family. He intends to bring two draughtsmen back with him from Italy, Laurent Benoît Dewez, a Liègeois, and the Italian Agostino Brunias. Robert points out that neither of the two young men speaks English, only French and Italian, so they will not get led into the lazier English ways of asking for more money and shorter hours. As Robert puts it, 'so have no chance of being soon debauch'd by evil communication!'

Clérisseau has confided in him that if only he were guaranteed a small annual salary so that he did not need to take pupils, he would be willing to be at Robert's service anywhere. Robert thinks this is a good idea. He does not want to lose Clérisseau to Italian pupils, so he suggests to his brothers that they should pay the Frenchman a retainer to help them in the London office as and when they need it, and he could then be available to accompany James on his tour to help him as he had Robert.

Objections are put forward, both to Robert's insistence on staying longer on the Continent and to his financial proposals. John, James and some of his sisters think his ideas too grand and that he should be content to start with less. In the event, Robert stayed in Italy as long as he needed, established himself in London in record time and was soon earning sums far in excess of what his brothers in Scotland had imagined possible. Robert spent the rest of his life working at high pressure and repaid in full for his gamble.

His common sense and far-seeing assessments of his family's abilities and his own conflicted with his genuinely sympathetic feelings and love for them. His clarity of thought and action were shown throughout his life and often made things difficult for him. In this case he knew that John ought to have his chance, but equally that he was not of the stuff of which innovators were made. Resentment lingered on in John's family; not perhaps in John himself, but certainly in his son, who felt all his life that his two uncles took advantage of his father and spent his money without sufficiently consulting him.

In the autumn of 1756 Robert felt that time was running out. He redoubled his efforts to cover all the sites and buildings he needed. He was particularly anxious to complete the thorough survey which he was carrying out at Hadrian's Villa (near Tivoli) and the Baths of Caracalla and Diocletian in Rome. He made hundreds of drawings which he originally intended to publish. They provided him with invaluable source material when he was in practice.

He writes to James on 11th September: 'I am to show the Baths in their present Ruinous Condition and from that to make other designs of them as they were when Intire and in their Glory. In which project Lord Burlington's [13] book has been of Unspeakable Service as he is vastly exact in his Measurements and in Palladio's [14] time they were much more Intire, so that I get great light from him. My other Studys are the drawings of what good Buildings are in Rome, either within or without.'

Robert has his eye to suitable qualifications. He writes to Jenny on 16th October: 'I intend to be made professor of Architecture, Painting and Sculpture in the Academy of Saint Luke in Rome. The Cerimony of which and getting out my Diploma will cost me 25 Guineas at least but is extreamly honourable and showy in all Books or things you may Publish. I shall obtain this easily and Grandly as I will follicite my good friend the Cardinal Albani to ask it in person. I hope also to be made member of the Academy of Florence in passing through that City which Sir Horace will push with pleasure. At Bologna I shall be received fellow of the Institute of that City also coveted by all the great men of the arts, and these three with what additional titles I may acquire in England will be very sufficient to show the person that has been honour'd with all of them was not altogether without merit in his profession.'

Robert was not boasting unduly. He obtained his various honours and was acknowledged as a man of ability and renown as he travelled through the cities of northern Italy. He had indeed made his mark in two and a half years since he had entered the country. If that had not been so his string-pulling would have been in vain.

One thing only Robert deeply regrets, that he has had to work in Rome for so long and has not had the time or money to go farther afield. This he leaves to James and writes to him on 24th July that he has covered Rome fully and James will be free, if he desires, 'to view Rome as a Gentleman would do for his pleasure, or what is better have given you the time to search for other things in Calabria, in Sicily and in Greece where were I not oblig'd to return to England, or if you had come abroad at the time I wrote you, we would have been just now, as my heart was sett on it'.

He goes on: 'But this I think of No More but leave it to those whose better stars conduct them to that Glorious Countrey. To view the Temples of Athens, of Thebes and of Sparta; The field of Marathon and Straits of Thermopylae and though the Thought is altogether imaginary yet it is pleasing to be where harangu'd Demosthenes and where Pericles council'd. I never go near the Capitol or near the Forum Romanum where harangu'd Cicero, Cesar, The Consuls, The Tribunes but I am struck with a respectful horror mix't with pity. The total extinction of all thats great and Virtuous, nothing but depravity of Sentiment, Lowness of Manners and Mercenary aims reigning in their Stead.'

Again, on 23rd October to Nell: 'At Venice and Vicenza I shall have more time than I expected for my Jaunt into Dalmatia and Pola in Istria. If you know with what sad heart I return without seeing Greece, especially to be on the very coast of it.' [15] 'I shall like Johnie still live in Hopes to see Athens and Sparta and look wishfully on Egypt and the Holy Land . . . but perhaps the time may come when I have 5 or 6 Thousands a Year that I may spend a Year or Two for the Good of the Publick and advancement of our Art.'

Alas for Robert. He got his income but never again had time to pause in his work.

The year 1757 finds Robert hard at work trying to beat the clock. He has a number of distractions: the New Year Carnival in Rome comes round once more and he attends the opera, concerts, plays and dances.

In February he was taken ill with symptoms of severe headache, toothache, a bad cold and a temperature. This in itself seems a normal malady which may have been due to a virus infection, sinus problems or merely to a bad cold or overwork. What is interesting in his subsequent account, written on 12th March to his sister Peggy, is the medical attention given to him and his acceptance of this as normal. To modern ears, it sounds rather as though the cure was worse than the malady. Describing the symptoms he says: 'I was instantly plagu'd with a severe Headack and so stuff'd in the brain and stop'd at the Nose, that water of Brandy, Pudding and Dry'd Skate, had the same taste in my Pallate.' He goes on: 'This cold dayly increasing I resolved to bleed for it which accordingly I did in great abundance at the left arm.' In addition he took a vomit powder and was astonished the next day to find his symptoms worse than ever. He sent for the doctor again and suggested to him that the application of leaches to the seat of the pain, his temples, would help. But the doctor 'Spying a good Vein thought his Lancet would more quickly free me of pain, which accordingly he plunged into the throbbing vein and soon reliev'd me of the excess of my Torment, not without the formality of a Through faint and carrying to bed.'

Still no cure; next day all was the same, so the doctor hopefully pulled out a tooth but without altering the symptoms, and Robert began to have morbid fears of brain tumours and other possibilities.

The doctor made a final effort and suggested blistering. For this he applied a plaster and brought up a large blister between the shoulders. Robert says: 'The Monday morning it was found to have run out most excessively and the blister was kept on to make it run more, which it continued to do almost all Monday and Tuesday.' With the added advice to take a 'Draught of the Salt of Wormwood' morning and night the doctor departed. By Thursday the pains had gone, and a weak Robert was advised to take a few glasses of claret to restore his strength. After about ten days he was up and out once more, leaving us to wonder if he had recovered because of his medical attentions or in spite of them.

During his incarceration in his room many kind visitors came to entertain him. Among these was a young lady, Miss Molyneux, who, related to the Bury family and in Rome to tend her sick sister, came with others to cheer him. At this time Robert seems to have come as near to falling desperately in love as, so far as we know, he ever did. Miss Molyneux describes him as 'that gay, chearfull and frolicksome Mr Adams', and also admires his brilliant drawings and academic studies. Robert describes her: 'I never saw so agreeable a Woman or so accomplish'd, with an inexhaustible fund of good sense, and most pleasing address, and most engaging manner. . . .

If my heart was not as hard as Iron I would most undoubtedly be head and ears and Desperation in Love. But thank God my plans and Elevation of Baths have a surprizing effect to keep down that Passion. Besides that I am not so vain as to think a lady with 900 pounds a Year's portion who has refused the best Noblemen in England to attend a sick sister would ever think of so poor a Divil, and thats another check to Ardent Love. Yet I must acknowledge that did I give way to my inclinations, I cou'd soon be intoxicated.'

But at the end of March the family set off to spend the summer sea-bathing at Naples. Robert will soon be on his way north and towards England. He sighs for her wonderful qualities and graces, especially the fact that she is so clever and has such a brilliant brain, but, knowing the pride of men, pretends that she has not and that they are the intelligent and cultured ones. To Robert this was unusual in the women he had met and he was most deeply impressed.

On 30th March he gives a final sigh for Greece and puts forward a last feeler. He dined one evening with the Abbé Grant, Gavin Hamilton and Clérisseau at a villa occupied by Hamilton on the slopes of Monte Gianicolo (the Janiculum of ancient Rome). From here [16] there is a magnificent view of Rome, and especially of the Tiber, Castel Sant' Angelo and St Peter's. Sitting in the gardens they discussed 'Greece and the Grecian Islands which if I had Cash I would go and see with pleasure', and, hopefully, 'if John would sett off directly and meet me at Vicenza we would go at his expences in a Vessell from Venice directly to the Greek Islands which is a pleasant saill of 8 days and from that we'd go to Athens. In short taking Clérisseau and my two Draughtsmen with us two, we would finish a very tolerable work to Rival Stuart and Revett's [17] in three months time and return home laden with Laurel'. Robert was quite right, but his money was running low. No suitable reply came from John, so, early in May, he leaves Rome, having packed up his vast quantity of drawings, books, paintings, sculpture and casts for shipment to England.

His brothers, as always, are still urging him to economize and suggest that, instead of paying for his two draughtsmen to travel with him to Venice and then to Dalmatia, he should send them direct to London. Robert points out that this would be a stupid economy as they would kick their heels in London and not earn their keep; the two of them, together with Clérisseau and himself, would get far more work done and so make the investment of the trip much more worth while. Robert was right of course; the work that they all accomplished in those weeks was prodigious, and proved invaluable in his later designs.

The four of them travelled north to Florence, stopping at Viterbo and also at Ferentino to see the Etruscan remains, staying awhile at Florence, then moving on for a week at Bologna and from there to Padua, which they reached by 23rd June. Robert collected his diplomas and honours as he went, and despite the intense heat visited picture galleries, churches and many other buildings. He describes the Basilica of St Antonio: 'Yesterday I paid a visite to the Shrine of the Famous St Antonio di Padova, surrounded day and night with 50 burning Lamps. His Body is conceal'd in the altar, over which messes are rung off From Morning to Night and all that believe in him are Saved. By this Saint Swear all Ostlers, Postilions and Low people, and the most reprobate Catholick sometimes in his ails and angers, sends all the other Saints to the Divil but always excepts St Antonio. The Tongue of the Saint is not in the Grave with his body but lock'd up in a Very Magnificent Chappell Built purposely for that and some other Holy relicts.'

Robert sends the two draughtsmen ahead to organize his accommodation in Venice. On 1st July he and Clérisseau resume their progress towards the city via the Brenta Canal, visiting Palladio's villas and palaces. Robert writes: 'Each side of the River, which is about 18 miles to Venice, is lin'd with the villas of Noble Venetians mostly by the Celeberrimo ed' Illustre Palladio.' He is being received all along his route now as a person of note and talent, invited to dinners and parties and enjoying the appreciation. Even he, though, with his not inconsiderable appetite for works of art, finds Florence, Bologna and Padua a little too full of them. His sensations are like those of many a keen tourist. There is so much to see in a limited time, and there are just too many 'Pietàs', 'Virgins with Child', 'Assumptions' and 'Ascensions'.

On 6th July Robert is writing from Venice, which he describes as a 'region of water, Gondolas and Voluptuousness'. With characteristic enthusiasm and enterprise he immediately begins arrangements for his trip down what is now the Adriatic coast of Yugo-slavia. For over a year he has been planning this last research problem. He has become interested in the domestic architecture of ancient Rome and wants to explore a site not yet the subject of research and publication, so that he can present such work as his original contribution to the subject. This will bring him honour as a scholar and architect, thus giving him a reputation to begin practice, and will also provide useful new source material for his own house designs. He feels that Roman domestic architecture should be more suitable as a basis for designing English homes than Classical temples. In 1757 little work had been done in excavating and studying such remains, and, inevitably, most of such buildings would have suffered more in the course of time than the very important places of worship and civic centres. Excavation at Herculaneum had barely started, Pompeii was an enterprise of the future and almost nothing had been discovered of the imperial palaces on the Palatine Hill in Rome.

Robert hit on the Palace of Diocletian at Split, a large, important scheme which he had heard had survived fairly well and which had not yet been studied or written up. It was an example of late Roman design, built about A.D. 300 and almost completed in about ten years. It was beautiful and luxurious, designed both as a status symbol and for ease of living, fit for the declining years of an emperor.

As Hadrian's Villa is much more than a villa, so Diocletian's palace was more like a town designed as a fortress. The rectangular site measures about 700 feet by 580 feet and enclosed much of the medieval town of Spalatro. The palace faced south, out to sea, and was surrounded by walls with a chief gateway in the centre of each side. The two principal entrances still exist, the Porta Aurea (golden gate) on the north façade and the Porta Argentea (silver gate) on the south. This latter is connected to the interior of the palace by a series of underground chambers.

In 1757 Split was part of the Venetian republic, but was something of an important outpost in view of the Turkish influence farther south, which was still considerable. Robert therefore needed special permission to go to make studies and drawings there, and influential friends in the Venetian Senate promised to obtain it for him.

By 6th July he had hired his felucca, then spent a few days

organizing necessary supplies for himself and his companions, Clérisseau and his draughtsmen. He writes to Peggy: 'I have today hired my Boat, we coast it all the Way and lye ashore every night, and I think of setting sail Sunday or Monday after being provided with my instructions. And in the mean time am laying up stores of Wine, Bread, Tea, Sugar, Tongues, Hams, and other necessarys for Gentlemen Voyagers, and expect to have a very pleasant trip of it. It is true the weather is rather too hot but our Boat is to have a Double Canvas over it so that we shall be in a kind of Room all the way and we carry Bed and sheating and other Apparel. Poor Brunias, who never was without the walls of Rome till he came with me and never saw the sea till he saw Venice is sick at the very thoughts of the voyage and is laying up store of Venice treacle to stop his spewing.'

They set sail on 11th July and arrived at Split on the 22nd after a pleasant, though very hot, voyage. Robert records his impressions on first sighting the palace: 'As we entered a grand bay, and sailed slowly towards the harbour, the Marine Wall, and long Arcades of the Palace, one of the Ancient Temples and other parts of that building which was the object of our voyage, presented themselves to our view and flattered me, from this first prospect, that my labor in visiting it would be amply rewarded.'

He writes to James on 6th August and tells him how the work is going. He finds a fair proportion of the palace reasonably intact, but his intentions to draw measured plans and elevations, as well as con- jectural restorations, are hampered by the fact that houses had subsequently been built onto and into the palace itself, intermingling ancient and modern inextricably in places. As in Rome, at the Colosseum for instance, the palace had been used by medieval builders as a quarry, and parts had been removed for building materials. But with the knowledge he already possessed from his work in Rome, and from intact parts of the palace, he was able to make reconstruction drawings of fair accuracy.

According to Robert, the town got its name from the old palace. When the materials were re-used in the Middle Ages the inhabitants took the name from *palatium* (palace), and this was gradually cor- rupted into Spalatro. It later became Spalato (Italian), which has now been altered to the Serbo-Croat Split.

He was disappointed to find that the domestic part of the palace, the living quarters, had been so extensively destroyed. The main areas of preservation comprised the fortifications and temples as well as the underground halls. He was the first to make a scientific reconstruction of the palace, and his work is still shown to be accurate, needing only minor alterations to incorporate the information obtained by later excavation.

The overwhelming impression which strikes a modern traveller is that the palace is just like Robert's drawings. The once magnificent south wall and colonnade (Robert's Marine Wall) are a little disappointing, for shops and houses now line the whole length of the harbour to a much greater height than in 1757, and obscure the lower part of the Roman façade; but the underground rooms, the peristyle courtyard and the Emperor's Mausoleum [18] are almost exactly as he saw them. This can be judged by comparing his and Clérisseau's drawings with present-day photographs. This completeness and the quality of the Roman work usually astonish English visitors, because most books available in this country give the impression that the palace exists only in a fragmentary condition. It is exciting and pleasurable to find that this is not so (Plate 10).

Built in limestone, the rectangular palace contained the state apartments in a long gallery on the south side facing the sea. It is this façade that still incorporates much of the original, magnificent colonnade and is the first part of the palace visible as one approaches by boat or walks along the harbour. Within the enclosing walls, pierced by the four gateways, were temples, baths, living accommodation, reception halls and gardens. The Porta Aurea on the north side was the principal entrance and is still in a good state of preservation. It shows clearly the late Roman characteristics of design, the so-called decadent features, such as the relieving arch stressed over a lintel or columns supported only on corbels.

The palace is entered via the underground tunnel in the south façade, and one passes through the now restored vaulted chambers which supported the state apartments on the upper storey. These were almost totally destroyed (much to Adam's disappointment), and the underground chambers owe their survival to use over the centuries as the city's refuse dump. These halls, which vary in shape from circular to octagonal, rectangular or apsidal, are of brick and stone, all vaulted in domical, barrel or groined forms in Roman concrete and brick manner.

Emerging from the underground halls one comes out into the peristyle above, which was the large open court of the palace, giving access to all the state apartments. It was also used as an open ceremonial hall and is surrounded by a Corinthian colonnade, still in magnificent condition. The only difference between Robert's drawings of the peristyle and a modern photograph is that the courtyard and pavement are now covered by café tables, where the visitor can enjoy the unique surroundings while refreshing himself in the hot sunshine.

Adjacent to the peristyle is the Emperor's Mausoleum, an octagonal building with encircling colonnade of Corinthian columns. The Imperial mausoleum was transferred in the seventh century by the Bishop of Ravenna to the temple on the other side of the peristyle, now a baptistery, and the building adapted as a Christian cathedral. It owes its preservation to this adaptation; in the Middle Ages a campanile was built beside it and a choir was added at the other end.

The cathedral has not obscured the mausoleum, which is a highlight for tourists. The exterior is complete with its approach steps and doorway, while inside the original domed roof can be seen with its brick relieving arches above the richly sculptured entablature. Medallion portraits of Diocletian and his wife are included in the decorative frieze. Below, Corinthian columns support the entablature. Between these are niches. Apart from the congregation and church furniture, it all looks exactly like Clérisseau's drawings of 1757.

The Temple of Jupiter near by is another important monument, which has survived better than the other temples here. There is a beautiful decorative doorway, its carving in superb condition; inside is a barrel-vaulted, coffered ceiling, its caissons finely enriched with flowers and heads.

Apart from the problems of the work itself, there were other difficulties. The Venetian Governor was totally unused to receiving a group of young men who, armed with measuring rods, settled down to draw in detail parts of his town, notably the fortifications, and even did a little digging too. The promised written authority had not arrived from the powers that be in Venice, and the Governor was on the point of arresting Robert and his party as Turkish spies when, fortunately for them, General Graham, an old friend and commander-in-chief of the Venetian forces, appeared in the city. He vouched for Robert and a compromise was made. The party was allowed to carry on with their work but, to appease the Governor's dormant suspicions, they were to be accompanied all the time by a Venetian officer.

This had an inhibiting effect, and Robert made haste to carry out his survey as quickly as possible in case he was stopped again. In five weeks the work was done, a truly superhuman effort on the part of four draughtsmen. His book, published in 1764 (*see* Chapter 3) testifies to this. Robert's own comment in the preface reads: 'The fear of a second interruption added to my industry and, by unwearied application during 5 weeks, we completed with an accuracy which afforded me great satisfaction, those parts of our work which it was necessary to execute on the spot.'

Despite the hard work and protracted concentration, Robert seems to have enjoyed his stay in Dalmatia and was keenly interested in life in this more remote part of the Venetian republic. He tells James that the cost of living was very low, with beef at a halfpenny a pound, fowls costing twopence-halfpenny each and hares threepence. He says that other items are in proportion, so that one could live like a prince for fifty pounds a year. This was fortunate, since there were no inns, hotels or lodgings. They rented a house, but had to furnish and equip it, as it contained nothing beyond its bare walls.

In compensation there was entertainment every evening in the form of a play or opera given by repertory companies from Venice. The weather stayed hot and dry, typical for August on the Dalmatian coast, and a procession carried the Madonna through the streets every evening in prayer for rain which, when Robert set sail on 28th August, had not yet come.

They arrived back in Venice on 11th September and stayed for some time longer. After this point Robert's letters are scanty, with long intervals between. It is not certain at what date he left Venice, but he visited Vicenza and Verona before crossing the Alps. Here he studied the works of Palladio in the master's own city and found them interesting. He was perhaps more deeply attracted, partly

13   *Fireplace panel detail, 20 St James's Square, London*

14   *Wall panel, ante-room, Syon House*

15   *Fireplace, drawing-room, Syon House*

Opposite

16   *Doorcase, drawing-room, Syon House*

17   *South front, Kedleston Hall, Derbyshire*

18 *Bridge, Kedleston Hall*

19   *Chimneypiece, hall, Kedleston Hall*

20   *Sofa detail (Linnell),*
drawing-room, Kedleston Hall

21   *Cast-iron stove, saloon,*
Kedleston Hall

22 *Door furniture, saloon, Saltram, Devon*

23 *Ceiling detail, drawing-room, Hatchlands*

because he was less familiar with them, by the palaces and fortifications of Michele Sanmichele in Verona.

By 17th November he is in Augsburg, in Bavaria, where he writes to Betty: 'After Fifteen days' journey through the Tyrol I have got this far into Germany [19] where I proposed to rest 2 days after the fatigues of a Rude and Tedious Voyage.' He goes on to say that the recent floods had carried away about twenty miles of the main road through the Tyrol and he had to take a minor route, flanked by snow-covered peaks, and was forced to stay at small, rough country inns.

Donald and the two draughtsmen are still with him, but Clérisseau had parted from them at Vicenza and returned to Venice where he would stay for the winter. Robert had made a verbal agreement with him that he would receive a retainer of £100 per annum, and the Frenchman would make his services available whenever James came to Italy for his tour. Robert had also given him a sum of money and a parting present, but could do little more as his finances were low and, anyway, he expected James to travel in the very near future.

Robert proposes to set off for Frankfurt on 19th November and expects the journey will take about five days. Thence he will continue by post-chaise, or by boat up the River Rhine, according to weather conditions.

Having made himself fluent in French and Italian over the last three years, he is now disappointed to find himself once more inarticulate. He writes: 'I am once more in the miserable situation of understanding nothing and no body. Nothing but German gibberish reigns here, and were it not for my Liegois [20] who is himself Flemish and Speaks German we should be à plaindre as the french say.' 'I am convinced,' he goes on, 'it was the Divil who invented the German Language and that is what I most dread in Hell. For some days past I have been in some doubts if I was not already upon the Borders of Acheron and nothing but my firm persuasion of the Damned Spirits being much livelier than these heavy Germanick bodys cou'd have convinced me of the Contrary.'

Though weary from journeying and with little time to spare, Robert characteristically is still thinking of his work and has his eye to the main chance. He says: 'This town of Augsbourg is famous for the numbers of engravers to be found in it and the cheapness of their work. As we may sometime hence have works to be Done and

Books to be publish'd, I am to reconnoitre these youths with some exactitude, as I have no notion of paying £20 in England for what will be done as well here for 20 shillings.'

The winter was setting in in northern Europe and floods delayed him again and again, but he eventually reached Antwerp, where he stopped to look at the paintings and buildings. He writes to Nelly from Rotterdam on 17th December: 'Antwerp I saw with pleasure. The pictures are very fine, with respect to effect and colouring, But in drawing defective. It is otherwise a very Nobility and the Gothick tower [21] is Magnificent.' But Robert was tiring. He had travelled almost constantly since May and had worked at fever pitch. He no longer wanted to stay and look at works of art alone. He longed, above all, to get home to Britain, to see his family and to start work and prove himself.

The last letter in this series is written from London to his mother on 17th January 1758: 'Sunday afternoon I sett sail from Helvoet-sluys, and after a most agreable passage arrived at Harwich on Monday morning.'

Standards of comfort on Channel crossings were obviously different in 1758 from what they are today. On a journey which Robert describes as 'agreable' he 'spew'd the whole night in the packet Boat but I suppose it will do me much good in the Main'.

The night's experiences had not left him unaware. He was delighted at Harwich to get his drawings through the customs without difficulty. He says: 'I was very lucky at the Custom House of Harwich, where the Collector who is a virtuoso and loves drawings, by seeing mine, let me pass everything free which otherwise must have cost me £10 or £12 sterling.'

The tour is over. Robert is home, or, at least, in England. He signs himself in his letter 'I ever am my Dearest Mothers British Boy and shall remain so'. He had been away for three and a quarter crowded years. He never travelled outside Britain again, but this first-hand experience, added to his unique abilities, enabled him to create the 'Adam style'.

NOTES

1 Boswell's *London Journal, 1762–1763*. William Heinemann Ltd, 1950.

2 A vest in the eighteenth century was a gentleman's waistcoat, and in 1754 reached either mid thigh or knee-length. It was usually richly patterned and was allowed to show, as the coat was either worn open or only one or two buttons were fastened at the waist. The vest was therefore the most important decorative item in a well-dressed gentleman's wardrobe.

3 These refer not to underwear, but to the ladies' brocaded stomachers or *échelles* worn in the front of the gown bodice.

4 Later carried out a great deal of work in a number of Adam houses.

5 Allan Ramsay, the Scottish painter, son of Allan Ramsay the poet who was a friend of William Adam.

6 Such cheeses today weigh about thirty-five to forty kilograms and cost about £1 per kilo. About the same, taking the cost of living into account.

7 Sir John Summerson, *Architecture in Britain, 1530–1830*. Pelican History of Art Series, Penguin Books, 1953.

8 At this date dinner was the main meal of the day, taken about 3 p.m.

9 Giovanni Battista Piranesi (1720–78), the Venetian draughtsman, famous for his drawings of views of Rome with dramatic, romantic landscape backgrounds. Passionately devoted to Italy and to the Roman heritage, he was the chief opponent of the theory that classical architecture originated in Greece. *See* page 12.

10 The Seven Years War.

11 A reference to the Highland forts where John is employed and which provide the basis of the family income.

12 Mrs Adam died in 1761, so the problem of where she would live solved itself.

13 Leader and patron of the Palladian School of Architecture in England from *c.* 1720.

14 Andrea Palladio (1508–80).

15 He is referring to the easy journey by sea from Split to Athens.

16 Now the site of the memorial to Garibaldi and the Thousand.

17 *The Antiquities of Athens*, James Stuart and Nicholas Revett.

18 Called by Robert the Temple of Jupiter but now part of the cathedral.

19 Reluctantly Robert had to travel home via Germany instead of France, owing to the Seven Years War. He was disappointed not to stay in Paris.

20 Laurent Benoît Dewez, one of his draughtsmen.

21 Antwerp Cathedral. One of the finest Gothic towers in Europe.

3. MAKING A START

ROBERT wasted no time. At the age of twenty-nine, with his finances at a low ebb, he had as quickly as possible to establish his reputation as a young architect of fashion and promise. A number of his friends and acquaintances – many of whom, such as Charles Hope and Allan Ramsay, had been with him in Rome – were convinced of his outstanding talents. Before his return they had already canvassed their friends and relations on his behalf. Wealthy men, including more than a sprinkling of the leading aristocracy, were showing interest in what this young prodigy might do. But, to display his work, Robert needed a house.

James had joined him in London; the two brothers set up home in a furnished house in St James's Place, and every day Robert sallied forth to visit possible clients and showed them his drawings.

James describes their new life to his sister Nelly in Scotland on 1st February. The younger brother is excited at being in London and spending his time with the returned traveller, who appears so sophisticated and knowledgeable. From working in Scotland it is a wonderful change. He meets new friends and is learning a whole new background to his profession. He writes: 'I am just now come home after having paid a good many visits along with Bob, and I have parted with him as he had yet another to pay before he shou'd end the Labors of the Day. . . . At present we are in a furnish'd house in St. James's place at a damn'd high rent, which we take by the week till something passable casts up, but we found it impossible to be longer in a vagabond situation. Our family therefor consists of 2 Masters, 2 Draughtsmen, one Man and one Maid, and all upon Board wages.'

They are hard up and the furnishings are inadequate, so James begs the family to send them some sheets, pillow-cases and tablecloths. He says that it does not matter if they are of a coarse quality as 'anything passes down with batchelors'.

Later in the day James continues: 'Bob and his Italian [1] are quivering away at this Nondum Pace to such a degree that I can't write a word. . . . I am so fond of Bob's Italian airs that I'm insensibly making the most absurd attempts upon them, to the great amusement of the traveller, who laughs me to scorn.

'Bob still continues to pay his respects to the great and as he has now got a place for showing his things, he is ready to admit strangers.'

Robert had been fortunate in the year of his return from Italy: he now had a first-class opportunity to make himself the doyen of English architecture. Colen Campbell, William Kent and Giacomo Leoni were all dead by 1750, and the lone wolf, James Gibbs, followed them in 1754. Lord Burlington died in 1753, and the second generation of Palladian architects continued his work. Chief of these were Sir Robert Taylor and James Paine in London and John Carr in Yorkshire. Taylor, at forty-four, was the eldest of these, but his work, though sound, was not very original and Palladianism was on its way out. Robert therefore might hope for a breakthrough to something different. Men such as Henry Keene, James Stuart or Nicholas Revett were not likely to take up the challenge.

This left William Chambers who, as Robert had known from the beginning, would be his stumbling-block. He was encouraged, if only in a negative way, to see Chambers in London. James describes how 'Chambers was to wait on Bob, and missing him left his name. We called on him, found him Drawing in a poor mean lodging up a long dark stair. He show'd some of those Designs he is going to publish which are wretched.[2] He mentioned the prince [3] more than once and showed us a Design of his, simple enough. You may believe however it shows his love for the Art. We did not reckon it very polite, the repetition of so great a name but Bob was excessively civil to him'.

Allan Ramsay had already proposed Robert's name as a member of the new Society of Arts in St Martin's Lane, founded in 1754, and on 1st February Robert was elected.

He quickly found a suitable house in Lower Grosvenor Street. He moved in with James, the draughtsmen and servants, and before long his two sisters came to run the household for him. Robert asked John for a loan to help him buy the house, which John granted, at a 4 per cent rate of interest. This spacious house remained the London home and office of Adam Brothers until their removal to the Adelphi in the 1770s.

By the summer of 1758 James had returned to work in Scotland, leaving Robert settled in at Lower Grosvenor Street, well organized in his domestic and business arrangements. Important clients were beginning to show tangible signs of interest. Lord Hope had been a great help to him in this respect, and new inquirers included the Duke of Argyll, Lord Findlater and Lord Mansfield. There was even a hopeful murmur from Lord Leicester but, not surprisingly, nothing came of this. After all, Kent's masterpiece at Holkham was not long finished.

It was just before this that the unfortunate first interview with Lord Bute occurred. Robert had been building his hopes high in this direction, and when his friend John Home, now Lord Bute's secretary, offered to introduce him, in company with Dr Alexander Carlyle and William Robertson (both Scots), Adam jumped at the chance. At that time Lord Bute had it in his power to influence considerably the career of a young architect, being principal adviser to the Princess of Wales, mother of the heir-apparent, Prince George. He had already arranged the appointment of Chambers as tutor to the young prince.

Carlyle reports the incident in his autobiography. The earl received them briefly and coldly, clearly ready to go out and anxious to terminate the interview as soon as possible. Robert, normally even-tempered, was stung by this rudeness: 'What! had he been presented to all the princes in Italy and France, and most graciously received, to come and be treated with such distance and pride by the youngest earl but one in all Scotland.' When, a short while later, Lord Bute returned the copy of Piranesi's book which he had sent him, Robert was coldly angry.

But, as Carlyle reports later: 'They were better friends afterwards and Robert found him a kind patron, when his professional merit was made known to him'; and, again, referring to Bute: 'He was a very worthy and virtuous man – a man of taste, and a good belles-lettres scholar, and that he trained up the prince on true patriotic principles and a love of the constitution. . . . But he proved himself unfit for the station he had assumed, being not versatile enough for a prime minister; and, though personally brave, yet void of that political firmness, which is necessary to stand the storms of state.' In retrospect, this would appear a fair summing-up of Bute when he held office in the early 1760s. Certainly Lord Bute was proud and not easy to know. He found it difficult to unbend and was totally lacking in the charm and ease of manner which Robert possessed to such a degree.

Once they had begun to understand each other, and appreciate each other's worth, Bute became, over the years, one of Robert's staunchest patrons, a fact recorded in the subscribers' list in the Spalatro volume, where ten copies were ascribed to his lordship.

It was as early as 1758 that two of the future owners of Adam's most famous houses came under the spell of his designs. These were Edwin Lascelles, for whom Robert did much work at Harewood House, and Sir Nathaniel Curzon, owner of Kedleston. Lord Mansfield later became a third important client at Kenwood.

In his letter to James on 17th June, Robert says: 'Lascelles' house is now well advanc'd, I have made some alterations on it, But as the plan did not admitt of a great many that has prevented the fronts from being much chang'd likewise.' He goes on to describe the alterations in detail and his ideas for ornamentation (*see* Chapter 4).

James reports from Edinburgh on 25th June that John has still not made up his mind whether to go to Italy or not. He is now consulting Lord Hopetoun and others to decide for him whether the advantage of the trip will be worth the expense. It is early November before he finally makes the decision not to go, and James definitely begins to lay his plans to set off at the end of 1759.

Robert, on hearing of this, sums up the situation with his customary speed and clarity, and also with an eye to his own advantage. John had planned to take with him George Richardson, a qualified draughtsman who had been with the firm in Scotland for some time. Robert now needs a good extra draughtsman, and James will need one on his tour. He writes: 'Now I see you are fixt as to your Travelling which is a Satisfaction especially as you have a twelve month to settle everything and prepare for it. What strikes me is the loss you will be at for a draughtsman, and as I know how difficult it is to pick up one that knows anything, either in England or Italy, I think if you cou'd get Johnie to agree to deliver over George Richardson to you immediately which he cannot refuse from his own intention to have taken him. In that case I wou'd have you send him directly to me and I shall promise to deliver him over to you in a fair way to doing well.'

Robert continues with some elder-brotherly advice to a future member of his firm: 'I have sent by Jenny the Book of Ornaments, which will be of Great use to you to draw after, particularly those that have the Griffins and foliages as it will fix the antique manner in your head before you see them. I have likewise made Brunias copy over the large drawing by Pietro da Cortona which is one of the best things for Setting one's hand to these things that I know and I would have you copy it with care.'

Clérisseau, waiting in Italy, is having financial problems, as the next brother is so long in coming to employ him. Robert agrees to continue paying the retainer, out of his own pocket if necessary, but he hopes that John and James will relieve him of the burden, as he is finding the lack of money a problem as yet. He is discovering that a long time may well elapse between acquiring the favour of a client and actually receiving any money. On 11th August he complains: 'Nobody thinks of paying and when they do, give nothing worth taking, so may the Divil damn them altogether, I'll turn Soap boiler and Tallow Chandler.'

One of Robert's problems is that he has made such a clear impression of a self-confident, well-to-do architect that he does not look as though he needs money. The Duke of Argyle had given him a twenty-pound note to give to his Italian draughtsman, but Robert thinks that he needs the money more. After all, he pays the bills.

The Spalatro volume was being produced slowly – too slowly. Bartolozzi and Zucchi were engraving plates in Italy under Clérisseau's supervision, and Robert's draughtsmen were working on it in England. But it was a long task, for Robert was a perfectionist. The drawings had to be of first-class quality. They were.

He decided that it would be a good investment to send out some complimentary copies, and compiled a list of suitable recipients.

Aiming high, he headed his list with Frederick the Great, King of Prussia, who, as Britain's ally in the Seven Years War, had held at bay so successfully the combined weight of France, Austria and Russia. Included also were the Pope and the College of Cardinals, and Elizabeth, Tsaritsa of Russia.

Adam's first commission, for General Bland's house, is now being carried out. The client is very pleased with it, but Robert is critical of the workmanship, particularly the stucco: 'It is not executed in the antique taste as it is impossible to get English workmen who will leave their angly stiff sharp manner. However as they know no better in England they cannot be so vext as I am myself.' Robert's answer to this, later, was to build up a team of craftsmen, mainly of continental origin (*see* Chapter 4).

Suddenly, one day in 1760, King George II died from a heart attack. It seemed to many – artists, politicians, lawyers, architects – that a new era was opening up when the young George III, his grandson, acceded. This youth, the third generation of kings from Hanover, tried to be more English than the English. His pride in the country's traditions and achievements was deep and sincere. He was young, energetic, idealistic, and he showed promise of interest in the arts and in becoming an enthusiastic patron. 'We shall see great things', was the feeling among musicians, writers and artists.

Perhaps he would build a great palace, fitting symbol of a monarchy now ruling a great empire. He would encourage composers and commission great portraits. He would reinforce and assist development of the democratic system of government.

In effect George III did none of these things. Compared with Charles II, he was a poor patron. He distrusted politicians and did his best to restore the power of the monarchy and do without a Cabinet. He was a great disappointment to those men who had hoped for so much, and, most of all perhaps, disappointed himself. He too had imagined that his ideas would bear richer fruit.

The king built no palaces, to the deep regret of Adam in particular, who had hoped to raise a great Roman pile of Palatine scale and splendour. Horace Walpole complained that the king's taste rose no higher than Handel and Benjamin West, barely noticing Reynolds and Gainsborough, who were giving of their best.

It is true that the king's patronage extended on so narrow a front that even Sir Joshua Reynolds, accepted as the leading portrait painter in the land and the Royal Academy's first president, had to press George III to sit for his portrait as a personal favour.

In the early years of his reign George III was still strongly influenced by Bute. John Stuart, Earl of Bute, had gained favour with the royal family through George's father, Frederick, Prince of Wales. When the latter died in 1751 Bute was appointed by the Princess of Wales as tutor to the boy, who admired and respected his abilities and judgment. With the accession in 1760 Bute rose quickly to power. He advocated a speedy end to the Seven Years War and gradually eased himself into Pitt's place, becoming Prime Minister in 1762.

Though able, he was not the man for the task and soon became very unpopular. This was partly because he was a Scot, and feeling against the influx from Scotland was running high in the 1760s. The talented Scots were accused of worming their way into high positions in the country, then making sure that they employed only 'North Britons'. It was pointed out that, from Bute downwards, the Courts of Justice, government service, the arts and medicine were all ruled by the Scots.

This antipathy towards everyone Scottish, which by 1765 had grown to an unreasoning extent, made many able Scotsmen disgusted with the discrimination, and a number of them left the country. They were slighted and often ignored. Boswell comments in 1762 on how difficult it was to get acquainted with people of fashion in London, and John Home, the Scottish dramatist, found that even Garrick, a friend of many of the Scottish fraternity in London, dared not present his play at Drury Lane under the author's own name. He used a pseudonym and the play was a great success. When, however, the identity of the author leaked out people ceased to go to see it.

Largely because of this, but also due to common customs and acquaintances, Scots in London tended to form a closely knit circle. Robert Adam was no exception. His friends, at least in the first year or so, were fellow exiles: Alexander Carlyle, John Home, William Robertson, Adam Smith, Sandy Wedderburn and Adam Ferguson.

Carlyle recounts how a number of them used to meet once a week in a coffee-house in Savile Row. 'We met every Wednesday at 3

o'clock. There were Home and Robertson, Wedderburn, Jack
Dalrymple, Bob Adam, Ferguson and myself, As Ferguson rode
back to Harrow, we always parted between 5 and 6 o'clock; and
it will hardly now be believed that our reckoning never exceeded
5/- a-piece. We had a very good dinner, and plenty of punch etc.,
though no claret for that sum.' (Carlyle is writing his autobiography
in 1800 and looking back nostalgically to former prices.)

Despite the anti-Scottish feeling, Adam had tremendous success
during his first year or so in London, acquiring wealthy and important clients. Most of these were already engaged in building or
altering their houses, but were so attracted by Robert's new style
and ideas that they cast aside the architect in charge and appointed
Adam to carry on with the work. It says much for his talent for
tactful persuasion and the pleasant ease of his relations with others
that, in every case, the displaced architect (who was sometimes a
much older man) bore no apparent grudge against Adam and, in a
number of instances, continued to work amicably under or with
him. Two such were John Carr and James Paine.

Some of Adam's patrons were Scots – Mansfield and Bute, for
example – but most were not. He also made lifelong English friends,
the two most famous of these being David Garrick and Sir Joshua
Reynolds. These three men were all innovators in their respective
professions: the stage, painting, architecture. They all represented
a high quality of endeavour and set new standards of taste and
perfection.

By 1759, though he was still showing his drawings, talking about
his ideas and interviewing clients, Robert's career was under way.
He was putting his schemes into practice.

One of his earliest commissions came from the Admiralty,
probably through the influence of Admiral Boscawen. The Admiralty building in Whitehall had been designed by Thomas Ripley
in the 1720s. Ripley died in 1758 and the Admiralty wanted a screen
and gateway to provide a suitable entrance from the street. They
were anxious to have an impressive and tasteful façade, for the
building behind was unquestionably dull in the extreme.

Adam made the designs in 1759, and the work was carried out in
1760. It was his first public work and was widely acclaimed; its
admirers included Horace Walpole and the Lords Commissioners

themselves. The screen, slightly altered, still exists in Whitehall, next to Kent's Horse Guards and opposite Inigo Jones' Banqueting Hall. This group comprises the three classical works of quality in the street. Robert used the Tuscan order (the Roman variant of Doric, where the columns are not fluted). There is a central gateway with pedimented terminal pavilions joined by the Tuscan colonnades. His original design (published in the *Works*) shows large-scale sculptured figures in niches, which do not exist, and tympana enrichment which differs from the work as carried out. The actual sculptural decoration was executed by Michael Spang, who worked for Adam on other occasions – at Kedleston, for instance (Plate *8*).

Admiral Edward Boscawen, commander of naval forces at Louisburg in Canada, returned home in 1759 to Hatchlands. This house near Guildford, purchased by him and his wife in 1750, was originally a moated grange of Chertsey Abbey, but had been rebuilt earlier in the eighteenth century in simple, red-brick, Georgian style.

They commissioned Robert Adam in 1759 to decorate the rooms on the south front, and it is chiefly the drawing- and dining-rooms that remain unaltered. It was his first large commission, and he was able to try out his ideas, based on what he had studied in Italy. Characteristically he did just that. His confidence and ability are shown by the fact that he did not play safe at this first opportunity by designing in a more traditional, tried manner. The decoration of these two rooms is immature compared with his great interiors of the 1760s, but it is different both from his father's work and from his own at Hopetoun in the early 1750s. The architectural and ornamental stucco detail is still in high relief, and the motifs large scale. The design is, however, original, totally different from the Palladian and rococo interiors and distinguishably Robert Adam.

In the library (the Adam drawing-room) the ceiling is much the finest part. The handling of the compartmenting and decorative sculptural work is virtually identical with Robert's drawings from Raphael villas in Italy (Soane Museum). The nearly square ceiling has a circular centre-piece. It is then divided into sections by moulded ribs which radiate from the central rose to the outer circle. The large-scale, high-relief sculptural decoration comprises figures, merfolk, marine trophies and Neptune – presumably nautical in deference to the admiral. The existing colour scheme, probably not far from the original, is in warm cream and pale green with gilt touches on the enrichments.

The large, rectangular drawing-room (originally the Adam dining-room) is beautifully situated, facing south on to the gardens, and with a semicircular bay in the centre of one long wall, opposite to the fireplace on the other. A full-scale entablature surrounds the room. The scheme of this, like the ceiling, was last decorated in the late nineteenth century, but in the clean Surrey air and lovingly cared for it is still in mint condition. It gives a warm, peaceful glow to the room. The background is softly hued in off-white cream, green and peach, the sculptured ornamental stucco in white and the enrichments lightly touched with gilt. The only exception to this sparing use of gold is in the rich frieze with its continuous band of anthemion and dolphins alternating with floral sprays.

On the ceiling an elongated octagon is set into the rectangle, and the centre-piece is a reeded oval. The interest lies in the spandrel corners, ornamented by male figures standing between dolphins and arabesque whorls. The bay decorative scheme contains shells, sea-horses, scrolls and anthemion. This ceiling shows especially the universal quality of Adam's handling of stucco ornament in scale, form and delicacy. Here is the germ of Adam's genius (Plate 23).

The quality of materials used by Robert in these early houses is very high. The wood-carving particularly is beautifully done, and the decoration is all in carved wood, and not stucco or composition as in so many of his later works. Window shutters and frames, dado rails, wainscot and door-cases are all finely carved in classical detail, heavier than his more typical work later and more solidly, squarely proportioned. This applies particularly to the mahogany doors and the carved cases. The former are polished with carved panels and the latter painted white with gilded enrichments; there is no order. Of special interest is the white marble fireplace with flanking caryatid figure supports (Plate 11). These were Adam's favourite early designs. They appear again at Harewood and Croome. On the centre panel is a carved two-horse chariot driven by a classical, winged Boadicea. The rectangular mirror above has a classic Adam frame.

Contemporary with Hatchlands is Robert's work at Shardeloes, near Amersham. Here also he was feeling his way, breaking away from earlier traditions, yet not fully sophisticated in his later, mature approach. Owned for many years by the Drake family, this fine house and stable block has now been divided into flats and maisonettes. The Adam *décor* of ceilings, walls and fireplaces has been fully preserved and redecorated.

The house was built by Leadbetter in 1758 and, as at Hatchlands, Adam was given the task of decorating the interior. Here also he used quality materials, polished mahogany doors and carved woodwork on walls and window-frames. The Roman Doric hall was the first that he tried out in this style; there were many to follow. He thought it a suitable order for entrance halls, presenting a dignified, formal manner with characteristic ornament and proportions to accentuate it. (*See* Robert's views on this order in his letter to Lord Kames, pages 108–9.)

On the ground floor the rooms are all eighteen feet high. The hall, which later became the saloon, is the largest room – thirty feet square – and this was entered from the central portico on the east front. The main reception rooms run *en suite* from this; a drawing-room, dining-room and library. The treatment of all these rooms shows an advance on Hatchlands towards the Adam style. In the dining-room (where Robert always thought the walls should be stucco ornamented in preference to using hangings or tapestry, in order to avoid retaining the odour of food) he introduced his characteristic relief panels.

This classic Adam feature can be seen in nearly every house he designed. At Shardeloes the ornament is in higher relief than later works – No. 20 St James's Square, for example – and the handling is less expert. His usual treatment of perfectly symmetrical arabesques intertwined with putti, vases, urns, anthemion, flowers and drops were designed with one or more focal centres. These were most often circular (though there are octagons and ovals) and could be paintings or Wedgwood-type sculptured cameos. Here is an early instance of such wall decoration.

Here too the ceiling is an early instance of a later classic Adam pattern. Rather on the lines of the eating-room at Osterley, a moulded oval motif, threaded and garlanded with foliage, forms the centre of the design. Less successful than his later version, the other motifs interposed create a certain incongruity.

The drawing-room ceiling is in lower relief and more typical of his established style. Its centre-piece is circular, and fans are introduced at the corners. Arabesques and paterae decorate the area outside the circle, which is closely surrounded by swags and drops.

The Shardeloes fireplaces are restrained and simple. The console design, with high-relief sculptured central panel, is used; also the classical form with Ionic columns and a swag and paterae frieze. White marble with coloured marble inlay is the material.

The library has something in common with Adam's much later interior at Mellerstain. Though the wall *décor* may have been altered to its present form by James and/or Samuel Wyatt *c.* 1775, the ceiling still exists to Adam's design; the work was carried out by Joseph Rose.

Robert's career was gaining impetus. On 7th December 1761 he and Chambers were appointed 'Joint Architects of His Majesty's Works' at a salary of £300 a year. In 1762 Piranesi's work *Campus Martius* was published, wherein he dedicated the plan to Robert: 'Roberto Adam Britann. Architecto Celebirrim.' A medal was engraved on the plan. It displayed the heads of Adam and Piranesi with the inscription: 'Io. Bapt. Piranesius Robertus Adam. Architecti'.

Early in 1761 Robert was still chasing up his plates in Venice for the Spalatro volume; they were progressing too slowly without him on the spot to chivvy the engravers. James, who was there for several months in 1760, had got things moving and supervised the work, but when he left at the end of the year Bartolozzi, Zucchi and Santini slipped back once more into the usual Venetian way of spending the winter: doing nothing. In February 1761 Robert writes to his agent, Mr Duff: 'As I have heard nothing lately from you about my Plates of Spalatro which my Brother left to be completed at Venice I beg you will do me the favour to enquire strictly about these, and let me know the Progress that is made in them.' He then lists in detail the plates concerned and begs Duff to send them by whatever route he prefers, via France or by Germany and Holland. He does not mind so long as he gets them soon. It is no use. The Italians will not be hurried. It is 1764 before the book is published.

James set off in May 1760, accompanied by the draughtsman

George Richardson, on his Grand Tour. He was away till 1763, visiting many of the places that Robert had seen. But he did not follow his brother in taking a similar opportunity to acquire the background knowledge that might have helped him to design great buildings. He thoroughly enjoyed himself and was most appreciative, though less comprehending, of all the great works of art he saw; but he travelled always as a gentleman on the Grand Tour, not, as Robert had done after his first few flourishes, as an architect bent on study and the pursuit of knowledge. Clérisseau, seeing through him from the first, both despised and took advantage of him, a thing he had never attempted with Robert, whom he respected and admired.

James crossed to The Hague and travelled in a leisurely manner by way of Brussels, Paris, Lyons, Turin, Milan and Padua to Venice, where he settled in by 25th June. His comments are more superficial than Robert's, and, as an elegant dandy, he disapproved strongly of France, especially the capital, which he thought dirty and disreputable. He liked the fashions, but found this elegance incomprehensible among such filth.

Visiting the Certosa di Pavia he was intrigued and surprised by the ceramic work on the early Renaissance façade, which he likened to marble, so fine and hard was it. 'Even the Corinthian Capitals are in Clay,' he exclaimed.

James settled down in Venice, acclimatizing himself to 'this Aquatic City' and its strangeness. After a while Clérisseau persuaded him to study some buildings and make some drawings, and also began to plan his trips.

Before he left England James agreed with Robert that he would try to cover the areas which his brother had been unable to visit; his work would thus complement Robert's, and their combined experience and data would prove invaluable. He was planning therefore to travel down the Adriatic via Pula to Greece and, on a different excursion, to visit Paestum, Calabria and Sicily. But he carried out only a fraction of the journey: the frustrations and difficulties inherent in eighteenth-century travel and in planning and achieving such projects were sufficient to deter him. Without Robert at his side his determination melted away and he returned to the pleasing life of a gentleman of leisure on the Continent.

In September he set off in a felucca to Pula, accompanied by

Clérisseau and Richardson. He had neglected to obtain permission for his studies and drawings, so returned empty-handed.

Early in October he was in Vicenza, where he spent some time, then travelled to Verona. His strictures on Palladio's work were scathing, especially on the 'Basilica' and the Teatro Olimpico (generally regarded as Palladio's outstanding works here). He awarded faint praise to the Villa Capra (the Rotunda), which had been the inspiration for 'Palladian' villas in England, notably Lord Burlington's Chiswick House and Campbell's Mereworth Castle. James sums up his days in Vicenza: 'I have been employ'd in examining the works of the celebrated Paladio, who is one of those fortunate Genius's who has purchas'd reputation at an easy rate. I am now fully satisfy'd that I have it to say that I have seen his work here, but by no means incline to spend more time on him and therefor I proceed to Verona tomorrow morning.'

James spent more time at Vicenza with the Italian nobility and town officials than in studying Palladio, but as they were insistent that he must see the works of Sanmichele in Verona he went off to do so, remembering that Robert also had been most impressed by his palaces. Having given a perfunctory glance at these James expressed his surprise that Bob should have felt as he did. Contrasting James's comments on what he saw during his whole tour one cannot fail to mark the superficiality of his remarks, compared with those of his elder brother, and the shallowness of his comprehension.

They all returned to Venice towards the end of October, and by 8th November were off to Florence. They travelled up the River Po, then visited Ferrara and Bologna en route. Florence really thrilled James. Like Michelangelo before him, and countless travellers since, he found the Ghiberti 'Gates of Paradise', the east doors of the baptistery, especially wonderful.

One of the tasks which James carried out assiduously for Robert was a search for marble columns, scagliola paving or pieces of antique statuary which his brother needed for certain houses he was designing in England. This is an instance of how James, when given a direct commission with precise terms of reference, was conscientious and capable. It seems likely that, had he been in Italy at the same time as Robert, he would have made much better use of his time and gained greater satisfaction from his tour.

From Florence he writes home on 13th December 1760 to report his progress in finding some ancient porphyry and granite columns and urns which Robert wants for temples in the grounds at Kedleston. He has found a number of other items, and asks for Bob's instructions as to whether or not he should buy them.

They take a trip to Pisa and spend some time in the Piazza dei Miracoli. James is fascinated by what he refers to as 'freezes and columns and other fragments of greek workmanship' in the cathedral and baptistery. He thinks these very fine and of 'an Elegance and perfection almost Roman, tho' they preserve so much of the Greek character as to leave their native country indisputable'. James goes on to say that he and Clérisseau have made detailed drawings of this ornament.

One wonders if Robert would have known better. The baptistery and cathedral at Pisa are Romanesque, but the sculptured panels on the baptistery font, described by James, are by Nicola Pisano, carried out in 1260, and in the Gothic phase of building, but their classical proto-Renaissance character is unmistakable. This is presumably what led James astray, but there was nothing ancient or Greek about Pisano.

James suffered the same bitterly cold weather in Tuscany that Robert had experienced. He was equally surprised and indignant. He writes on 26th January: 'The Arno has frozen to that degree, that I have not any winter in England suffer'd more from cold, because the houses are not made here in expectation of cold, but I keep a strong fire and a stout under Westcoat, as thick as two English Flannels.'

James's understanding of his own abilities and usefulness to the Adam firm, in comparison with Robert's, are shown in his letter of 2nd February 1761. He is replying to news of Robert's professional achievements in London. He exhibits no rancour, but some humour, at this realization: 'You may assure Bob, I shall also pardon him for superior merit. I am much less ambitious than Caesar, I am contented to hold a second place.' A little further on: 'I have ordered another parmezan Cheese for you.'

The party reached Rome at the end of February and settled in at Robert's old quarters in the Casa Quernieri.

It was not long before friction between James and Clérisseau became acute. Their personalities, training and approach to life were all so different, and it was inevitable that they would get on each other's nerves and see the worst in each other. Clérisseau saw James as foppish, indolent, pleasure-loving and snobbish. James thought Clérisseau vain, artful, none too scrupulous and in the habit of discussing his 'betters' behind their backs. Clérisseau's inability to learn any language other than his own and his poor attempts to write even French, together with his apparent lack of knowledge or interest in any subject save architectural history, made him a bore to James. Clérisseau, in his turn, despised the young dilettante and thought him all words and no action.

Those characteristics in both men were true, but showed only one side of their respective personalities. During 1761 they both wrote long letters to Robert, complaining of each other. As time passed James began to speak Italian fluently and to enjoy himself in society. He did less and less work, merely informing Clérisseau and the draughtsmen what he wanted done. Matters came to a head. James accused Clérisseau of withholding copies of Robert's drawings in order to pass them off as his own, and he advised Robert not to trust the 'artful deceiver'. Clérisseau countered with indignation that his work was far better than either James's or Robert's, and that neither could have got anywhere without his help.

After some hotly spoken words, James and Clérisseau settled down to an uneasy truce. We have no record of what Robert thought of the long letters of recrimination which he received from both contestants. Knowing both intimately, he was probably amused.

At the end of August James and his *entourage* set off for Naples and all points south. August is an unsuitable time of year to travel in the *mezzogiorno*, even today. In 1761, without air-conditioning, an *autostrada del sole* and aerosol sprays against mosquitoes and flies, it was almost suicidal for a party of northern Europeans and, if James had only organized himself a bit better, unnecessary.

Having made the journey, he complains bitterly of its discomforts. Even so, he carries out a fairly energetic programme, visiting Herculaneum, Baia, Pozzuoli like Robert, but goes on to see the excavations at Pompeii which he finds most interesting. The drawings made here of the stucco wall decoration were, no doubt, invaluable to Robert, who had been fascinated by such work at Herculaneum.

James may have been shallow-minded and lacking in balanced judgment and criticism, but he had a fair knowledge of the history of his subject and, all along, he was absorbed by the ancient Roman work, though dismissing Italian Renaissance and Baroque with scant ceremony. Thus he was most impressed by the Trajan Arch at Benevento, but unmoved by Vanvitelli's yet unfinished royal palace at Caserta, begun in 1752.

He started to make arrangements for the trip to Sicily, but these involved a long wait for permission from a government that was no model of efficiency. When, eventually, limited approval was given, permitting him to visit and draw but not to dig, he had tired of the idea and could not face the journey. He settled for Paestum instead.

The ancient Greek site Poseidonia, called Paestum by the Romans and Pesto by modern Italy, is now easily accessible by road or rail. It lies near the coast, about twenty-five miles south of Salerno. It was difficult to reach in November 1761, when storms and floods made the poor roads impassable. James and his party had to turn back, and they eventually reached it by boat from Salerno. They were disappointed in what they saw.

These three archaic Greek temples, dating from the sixth and fifth centuries B.C., are prized today as almost unique specimens of this early time. In the mid-eighteenth century few European students had seen them, and James's reaction was not uncommon among his contemporaries. He thought them unworthy of the trouble they had taken to get there, and could not see why they should be so famous. He felt them to be 'an inelegant unriched Doric that afford no detail and scarcely produce 2 good views'.

James returned as quickly as possible to Naples and thence, in December, to Rome, where he stayed till 1763, making no more trips and doing little work.

He was abroad for slightly longer than Robert. He had more assistance from draughtsmen and body servants. He spent more money, discussed many ideas and lectured to all who would hear him. He was charming and well liked, always a popular guest and host and, perhaps because he lacked Robert's dedicated singleness of purpose and had plenty of time to spare, people found him more *simpatico*.

He had achieved hardly anything in three and a half years away, but the atmosphere and knowledge had been absorbed, and he had read widely. On his return to London he worked steadily and consistently for Robert for thirty years and remained always his loyal second-in-command, willing to do anything that his idolized elder brother asked of him.

Robert's celebrated letter to Lord Kames has been quoted in full or in part in a number of publications because it is the only record we have of his views at this period on architectural form and how it should be used. By March 1763, when he wrote the letter, he was well established in his career, was building several of his great houses and had had time to crystallize his ideas on how to employ in the design of country houses the material he had absorbed in Italy. A decade later he gives us his ideas once more in the *Works*, but by then they had evolved further. The salient parts of the letter to Lord Kames are quoted here for readers who are interested in the architectural problems of classical design.

Lord Kames, a colleague of Lord Auchinleck, James Boswell's father, was a notable figure in Scots law. He was also an enthusiastic and informed student of architecture and had known the Adam family for many years. In 1763 he was sixty-eight, but still energetic and wanting to be *au fait* with the classical problems of the day.

Robert's letter, giving his views in answer to Lord Kames's queries, make clear his belief (which he held all his life) that a great architect should not hesitate to alter the classical rules of proportion and detail if, by so doing, he could interpret more accurately and with spirit the essence of the classical order. He is convinced by his studies that this is what the ancient Greeks and Romans did, and that only the modern world creates strict rules, rendering the whole style sterile. He is in particular answering Lord Kames's queries on the use and handling of the different orders.

'If you wish that the Doric Order should appear Simple and Solid, you ought not to flute your Columns, nor carve any of the Mouldings of your Capitals and Bases. Keep the Entablature of the plainest kind, no Guttae to your Mutules nor no Ornaments in your Metopes.[4] In which case you will find no one part too much or too little ornamented for the Others, and I have already experienced this in many Buildings I have executed. If you flute your columns, you must then enrich your Capital and Base, Carve your Cornice and put ornaments in the Metopes of the Freeze. This degree of enrichment I would seldom use without Doors. But it is very proper in Halls,[5] Insides of Temples etc. I have ventured to alter some parts of this Order particularly in its Mouldings rejecting some of the Common ones and adopting or substituting others in their Stead. These alterations most people have allow'd to be much for the better. But it is a dangerous experiment for mere Retailers of the Art who have neither Eyes nor Judgement.

'The Capital of the Corinthian Order demands Delicacy and Richness in every other part belonging to that Order and when that necessary profusion of ornament cannot be afforded the Architect ought to reject it altogether. The Fable of Calimachus,[6] the Basket of Acanthus leaves, I never had any faith in. The Egyptians had a kind of Corinthian Order and in many parts so similar to that which the Grecians executed, that we cannot doubt of their having only Chang'd, and improved, as they imagin'd, many parts of the Egyptian Capital. If Your Lordship will look into Norden's Anti- quity's of Egypt you will see the Capital I refer to. I own that their appears an absurdity in supporting any weight by a combined Cluster of light foliage. But if you suppose a Column to represent a tree I shall suppose a palm tree which grows of a pretty equal thickness and of which the Branches grow near the top and that part of the top of this Tree is cutt off and the Branches or Leaves left, you will find that Tree able to support a weight and these Branches by no means impairing its Strength nor in any danger of being Broke off, they will bend down their heads with the Beam or Entablature that lies upon them together, as those of the Corinthian Capital do, but have no connection with the support of that weight and this I take to be the true rise of a Corinthian Order.

'The Ionic Order ought only to be used in Gay and Slight build- ings as the meagreness of its Capital never fills the Eye sufficiently on the outsides of Solid Architecture.[7] I always thought this Order destined for insides of Houses [8] and Temples. But the universal practice to the Contrary in all Countrys shows how much I stand Single in this opinion.

'If a Building was not so immensely great as to demand Variety of Orders I would omitt entirely the two Mongrel Orders, the Composite and the Tuscan and God knows, our Confined ideas of

Magnificence in a Building does but too little require that variety. The Composite Capital is by no means so fine as the Corinthian and the Doric Order can without great variation supply every purpose of the Tuscan.

'I flatter myself that the Arts in general are in a progressive state in England. If the King builds a palace [9] in a Magnificent and pure Stile of Architecture, it will give a great push at once to the taste of this Countrey, as it will not only furnish Ideas for Lesser Buildings, but show Effects both of External and Internal composition which this Countrey is as Yet entirely Ignorant of. If it is done Meanly or in Bad Taste, I should apprehend the Worst of Consequences. Painting and Sculpture depend more upon good Architecture than one would imagine. They are the Necessary accompanyments and a Building that makes no provision for them I would at once pronounce to be wretched.' One wonders what Robert would have thought of the utilitarian structures of today, stripped of all ornament.

This is one of the criticisms levelled at Adam by his detractors; not the fact that he regards painting and sculpture as essential to his architecture, but that he treats them as subservient. In his buildings he always designed their place – walls, ceilings, niches, etc. – and even drew in the form. To Robert they complemented his architecture. They were less important in their own right. What such critics ignore is that, in a scheme combining the visual arts, one is always supreme, the others are background. Since Robert was an architect, architecture came first.

Robert's Spalatro volume was finally published in 1764. Great interest attended its appearance, for by now he had become what he had intended from the beginning, the most popular and fashionable architect in Britain. Patrons were queueing up to employ him; they all knew that his studies in Split represented his original contribution to architectural history, and that a number of his novel ideas derived from his research into Roman domestic building there.

It is untrue to imagine that all his designs were based on Diocletian's late Roman palace. He used ideas and forms from many places. It was the early nineteenth-century historians who tended to condemn him for what they believed to be his limited source material. But such a study was new in 1764, and no comparable survey of the palace had been done before. Interest was also aroused because it was expected that Robert would take the opportunity to state in print his ideas on classical design as applied to eighteenth-century architecture. This he did.

The volume is a beautiful production, with finely drawn and engraved plates illustrating both views of the palace and its surroundings from the sea and landward sides, and measured drawings of all the architectural forms and detail. The plates are by Bartolozzi, Santini, Cunego, Zucchi and Clérisseau, all Italians except for the Frenchman. Robert wrote the descriptive text, giving full details and measurements of each part of the monument (Plate *10*).

The quality of the production far surpassed any equivalent volume published in England in the eighteenth century; the list of subscribers is testimony to this. There are over five hundred of them, headed by a selection of the aristocracy that reads like a page from Debrett. After the names of the nobility and most of the great libraries, subscribers of interest listed include the Hon. Horace Walpole, the Archbishop of York, Joshua Reynolds, David Garrick, Allan Ramsay, Michael Rysbrack and the Rt Hon. Robert, Lord Clive. The twenty-eight foreign subscribers include the Duke of Parma, the library of St Mark in Venice and the Venetian Ambassador.

The frontispiece of the book, by Bartolozzi, shows a view of the approach to the ruins with, in the foreground, two young men at work, one drawing and one supervising, both dressed in tricorne hats, knee-length coats and vests, breeches and stockings. Near by, and less incongruously attired in Eastern costume with turbans and flowing robes, are some local citizens.

The title page reads:

> RUINS OF THE PALACE
> OF THE EMPEROR DIOCLETIAN
> AT SPALATRO IN DALMATIA
> BY R. ADAM F.R.S. F.S.A.
> ARCHITECT TO THE KING
> AND TO THE QUEEN
> PRINTED FOR THE AUTHOR
> MDCCLXIIII

In his dedication Robert is still clearly trying to impress the young monarch, adding some judicious flattery and hoping that a commission for a great building will be forthcoming. It reads:

TO
THE KING

I beg to lay before your Majesty the RUINS OF SPALATRO, once the favourite residence of a great Emperor, who, by his Munificence and Example, revived the Study of Architecture, and excited the Masters of that Art to emulate in their Works the Elegance and Purity of a better Age.

All the Arts flourish under Princes who are endowed with Genius, as well as possessed of Power. Architecture in a particular Manner depends upon the Patronage of the Great, as they alone are able to execute what the Artist plans. Your Majesty's early Application to the Study of this Art, the extensive knowledge you have acquired of its Principles encourages every Lover of the Profession to hope that he shall find in GEORGE THE THIRD, not only a powerful Patron, but a skilful Judge.

At this happy Period, when Great Britain enjoys in Peace the Reputation and Power she has acquired by Arms, Your Majesty's singular Attention to the Arts of Elegance, promises an Age of Perfection that will compleat the Glories of Your Reign, and fix an Æra no less remarkable than that of PERICLES, AUGUSTUS or the MEDICIS.

I am,

May it please Your Majesty,

Your Majesty's

Most Dutiful Servant and Faithful Subject,

ROBERT ADAM.

In his 'Introduction' Robert points out that the 'buildings of the Antients' act as models for eighteenth-century architecture in the same way that Nature does for the other arts, and that few monuments remain of Greek or Roman magnificence save in public buildings: temples, amphitheatres, baths. He goes on to say that while in Italy he felt that his knowledge of architecture would remain imperfect if he were not able to study such a building. He had heard about Spalatro and knew that the palace remains, though tolerably entire, had never been observed accurately or drawn with taste. He had therefore prevailed upon Clérisseau to join him, and set out with two draughtsmen on 11th July 1757. He continues with a description of their experiences and problems with the Venetian governor, and describes the palace fully.

Soon after its foundation, Robert presented the new Royal Academy of Arts with a copy of his book. The Academy library still proudly possesses the volume, whose cover, in red leather and tooled gilt, is yet in pristine condition. Robert's note of presentation is still within it:

Mr Adam presents his compliments to Mr Chambers [10] and sends him a copy of the Ruins of Diocletian's Palace at Spalatro which he begs Mr Chambers will do him the Honour to present to the Royal Academy and Beg their acceptance of it, and of his sincere wishes for the prosperity of so great and usefull an Institution.
Lower Gros. Street   11th January 1769

In 1964, the Yugoslav authorities in Split staged a jubilee exhibition in the town to celebrate the two hundredth anniversary of the publication of Robert's volume. The exhibition displayed the folio, translated into Serbo-Croatian, and books which have been published on Adam in Yugoslav literature; also those showing the influence of the palace on world architecture, before and after his survey. A booklet was produced to commemorate the event, entitled *Robert Adam and the Palace of Diocletian at Split*, which tells the story of earlier investigations there and of Adam's own studies.

NOTES

1 Agostino Brunias, one of the draughtsmen who came home with Robert from Italy.

2 This sounds prejudiced as the 'Designs' were for Chambers's *Treatise on Civil Architecture*, published 1759, a work of considerable importance.

3 Prince George, later George III. Chambers had recently been appointed his architectural tutor and was obviously proud of the honour. Robert, equally clearly, was a little concerned about it.

4 Though Robert (page 109) advises against the use of the Tuscan order, that is really what he is describing here. The Roman Doric is the one with the fluted column shaft and the ornamented frieze.

5 Robert's favourite use of it.

6 Callimachus of Corinth was a bronze worker. He was credited by Vitruvius as the original designer of the capital from having seen a basket set over the grave of a Corinthian girl covered by a tile and surrounded by acanthus leaves. Robert is quite right in that there was an Egyptian prototype remarkably similar but using differing leaves. In fact the Greek Corinthian capital often has palm or lily leaves for the top row, acanthus leaves for the lower row and no volutes, as in the Tower of the Winds, Athens. Robert himself used such a capital on many occasions (page 133).

7 Referring to the exterior only of a building.

8 Robert used it in this way time and time again. The ante-room at Syon is the prime example.

9 Robert is still hoping.

10 The R.A. treasurer.

4. THE GLORIOUS DECADE

Robert's meteoric success in becoming the leading fashionable architect within a bare two or three years of his return to England has sometimes occasioned surprise. This was a remarkably short time in which to move from obscurity to fame. Most architects have to wait for a period nearer a decade, often impecuniously, while working up a reputation. There were three main reasons for Robert's speedy arrival: first, the economic climate of Britain in 1758; second, his own unique ability; third, the length and variety of his apprenticeship.

It was a suitable time to begin practice. Everything was in his favour. Britain, soon to be rid of the drain of the Seven Years War, had amassed a vast empire and had become a rich and powerful nation. This was reflected in the willingness and ability of land-owners to spend great sums in building and decorating their homes; both their country seats and their town houses.

Robert's capabilities are self-evident as one studies his existing work. The fact that he succeeded in manifesting and publicizing this talent was due partly to his charm, energy and determination, but mainly to his having something new to offer, something that appealed to his clients. This something, the 'Adam style' which he developed in the first decade, was evolved from the wide canvas of experience he had had over the previous ten years, first working in Scotland, then studying in Italy.

He drew on all these sources, and that is why his work in different buildings appears so varied and yet at the same time so personal. Robert believed in suiting the mode to the commission. In fully eclectic manner he took from the grandeur of imperial Rome found in thermae and triumphal arches, from the late Roman work of Diocletian's palace at Split, from the delicate stucco and fresco wall decoration he had studied at Herculaneum and which James had recorded at Pompeii, from the purity of Grecian ornament and orders, from Byzantine colouring and richness and from the tremendous scope of Renaissance and Baroque forms which inspired his theme of 'architectural movement'. He fused it all into 'Adam', different from any of them and fundamentally English.

To think of Robert Adam as only an interior decorator is to encompass only part of his achievement. He was an architect, fully and comprehensively. That most of his surviving work consists of interior decoration is due only to the fact that he was commissioned in a majority of cases to supply it. His clients did not doubt that he was equally capable of designing the exteriors of their houses, but more often than not those houses already existed. The patron did not intend to build another house; in fact in a number of cases he had only partly finished one, and Robert was asked to complete it. He was requested to take over from the architect in charge and, usually, this meant completing a façade or a portico, then handling the interior schemes.

What is most remarkable about his career is not that it got under way so quickly, but that the majority of his superb houses were begun, and many of them finished, in this decade of 1760–70. Those were the great years for Robert Adam. Everyone praised him; his career was blossoming, and it looked as though nothing could interfere with its progress. In this decade alone he was working on the houses of Syon, Osterley, Kedleston, Harewood, Bowood, Kenwood, Mersham-le-Hatch, Nostell, Newby, Croome and Lansdowne, apart from smaller commissions at Kimbolton, Moor Park and West Wycombe. This represents a staggering volume of work, all of high standard and much of it bearing the stamp of genius.

A study of the drawings in the Adam collection at the Sir John Soane's Museum makes clear the immense care and effort that Adam put into the designs for all his commissions. His ceiling and wall designs in particular show an incredible attention to detail. Many of the famous interiors are represented by two or three or even more alternative schemes, and some of these, especially the later ones, are in full colour repeated for different schemes. Where he intended a wall covered by alternating panels of stucco decoration and paintings, he not only draws the stucco pattern in detail but also the paintings. These were often of ruined buildings or classical interiors. One for No. 20 Portman Square, for example, shows a picture of a view of the crossing inside a building like St Peter's in Rome, with all the information delineated on the pendentive pictures and the vault caissons. This is only the guide for a painter to follow, not an architect's design. Again, for the music-room at Harewood, we can see similar paintings drawn in careful detail, some classical, some landscapes.

Adam's colour schemes shown in the Soane Museum drawings are not of course necessarily those finally used. Many of them, considered together, reveal his preference for certain schemes, certain colours and tones, for different surfaces and parts of a room; it is encouraging to see many owners in the last decade going to great trouble to discover what Adam intended for their particular house and room, then taking pains to use this scheme in redecoration.

Robert's idea was to tone the general background areas in light, fresh colours so as to cut down what he thought to be the 'glare' obtained in the all-white ceilings and walls. His favourite colours for use here were very pale apple and sage greens (sometimes with a darker shade of green to contrast) oyster tones, creams, warm pinks and, frequently, green and pink in the same scheme. The stucco ornamentation is most usually white, sometimes with touches of colour and gilt, but only here and there, rarely all over. The background colour of the small roundels and medallions is often a rich, strong colour. This is a small area, and a touch here gives value and brilliance to the rest of the scheme. Favourite colours for this are deep caerulean and ultramarine blue, purple, deep red and burnt sienna. The drawings which are coloured are equally detailed and careful, with hours of work in each one.

I. SYON AND KEDLESTON

(Descriptions of all the rooms in Adam houses are not given in the present study, but only the salient features of each building. An account of the houses as they are to be seen today can be found beginning on page 186. Houses which no longer exist are not fully discussed. They are referred to only where they were of exceptional interest and important in the development of the Adam style.)

To evaluate Adam's achievement it must be seen in the perspective of one building with another. His work in the decade 1760–70 was almost entirely in country house design, and about 85 to 90 per cent of it interior schemes.

Taking the Adam work in these houses, as they exist today, there are broadly three categories of standard. Naturally individual taste varies, and some prefer the atmosphere and approach in one house to those in another. Regardless of personal preference, two houses stand supreme as Adam masterpieces: Syon and Kedleston.

In both cases the house, or a large part of it, already existed, and he had problems in adapting it to what he desired to create. Both clients were wealthy, and the quality of materials, breadth of vision and superb standard of craftsmanship are uniquely high. In each house the client finally called a halt, and Adam could not (sadly for posterity) complete his full scheme. At Syon the rotunda was never built, at Kedleston the south wings. Both houses are still owned and lived in by descendants of the original patrons. They have been cared for and used through the centuries and have been hardly altered. It says much for Adam's quality of workmanship that, despite such use, their condition is now so good. We are fortunate that both are open to public view.

The first Duke of Northumberland was one of Adam's most enthusiastic patrons. He commissioned him to redecorate the interior of Alnwick Castle, the family seat in Northumberland, then to tackle the great town house and finally the London/country mansion at Syon. The Adam work at Alnwick was remodelled again in nineteenth-century Gothic; Northumberland House at Charing Cross, one of Robert's most palatial and colourful houses, was demolished in 1874 by the Metropolitan Board of Works to make way for Northumberland Avenue. We are left, deeply grateful, with Syon.

The religious house founded by Henry V was spared at the Dissolution because Henry VIII wanted it. James I granted it to the Northumberland family and, when Adam was given the task of turning the historic building into an eighteenth-century mansion, he was not permitted to alter the exterior or layout. Today the great

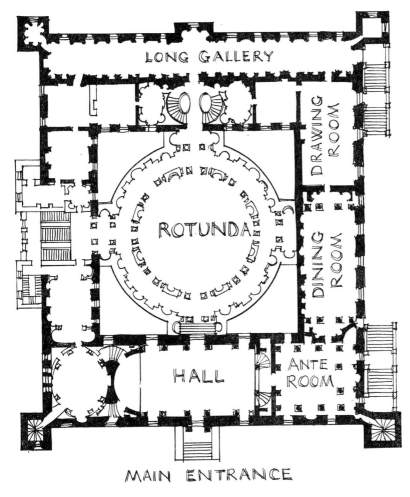

1   *Ground plan of Syon House. The Rotunda and other parts (left white) not built*

grim, rectangular block, its battlemented eastern skyline crowned
with the lion,[1] tail streaming out behind, is a landmark across the
river from Kew Gardens.

Inside is a different world: the creation of a travelled, cultured,
wealthy patron and a superb architect grasping his first opportunity
with both hands. There were problems in adaptation. The rooms of
the Jacobean house were the wrong shape for classical interiors. The
levels varied from one end of the house to the other. It was not
symmetrical. It was old and still based on medieval foundations.

Robert succeeded in producing a suite of rooms round the rectangular courtyard, leading one into another, giving long vistas when the doors were opened. The levels were adjusted almost imperceptibly, and the room proportions appeared to be changed by his skilful architectural handling.

All Robert's best interiors have two special characteristics: the rooms are designed to give *en suite* vistas, and each room, different in shape from the others, is treated in a contrasting manner. The eye is constantly stimulated yet the effect is never disturbing (Fig. 1).

Robert intended a great rotunda or domed pantheon to cover the original monastic court. This was to be supported on a circular ring of columns, and the great space, about eighty feet across, was to be used for important gatherings. All the state rooms would have access to it. The cost of Syon proved too great even for the Duke of Northumberland, so the rotunda was never built. Its lack destroys the coherence that such a central feature would have brought to the design. Walpole, among others, describes what it might have been like, when a temporary covering was erected over the court in 1768 for a reception given for the King of Denmark, where three hundred guests were comfortably dined and entertained.

There are five state rooms *en suite* at Syon. The entrance gives into the centre of the hall, and one progresses through the ante-room to the dining-room, drawing-room and gallery.

The great hall is modelled on a Roman basilica with apses at both ends; one is coffered, the other is screened and contains the steps up to the ante-room, made necessary by the uneven floor levels. Adam made a virtue of necessity. In his own words: 'The inequality of the levels has been managed in such a manner as to increase the scenery and add to the movement so that an apparent effect has been converted into a real beauty.' How right he is.

The scheme is cool and of Roman grandeur. There is no colour here. All is cream and white with black breaking into the floor pattern. The Roman Doric order is used, Adam's favourite for entrance halls, and seldom to more telling effect. The proportion of the room was too rectangular (66 by 31 feet and 34 feet high) for Adam's intentions. He reduced the apparent length by his apses and the height by the almost Palladian, richly decorated, deeply beamed ceiling.

The startling metamorphosis between the adjoining hall and ante-room assails the observer as he enters, like the *fortissimo* chords re-introducing the dominant theme of a symphony after the quiet movement. Adam too was handling an architectural symphony with colour and form. The ante-room at Syon is of unbelievable richness in colour; it glows and scintillates in the shafts of south-westerly sunshine as if made of precious stones. Here also is Roman grandeur but of a warm, imperial kind. It is a room which has no parallel. It competes on equal terms with any that the continent of Europe has produced.

Adam's architectural *tour de force* here is in creating the appearance of a cubic room; its actual size is 36 by 30 feet and 21 feet high. He makes a square floor area by his disposition of the columns. These are set round the wall on three sides, each supporting projecting entablatures and gilt classical statues. On the fourth, window, side they are set eight feet from the wall and carry a continuous beam with statues above the columns.

The eye is so absorbed by the riot of colour that it does not notice the deception. The colour is largely produced by the valuable natural materials, not by decorative means. The focal point of design is in the columns and pilasters, which are in *verde antico* marble from Greece: the former veneered, the latter solid.[2] The gilt sculpture and panels, the brilliant scagliola floor in tune with, though not a copy of, the cream and gold ceiling, and the bright, clear blue backing to gilt anthemion frieze act as a foil to the soft subtlety of the columns (Plates *12*, *14*).

The dining-room is sometimes described as 'ordinary Adam'. It is in contrast to both ante-room and drawing-room in colour, but not inferior in standard. Here is the tranquil mood, all cream and gold, except for the white chimney-piece and chiaroscuro wall panels. It is a beautifully proportioned room, almost a triple cube. At each end is a Corinthian screen fronting an apsidal recess.

The drawing-room once more denotes a marked change of mood. The rich colouring here is provided by the wall covering and ceiling. The former is of plum-coloured Spitalfields silk, patterned with grey flowers and ribbons, which gleams in a silvery tone.

The ceiling design was controversial from the beginning. Robert tried to obtain the effect of Raphael's vaulting ornament in the Villa

Madama, but the result evoked Sir William Chambers' disgusted comment that it resembled skied dinner plates. There is justice in the criticism. The motif components are in too small scale for the immense coved ceiling which is not a vault. It is then surfaced all over with regular octagons and diamonds, each with a tiny painted medallion in it. Adam's colour scheme in the Soane Museum shows vivid blue backgrounds, red in the circles and gilt bordering overall. The present ceiling is nearly like this, but there is more blue than in his scheme. If the scale is inadequate, this is the error of the architect. There is no fault to be found with Cipriani's paintings [3] in the roundels, which are exquisitely handled; indeed the detail is finer than the overall impression.

The superbly successful features of the drawing-room are the doors, doorcases and mantelpiece. Adam introduced here a new decorative medium, that of ormolu. It is used in the Ionic pilasters flanking the door, in typical Adam decorative motifs, on an ivory base. The rest of the doorcase is in cream and gold, and the finely polished mahogany doors with reeded panels are forerunners of what was to become the classic Adam pattern (Plate 16).

The white marble mantelpiece is decorated in delicate manner with ormolu; even the column arrises between the flutes are delineated in metal beading, as also are the base enrichments. It is Adam's finest mantelpiece of this type, aptly described by Mr Bolton (see Note 2, page 45) as having 'an overdress of lace thrown upon the white marble form' (Plate 15).

The Jacobean gallery, 136 feet long, 14 feet wide and 14 feet high, was an absurd shape for a Georgian apartment. Robert decided that it was useless to try to alter it, so he must conform to its purpose and style. He equipped it as a library, with bookcases lining one long wall, opposite to the windows on the other, but decorated it as a room for entertainment, chat and gaiety. In short, it could be used for its original purpose. The decorative scheme is all in subdued low relief and quiet, soft colours.

He divided the ceiling into circles, repeated the length of the gallery, encompassed in octagons and squares, the emphasis being on increasing the apparent width and cutting down its length. Along the walls he repeated a unit of four Corinthian pilasters with wide intervals to accommodate the doorways and chimney-pieces between. The opposite wall, with its windows already positioned, could not be fitted correctly, but as these same windows shadowed their side of the wall, the fact that the ceiling lines matched the pilasters on the other side and not the window one is barely discernible.

The bookshelves are framed by a subsidiary order of Ionic pilasters, and the all-over stucco decoration comprises all Adam's favourite forms: arabesques, paterae, anthemion, vases, drops and a typically Pompeian type of half-putti, half-scroll, symmetrical motif.

The gallery is sometimes thought to be too fussy and ephemeral, but the architect's aim was to dispel the impression of Jacobean solidity by decorative fantasy. It is still a typical long gallery, but it is no longer incongruous in an eighteenth-century house.

Kedleston was one of Adam's few opportunities to design the exterior of a country house, but even here he came into the affair half way through. Sir Nathaniel Curzon (later Lord Scarsdale) was, like the Duke of Northumberland, a cultured, travelled man who wanted a house in the latest mode. He took over a Queen Anne house, had it demolished and employed Matthew Brettingham to build him a new one. Brettingham was soon replaced by James Paine, who continued the work of his predecessor. He designed a central block with four wings and completed the north (entrance) façade in Palladian manner.

As early as 1758 Sir Nathaniel had been introduced to Robert. After seeing his drawings and talking to him, he was fired by the young man's knowledge and enthusiasm. This was really what he wanted. So Adam replaced Paine, who took his discharge very well; he was busy on other work and he admired Adam.

Robert's contribution to Kedleston therefore was the design of the south front facing the grounds and completion of the interior scheme initiated by Paine. A mere glance at the north and south façades of Kedleston sums up for the observer the fundamental differences between Adam and the Palladians. On the north is a heavy Corinthian, pedimented portico over a rusticated basement. On each side are flanking steps to the main entrance on the *piano nobile* which leads into the great hall. On either side are lower

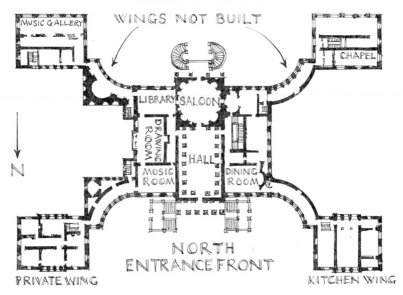

2   *Ground plan of Kedleston Hall*

ranges terminating in end pavilions, themselves miniature Palladian houses. It is strongly reminiscent of Holkham (begun 1734) (Fig. 2).

On the south Robert pursued his theme of 'architectural movement'. It is a simple block, again with rusticated basement, but with curving stairways to the *piano nobile*. The central feature is a triumphal arch, modelled upon that of Constantine in Rome, and the low dome of the saloon rises unobtrusively behind it. The whole design is elegant and original, but we can see it only in this truncated form, for Robert had planned curving colonnades, stretching out to corner pavilions, balancing those on the north side. His idea here was to obtain his 'movement' by the Baroque theme of convexity moving into concavity; here based on St Peter's in Rome. He wanted the convex dome to act as a foil and link to the concave colonnades. Alas, as at Syon, the expense became too great even for Curzon, and seeing the interior, that is not surprising (Plate *17*).

In the grounds Robert erected a number of buildings: the elegant fishing house, the orangery and the fine entrance screen from the road. His masterpiece here, though, is the three-arched bridge over the widened brook; one of his best. It is simple, beautifully proportioned and in true Roman style with horizontal parapet and roadway (Plate *18*).

There are many fine state rooms in Kedleston: the library, great drawing-room, dining-room, music-room and state bedroom. These are quality Adam interiors, mostly in his earlier style, but they do not compare with those at Syon. What are remarkable and quite unique are the vast Roman hall and the circular pantheon of a saloon.

It was these apartments that aroused Dr Johnson's famous strictures when he visited the house with Boswell soon after its decoration. He thought 'the house would do excellently well for a town hall; the large room with the pillars (the hall) would do for the judges to sit at assizes; the circular room (the saloon) for a jury chamber'. It is notable, however, that the Doctor was not an advocate of wealth and privilege. The comments of others, from Boswell onwards, have been very different.

The great hall, on the *piano nobile*, stands above a lower, entrance hall, used in normal circumstances. The apartment above was for formal occasions, designed on the lines of a Roman atrium, dedicated to honouring the ancestors of the house, and decorated with their statues, arms and trophies.

It is an enormous apartment, built in truly Roman imperial manner. The sixteen vast monolithic columns and four half-columns are of a local alabaster, dug from Lord Scarsdale's own quarries. Strangely they are usually described as green-veined, presumably because still-imperfect colour photographic processes show them this way. They are in fact marked in a warm reddish-brown on a cream background, with bases to match and the Corinthian capitals in white marble.

The apartment is lit solely from above, like the Pantheon in Rome, It has no distracting windows piercing the walls. There are three elliptical oculi in the ceiling, set in line on the long axis of the hall. The ceiling itself is in white and pale green, the entablature also white with a darker green background to the frieze. The grey floor is patterned with white-veined marble.

In Roman times the wall niches would have been occupied by statues of the family ancestors. They have classical gods and goddesses instead. Above are the grisaille Homeric panels.

Second only to the great conception and handling of the hall are the two magnificent wall fireplaces; white marble below and stucco relief with circular painting above. The grate, fire-irons and fender in burnished brass and steel are of Adam's finest quality (Plate 19).

The circular saloon, 42 feet in diameter and 55 feet high, leads out of the hall, making a sequence of state rooms unparalleled in the eighteenth century. The proportions are perfect and the craftsmanship is superb. Every detail was designed and drawn by the architect, and the Adam team were inspired to their greatest achievement here, from the exquisitely decorated cast-iron stoves (Plate 21) (part of Adam's hot-air heating system) to the delicate tablet girandoles, wall paintings and gilded door-frames to the dome itself. Here, above the cornice and decorative frieze, are diminishing octagonal lacunae, enriched with gold, culminating in a central oculus.

Everything on the walls, doorways, windows, niches takes the curve of the circle; all in a gentle scheme of cream and gold broken only by the deep grey/green scagliola pilasters and the dull, rich black of the elegant stoves.

2. HAREWOOD, OSTERLEY, KENWOOD

Edwin Lascelles, later Lord Harewood, was, like Sir Nathaniel Curzon, one of Robert's first patrons. As early as 1758 designs were being made for him (page 94 in Chapter 3), but although Adam did a great deal of work here most of the exterior was eventually by John Carr, and Sir Charles Barry made many later alterations.

Lascelles inherited the estate of Gawthorpe in 1754. Being, like Adam's other clients, a travelled man, interested in the current vogue of architecture, he decided to build a new house. He demolished Gawthorpe and, after turning down designs submitted by Sir William Chambers, commissioned the Yorkshire architect John Carr to build the house and a new village, which he called Harewood. Work began on the house in 1759, and historians have been arguing for many years about how much of the building was Carr's and how much by Adam.

It now seems fairly certain that the house was built largely to Carr's design. The entrance front definitely was and much of the south (garden) side; also the dispensation, size and shape of the main rooms. Whatever hand Adam may have had in alterations to the south façade was obscured by Barry's drastic refacing and uplift of 1843.

As at Kedleston, Robert was called in to work with and, in parts, take over from, an older man. Similarly the two architects here got on very well and worked harmoniously together. It is undisputed, indeed Carr says so, that Adam was responsible for all interior decorative treatment. But, since the rooms were already set in their shape and size, his scope was more limited than usual and his variation of apartments is less noticeable.

Some fine Adam interiors remain at Harewood comparatively unaltered. These comprise the hall, the gallery, the music-room and the staircase.

The hall is striking. The visitor comes up the steps into one of Adam's best Roman Doric entrance halls. Quite different, and possibly more successful than Syon, it uses many of the same features. Here the twelve Doric columns and four corner pilasters are engaged, fluted and enriched. The ceiling is deeply panelled and patterned and has a central circle; oval and circular paterae cover the remaining area. The Doric entablature has an unusually striking frieze of ox skulls, alternating with paterae and the whole threaded through with a key pattern. The use of the order is entirely in keeping with Adam's advice to Lord Kames (Chapter 3, p. 109), and, since he has enriched his order as well as taking liberties with it, he has included six doorways, two principal ones with entablatures echoing those of the main walls. Some very fine relief panels decorate the walls themselves: circular ones depicting arms and rectangular containing figure compositions (Plate 31).

The hall has recently been redecorated in an unusual and impressive scheme. The Soane Museum drawings for the ceiling show no colour directives, and the scheme may well be as Adam intended. The ceiling background is in a deep rust red and a soft mushroom with paterae showing Wedgwood blue behind the stucco decoration, which is all in white. The walls are a deep slate blue, doorways and panels white and the columns a very deep dark red. It seems likely that Adam would have been a little surprised but gratified.

The proportions of the gallery which takes up a whole wing of the house were obviously uncongenial to Adam: 77 feet long, 24 feet wide and 21 feet high, it savoured too much of Syon. It was far too long and too narrow and too low. His magnificent ceiling design, very typical of the established Adam pattern, helps to offset this by splitting up the length into octagons, lunettes, ovals, all decorated in low-relief stucco with Adam motifs, especially griffins, predominating. His Soane Museum drawings for this (there are several alternatives) are in exquisite detail and show his favourite colouring, not too far from the present one. The scheme is delicate: white stucco on pale green and pink backgrounds with small touches of caerulean blue, deep pink and burnt sienna on the tablets, circles, octagons and lozenge grounds (Plate 24).

The gallery is particularly noted, as is all of Harewood, for the successful co-operation between Chippendale and Adam. Most of the furniture was made by the firm of Chippendale in the Adam style. The three great Venetian windows along one side have curtain boxes and pendant valances carved in wood. The latter are so realistic that most observers take them for curtaining. Adam did not intend any further hangings. The pier glasses between the windows with console tables below are superb. The glasses have gilt frames incorporating Kauffmann paintings in the cresting, which is in keeping with the window cornices between.

Most of the furniture here is Chippendale, the frames to the Reynolds portraits are Adam, and the only inharmonious note sounds from the two Victorian fireplaces introduced by Barry to replace the single Adam one. This latter is now in the dining-room; it is one of his early designs and certainly not his best, but a great improvement on Barry's.

The music-room is charming and gives us one of the few remaining examples of what must have been numerous in Adam's day: an original carpet which echoes or matches the ceiling design. This was a favourite motif of Robert's, and here shows a circle within the square room and central star surrounded by paterae and swags. The circular paterae reflect the Kauffmann medallions in the ceiling. The wall decoration here is also a classic Adam method: rectangular panels of stucco design alternating with Zucchi paintings of Piranesi-type ruins.

One of the most characteristic and beautiful features of Adam houses is the staircase. Neither Syon nor Kedleston has a notable one. At Harewood the design is interesting, if not Robert's best. His difficulty here was that the stairwell is narrow. Adam, like Carr before him, planned a single type with flights rising up each side successively, but the client, as so often at Harewood, objected. Lascelles had definite ideas, and he caused Adam to make more alternative designs here than the architect was obliged to do any-where else. He insisted on the more impressive double ascent, though there really is not room for it. The typical Adam carved mahogany handrail and iron balustrade are good, but the narrowness of the well spoils the majesty of the staircase, which Adam achieved elsewhere.

Osterley House is only six or seven miles from Syon. It presents a contrast, being (mainly) Adam, but on a more domestic scale. Again the architect took over an old house, this time Elizabethan. His contribution to the outside is the magnificent portico on the east. It has been suggested that his inspiration here came from the temple at Palmyra and that he used information from Robert Wood's drawings. The detail, in particular, is reminiscent of the Erechtheion in Athens, and the doorway in the courtyard is almost a facsimile of that in the north porch there. The Osterley portico is a fine one, pedimented, with a double row of six Ionic columns leading into the square courtyard of the sixteenth-century house. Adam had raised the courtyard to *piano nobile* level, and this gave the grand entrance approach up twenty steps to the portico. On the rear elevation he built a doorway entrance with iron and stone approach staircase (Plate 25).

The whole of the interior at Osterley except the gallery is by Adam and there are many rooms: hall, dining-room, library, tapestry-room, Etruscan room and state bedroom.

The hall is quite different from those already described. It is large and rectangular, but the order is subservient, in pilaster form, and the whole is in low relief and in quiet tones. The capital is that Composite type inferred in the letter to Lord Kames (page 109), having a lower row of acanthus leaves, an upper of lily or palm, with reeding between and no volutes; an Adam special. The floor, of black and white marble, echoes the ceiling design in stucco, both with an oval centre-piece and banded exterior with paterae and panels. The hall is completely symmetrical. There is a coffered apse at each end, containing a fireplace and statued niches. Along the walls, between the mahogany doors, are panels of stucco trophies, like those at Syon, but not so fine.

Osterley has a beautiful staircase. Set in a narrow, stucco-decorated well, it extends from ground level over two storeys. At the first floor (level with the main entrance) is a Corinthian colon-naded screen and, on the floor above, an Ionic one. The balustrade is of iron with anthemion motif (like Kenwood and Newby); the handrail is carved mahogany, the stairs of stone.

The eating-room is attractive. Here is a ceiling like Shardeloes, but an advance on it – ellipses with intertwined vines. Walls are decorated with panels of stucco incorporating painted medallions alternating with paintings, in the Adam tradition for dining-rooms. The white marble fireplace has Doric columns and there is a fine steel grate.

The library is intimate and beautifully handled. The ceiling is an ordinary Adam low relief design, but the windows, Ionic-pilastered white bookcases, fireplaces and paintings create a soothing, elegant room; harmonious yet inspiring to work in.

Two apartments at Osterley are rare examples of a number which used to exist elsewhere: the tapestry room and the Etruscan room. In the former the walls are covered by Boucher-Neilson tapestries depicting 'Les Amours des Dieux'. There were six sets of these gobelins made for Adam rooms, but only those at Newby (page 135) survive *in situ*. The set at Croome (page 134) were sold some years ago to the Metropolitan Museum in New York for fifty thousand pounds. Here at Osterley the signature of James Neilson, the Scottish representative of the Gobelins firm, is woven into the tapestries. The colours are rich and warm, the detail is carefully defined and the craftsmanship magnificent (Plate 26).

The Etruscan room is one of a number of examples designed by Adam at Home House, Derby House, Harewood, Apsley House and Cumberland House. Most of these have been lost except for the work at Home House, No. 20 Portman Square, now the Courtauld Institute, which has been well restored. Adam's ideas on his sources reflected contemporary understanding and as such were inaccurate, but the style he created from these, like Wedgwood's ware, is a work of art in its own right. It is presented in earth colours: yellow, ochres, siennas, umbers, crimson and black. At Osterley it is largely done on paper by Angelica Kauffmann and other artists on the doors, walls and ceilings. At Portman Square the work is painted on the ceiling and door-cases and, on the mantelpiece, inlaid as well. The decorative medium is entirely linear, and motifs are more Greek and Roman than Etruscan.

Kenwood was designed for Lord Mansfield in 1767. Adam made some alterations to the exterior, including a portico built on the north front and based on the Erechtheion on the Athenian acropolis. This still exists, as does also the library which was his principal contribution here.

This apartment was designed not only for displaying books, but also as a room for entertaining. The rectangular form is shortened at each end by curved apses each fronted by a screen of Corinthian columns supporting only a bar entablature which does not hide the exquisite decoration of the half-dome of the apse. This apsidal finish to one or both ends of a rectangular room was a favourite Adam device, altering proportions as he needed and giving interest and mystery to the apartment. The dining-room at Syon and that at Newby are other examples.

The Kenwood library ceiling is barrel vaulted (not flat like the Newby one). It is divided lengthwise into three parallel sections, then subdivided horizontally. The panels are decorated in oval and lunette forms, painted with figure compositions. The surrounding stucco is in low relief and of exceptional standard, as it is also on the cornice and screen entablatures.

The present colour scheme dates from the turn of the century. Fortunately it is about to be redecorated, when the heavy warm colours and superabundance of gilt will be removed in favour of one of Adam's two original schemes, one predominantly in greens and one in blues, but both with white stucco and white columns instead of the present heavy purplish ones.

The library is beautifully proportioned and handled, the stucco decoration superb. It was one of Adam's best interiors, using quality materials before mass-production methods and low relief décor overwhelmed him in the 1770s (Plate 28).

3. BOWOOD, COMPTON VERNEY, CROOME,
KIMBOLTON, LUTON HOO, MERSHAM-LE-HATCH,
MOOR PARK, NEWBY, NOSTELL, WEST WYCOMBE

Adam started work on all these houses in the decade 1760–70, and much of it was completed. At Mersham-le-Hatch and Luton Hoo he had the handling of the whole scheme from the beginning; at the others the whole or part of the house existed, and he made additions and decorated some or all of the interior. In some cases very little of his work survives; at Moor Park, West Wycombe, Compton Verney, for example. In others there are suites of rooms and considerable parts of the house existing.

The problems arising from this large selection of houses in different parts of the country were varied and numerous. Robert was perpetually travelling from his office in Lower Grosvenor Street in London to counties as far separated as Wiltshire, Yorkshire, Kent and Worcestershire. In the 1760s this took time and money, and was a much more exhausting business than now. We may complain about conditions for commuters on British Rail, but it is generally possible to study one's notes for the day's work or read a book. To do so in a pitching, swaying stagecoach (unheated and unsprung) was difficult. Robert's letters to his clients always seem to begin with an apology for not having written earlier, but 'I have been in the Countrey for . . .' Physical stamina as well as a capacity for hard work and alertness to solve the individual problems of each house were essential qualities for the fashionable architect.

Luton and Mersham were Robert's opportunities in this decade to design new projects. Lord Bute purchased a brick house and estate in 1762, then asked Robert to build him a new house.[4] The great mansion of Luton Hoo [5] was an enormous project. Begun in 1767, it had a frontage of 244 feet and contained among its magnificent suite of rooms a great circular hall and a vast library: 146 feet long, it contained over thirty thousand books and an unusually valuable collection of mathematical and scientific instruments. Robert considered Luton one of his best works, and particularly so the library. Although it is by no means certain that Adam's engraved designs were fully executed, the library attracted a great deal of favourable comment from all who saw it.

In 1816 Smirke made drastic alterations and, tragically, in 1843 a disastrous fire destroyed most of the interior. The present house owes almost nothing to Robert Adam.

Mersham-le-Hatch, in contrast, is a modest house by eighteenth-century standards. The simple brick exterior, of central block and side pavilions, stands almost unaltered, but much of the interior furnishing has gone. It represents a pleasant pedestrian Adam, quiet, tasteful, in good quality, but lacking the spirit of greatness that we expect from this architect.

At Bowood and Nostell some excellent exterior work remains. The Earl of Shelburne (later Marquess of Lansdowne) was one of Adam's earliest clients. After building a mausoleum for the late Lady Shelburne, he was asked to alter and extend Bowood, which had been designed in 1755 by Henry Keene. This architect had built the main house and, at right angles to it, a long E-shaped office and stable block. Adam built new porticoes for the house, added a new range to join it to the office wing, then faced the latter with the famous colonnaded structure generally called the 'Diocletian Wing'. This contained a suite of rooms and an orangery.

It is the only part now remaining, as the house was finally demolished, after many later alterations, in 1955. It is said to have been called 'Diocletian' because the marquess, impressed by Robert's publication, had asked him to base it on the palace at Split. Adam does not say that this is so, and it is difficult to trace much similarity between the admittedly fine elevation at Bowood and the impressive but different crypto-porticus along the harbour at Split. The capitals, said to be inspired by the Roman palace, are unusual. Presumably of Composite basis, they have no volutes. They are related to a favoured Adam design, having a lower row of acanthus leaves, but above are no leaves, only spreading fluting and an echinus moulding enriched with egg and dart (see Glossary).

At Nostell, as at Kedleston, Adam followed James Paine, who here also had designed a large central block 160 feet by 80 feet with quadrant colonnades connecting to four small corner pavilions, each 50 feet square. This was a standard Palladian layout, but large and extravagant. The central block and two of the pavilions were built.

Adam was asked to decorate the rooms in the main house and, later, to design a new wing in place of the two unbuilt pavilions.

His interior work here is largely of the 1760s, but the new wing was begun in 1776. Work was suspended in 1785 and the interior decoration is late Victorian. It is interesting to compare Paine's exterior work on the main house at Nostell with Adam's adjacent wing. Superficially the same style in the Ionic order, the quality, proportions and detail are in great contrast.

Some structural alteration was made by Adam in the main block. In the centre he adjusted the east façade main hall over the lower entrance hall, used a central staircase up the middle of the house and designed the saloon on the west front. It is one of his best rooms here, with a particularly fine deeply coved ceiling made up from circles and lunettes. Between the windows are beautiful pier glasses above side tables, inspired by Adam and made by Chippendale. Indeed Nostell and Harewood are the two chief examples of houses possessing a quantity of Chippendale-made furniture based on original Adam themes (Plate 30).

At Croome Court Robert replaced a different architect, Lancelot (Capability) Brown, better known as the famous landscape gardener. The house had been begun in the early 1750s, possibly by Sanderson Miller, possibly by Brown. Certainly the grounds were laid out by Capability Brown, who acquired this name because of his habit of saying, when called in by a new client to express his opinion on the possible development of his estate: 'I see great capability of improvement here.' At Croome he created the winding lakes through the park and raised the hill for the re-siting of the 'Gothick' Church.

Adam and Brown met on a number of projects where the latter was laying out the parkland, at Bowood and Compton Verney, for instance, but at Croome, Brown was the architect. He had completed the house for the Earl of Coventry when Adam was called in. There is still some dispute as to which parts of the interior are his and which Brown's. Certainly the fine gallery is Adam: it is the best room in the house, 62 feet long, and takes up the west wing on the first floor.

It has a coffered octagon ceiling of Italian Renaissance type, a rich entablature with anthemion frieze and, below, stucco griffin and

24 *Ceiling detail, gallery, Harewood House*

25   *East portico, Osterley Park, Middlesex*

26   *The Tapestry Room, Osterley Park*

27   *The Adelphi Terrace, London,* *as it was in the eighteenth century*

28   The Library, Kenwood

29 *The hall, Newby Hall, Yorkshire*

30 *Fireplace detail, saloon, Nostell Priory, Yorkshire*

31 *Wall panel (Wedding of Neptune and Amphitrite), hall,
Harewood House*

scroll panels and grisaille paintings in Adam frames. The white
marble fireplace, with flanking female statues, is one of his best of
these early designs.

The house is now used by a religious order as a school for mentally
handicapped children, who have great respect for the Adam *décor*
around them. Doors, walls and all surfaces are in beautiful condition, but the Adam furniture has long since been removed.

William Weddell, the owner of Newby Hall, a lovely brick Queen
Anne house, consulted Adam in 1765 on his return from the grand
tour in Italy, because he had acquired a great collection of sculpture
there and needed a gallery to display it.

The house was a simple block, brick with stone dressings in
Dutch Palladian style. Adam, appreciating its quality, left the
exterior alone, but added two wings, one for the new gallery and
another to balance on the other side. In the centre of this elevation
he designed a classical porch.

Although he redecorated and replanned several of the existing
rooms in the house, of which the hall, library, tapestry-room and
staircase are very fine, it is the sculpture gallery which is unique to
Newby. It remains today as he designed it (Plate 29).

The gallery is based on Roman themes as seen by Robert in the
Rome catacombs and at Herculaneum. It shows the type of proportion he desired when given the opportunity instead of having, as at
Syon, Harewood and Croome, to abide by the existing ones. The
gallery is divided into three sections: a rectangular room at each end
and a central rotunda. Deep vaulted arches join the three compartments, which thus afford a vista from one end of the gallery to the
other. An oculus in the coffered dome of the rotunda lights the
central part, and sculpture is arranged round the walls on pedestals
in niches and larger exedrae.

Both apartment and sculpture are scaled perfectly together. The
ornamental detail is very Roman and of high quality. The gallery has
recently been redecorated similarly to the original scheme in white
stucco ornament on backgrounds ranging from shades of pale pink to
salmon.[6]

In this same decade, 1760–70, Robert acquired the services of
many fine craftsmen. Without the quality of their work he could not
have created the interiors which he did. Many of the team were of

135

Continental origin, mostly Italian, but some were English. Adam designed everything in detail for the decorative scheme: stucco, paintings, carved ornament, metalwork, ceramics. He demanded a high standard of craftsmanship and obtained it.

None of his workers was a great creative artist: that would have been no use to Robert. He made the designs, his architecture was paramount, the decorative scheme was a necessary adjunct to it. They were all technical experts in their craft and did what he asked of them. None of them worked for him alone; they were not his personal team. Some, like Biagio Rebecca and Joseph Wilton, worked in only one or two Adam houses; the rest of their work was for other architects such as Chambers or Wyatt. Others, including Angelica Kauffmann and Antonio Zucchi, did more for Adam than for anyone else. All the craftsmen liked working for him. He was pleasant, helpful, enthusiastic, but also demanding of their best. He paid fairly and obtained a just deal for them with clients.

Among the painters were Angelica Kauffmann, Giovanni Battista Cipriani, William Hamilton, Francesco Zuccarelli and Antonio Zucchi. Of these, Angelica Kauffmann was the best known and most colourful character. Born in Switzerland, she grew up in Rome and came to England in 1766, where she was made a founder member of the Royal Academy in 1768, an honour which Robert did not achieve. Possibly, however, she was an expert at exploiting her talents as a feminine artist in a man's world. Her painting was good, though not brilliant, her figure work indifferent; she had wit and charm and gaiety. Sir Joshua Reynolds, the Academy's first president, was one of the targets of her flirtatious activities, though she was more successful with Goethe. She had two husbands, the second of whom was Zucchi.

Like Chippendale, who also worked a great deal for Adam, Angelica was until recently credited with too much of the painting in Adam houses, such as the drawing-room at Syon House. But she was certainly the most prolific of his painters, and earned many thousands of pounds in England before returning to Italy with her second husband. Her funeral in Rome in 1807 was directed by no less a personage than the sculptor Antonio Canova.

Antonio Zucchi also did a great deal of work in Adam buildings, both in ceiling decorative panels, like his wife, and in easel paintings of landscapes and ruins. It was his brother Giuseppe who had accompanied Robert to Split in 1757.

Cipriani was a very talented member of the team. He specialized in monochrome panels in grisaille of figure compositions, especially of children. He worked in many Adam houses and also painted a quantity of ceiling colour panels.

Biagio Rebecca worked in several media. He was expert at imitating classical reliefs, also in painted decoration. In this latter capacity he worked more often for James Wyatt, as at Heveningham.

Francesco Bartolozzi was devoted to the antique world and expert at reproducing its craftsmanship. His engravings are of superb quality, as can be seen in Robert's Spalatro book, for which Bartolozzi did many of the plates. Very Italian in his charm and ease of manner, he earned a great deal of money and promptly spent it. Despite the enormous quantities of alcohol he consumed and the snuff he took he lived to the ripe old age of eighty-eight.

Michelangelo Pergolesi was a decorator who worked occasionally for Adam. Later he took to designing his own ornament in the Adam style and became one of the army of Adam's imitators whose work the nineteenth century accepted as genuine.

Robert's expert stuccoist was Joseph Rose. His work was of superb quality and, as at Syon and Harewood, was as good as any produced in ancient or Renaissance Rome. He worked in most of the Adam houses, but also made designs for other projects.

Among the sculptors and carvers were Joseph Wilton, Michael Spang and Thomas Carter. Their media were stone and marble, mainly on chimney-pieces or on exterior reliefs such as Spang's on the Admiralty Screen.

Much of the Adam metalwork came from Matthew Boulton, who was craftsman, inventor and business man. It was the development of his ormolu that Robert introduced at Syon in door panels, frames and chimney-pieces. As a decorative medium for marble or polished wood, Robert exploited its possibilities to the full in both furniture and architectural features. It was of course used by other architects and furniture designers.

Josiah Wedgwood and Robert Adam had much in common besides being exactly contemporary. Wedgwood was also an energetic visionary, obsessed with his work, a shrewd business man and a craftsman dedicated to raising the standard of the quality of his product. He aimed at purity of earthenware and made it into a work of art suitable for a queen's table, whereas previously it had been the poor relation of porcelain in the ceramics industry.

John Flaxman, the sculptor, worked for Wedgwood for many years and modelled the famous friezes, medallions and plaques, many of which still ornament the Wedgwood jasperware of today. Adam used these plaques as inlay to his chimney-pieces and furniture and imitated their design in stucco on many of his ceilings, as at Mellerstain. There was close collaboration between Wedgwood and Adam, but it was Flaxman's finely modelled classical relief figure compositions, together with the potter's purity processes, that made this ware so successful.

Adam designed much of his own furniture; several different cabinet-makers actually made it, not only Chippendale as it is some-times thought. On occasion Adam would accept the cabinet-makers' designs if they appeared to suit a specific scheme. Although the original conception was often Robert's, an experienced cabinet-maker was needed to interpret his designs in wood, paint, gilt, stucco and inlay.

Chippendale's firm was founded in the early 1750s and, after the publication of his famous *The Gentleman and Cabinet Maker's Director* in 1754, his reputation was made. His work until the early 1760s was in several styles: rococo, Gothic, Chinese, and his famous ladder-back and ribband-back chairs, for example; but after collaborating with Adam in so many houses he adopted Robert's neo-classical style. Like Adam, Chippendale was an eclectic. He did not invent any of these styles, he simply created his own version of them, which was successful.

Among the other cabinet-makers who worked for Adam were John Linnell who created, among other things, the fantastic gilded merfolk sofas at Kedleston, and William France who worked at Kenwood (Plate 20).

NOTES

1 After a model by Michelangelo. Erected here in 1874 after its removal from Northumberland House on demolition.

2 Since the later nineteenth century, biographers have stated that the column shafts in the ante-room at Syon were of verde antique marble, dredged from the River Tiber and sold to the first Duke of Northumberland for £1,000 per shaft, Restoration just after the Second World War by the marble specialist firm of J. Whitehead and Sons Ltd showed these columns to be of Greek *verde antico* marble applied in a very thin veneer to a core. It was presumed that some shafts of antique marble had been dredged from the Tiber and that these were cut into thin pieces and then used for the column veneer and the pilasters. The present Duke of Northumberland finds no record of transactions relating to the payment of £1,000 per column shaft.

3 For many years the paintings on this ceiling were ascribed to Angelica Kauffmann. The late Duke of Northumberland (father of the tenth duke) discovered that this was not correct when doing detailed research for his *Guide Book to Syon House*. He quotes from a letter written to Adam by the first Duke of Northumberland, saying that he is 'sorry there appeared any mistake between us about the price fixed for the Paintings, which I am persuaded it will be very easy to set right, but it proceeded to a great degree from what Cipriani himself told me, when I showed him the two paintings, one with a single, the other with double figures, which were done as specimens, and which I am certain he then offered to paint for the whole room at two guineas each picture and, to finish them in the best manner.'

4 The plans were not carried out, and Adam eventually transformed the old house, extending it instead of starting on a new building.

5 The Manor of Hoo was called after a medieval family of de Hoo living there. Hoo is a Saxon word meaning the spur of a hill, and the family, as was common, took their name from the property.

6 Robert's colour drawing in the Soane Museum shows more subtle colouring.

5. PROBLEMS

Robert's creative career divides itself naturally into three decades. The first, 1760–70, as described, was the period of expansion, of attainment, when everything was going right. His patrons were the aristocracy, not the Crown: George III never took to Adam, but almost all of the rest of the nobility did. His work was praised universally with hardly a dissenting voice.

The decade of the 1770s was different. All kinds of difficulties and drawbacks arose. Partly these were due to Robert's own characteristics: his driving ambition, his consequent impatience, his passionate desire to design a great architectural project. Partly they came from factors outside his control: the arrival of James Wyatt on the architectural scene, and the passing of the power of patronage from the aristocracy to municipal and government authorities.

He was now moving from the position of a rising young star into middle life. He reached the age of forty-two in 1770; younger men were reaping some of the honours he had missed, and, most important of all, he was changing his style and criticism of his work was growing.

He was not short of commissions. Indeed one of the basic reasons for his problems was pressure of work. James, William and a team of capable craftsmen were now working with him and commissions poured in.

The firm of Adam Bros. worked until after 1780 on many of the houses described in Chapter 4, and many new projects were begun. Because of this pressure Robert began to stereotype his designs and perfected a number of compositions, especially in stucco, in order to mass-produce the decorative motifs intended for ceilings and walls. The fine-quality materials used at Syon, Kedleston and other houses in the 1760s were seldom seen again. This was partly due to rising costs, which the client was unwilling to shoulder, but also to the time needed to work such materials. Stucco was cheaper and quicker than marble or wood carving.

National economic problems were also a factor in this abandonment of quality materials. The American War of Independence, which began in 1775, led speculators and property developers to cut back their enterprises – at least for the duration. When the war ended the U.S.A. had been created from an English colony. Things were never again quite the same for Britain. The British Army's fighting qualities were as great as ever in her history, but the long series of blunders by the military and naval command, together with political ineptitude, for which George III himself must bear a considerable responsibility, enabled what was initially an undisciplined, raw American force to win the day. America had been born, leaving Britain to fight half of Europe, ready as always to tear her apart when weakness was evident. That this did not happen was due, as so often in British history, to a number of individual great men.

In England the Royal Academy of Arts was founded in 1768, with Reynolds as its president and Chambers as treasurer, a post that he held until his death in 1796. The academy, as its title suggests, was at its inception very much a royal project. This is the only reason that has ever been put forward why Robert Adam was neither a founder member nor ever elected. He was consistently passed over in favour of younger, far less able men, first Wyatt at the age of twenty-four, then John Yenn, Chambers's pupil, and many others.

From the beginning, in 1758 when he was appointed architectural tutor to the young prince, Chambers had been George III's architect. Sir William Chambers was an able man, a gifted architect of the Roman Palladian school, but also a narrow, rigid personality. He disliked all that Adam stood for – his popularity, his gaiety, his light, elegant designs. This was not mere jealousy. Chambers genuinely felt that Robert was not a serious architect. He thought him self-opinionated and not true to the classical principles followed in Britain for so long and based on those of her first classical architect, Inigo Jones. Chambers would equally have disapproved of Wren for the same reasons.

Chambers, however, had the king's ear and, as long as he

continued to do so, Robert was out. The foundation of the Royal Academy was largely due to Chambers's influence with the king. Its purpose, in 1768, was to consolidate the arts and to act as an artistic opposition to bodies such as the Royal Society and the Society of Arts, both earlier foundations with a scientific bias to which Robert belonged.

George III also objected to Adam because he was a Scot, and Scots were still unpopular in England. Chambers too was a Scot, but made a point of stressing his birth in Sweden. Robert was proud of his nationality and saw no reason to hide it.

In 1768 Robert was elected Member of Parliament for Kinross-shire, defeating his opponent John Irwin by sixteen votes to three. He was a regular government follower. It could not be said that he supported Whig or Tory; there was no clear-cut distinction. M.P.s supported 'personal parties' such as those led by Lord Bute or Lord North, and Robert's loyalties generally lay with Bute and the Duke of Argyll.

Robert rarely spoke in the House. He was a conscientious member and attended regularly, but his main interest, as always, was architectural, and he valued his membership principally for the useful contacts that it enabled him to make. At the election of 1774, however, Kinross was not represented; its right to a seat alternated with that of Clackmannanshire. Robert did not seek another seat. He retained his political contacts, but his favouring of certain leaders in Parliament had lost him even more favour with George III.

Dr Carlyle writes of this period: 'I then lodged in New Bond Street with my aunt and resorted often at supper to Robert Adam's, whose sisters were very agreable, and when we had news of the House of Commons, of which he was a member, and which he told us in the most agreable manner, and with very lively comments.'

The Scottish fraternity were still meeting regularly for converse and discussion. Their favourite meeting-place in the 1770s was the British Coffee House in Cockspur Street, which had been redesigned by Robert in 1770, but is now demolished.

Robert had been sure during his years in Italy that his chief rival in securing patronage would be Chambers. In the 1770s this was not so. Chambers had been successful and he was the king's architect, but he had been little hindrance in the development of Robert's career,

except in so far as he had obtained the great public building commission (Somerset House) which had been denied to Robert because
of his lack of royal favour.

In the early 1770s there arose a much greater potential rival to
Adam: James Wyatt. Opinions vary about Wyatt. Some historians
think of him as an able eclectic, others as a mere plagiarist. It is
certain that he had great ability, and equally so that he used the
current styles and interpreted them in his own way, as Robert and
Chambers did with antique design. Wyatt, in a long lifetime,
designed in all styles: Adam, ancient Roman, medieval, Palladian. In
the later eighteenth and early nineteenth centuries his work was
chiefly Gothic, and he was dubbed by Pugin 'the Destroyer' for his
mutiliation of the medieval work in Salisbury Cathedral and its
replacement by his own interpretation.

In the 1770s he was an Adam imitator. He first came to public
notice for his rebuilding of the Pantheon in Oxford Street. He had
spent some years studying in Italy, and his Pantheon was based on the
prototype in Rome, but its interior decoration was Adam. It was
opened in 1772 when Wyatt was only twenty-six, and though it was
destroyed by fire in 1792 – the site is now occupied by Marks and
Spencers stores – it made his reputation at the time. The critics,
including Horace Walpole, switched their allegiance from Robert
to the new star, who then went on from strength to strength. His
excellent work at Heveningham is not easily distinguishable from
Robert's style, though later, since he had none of Robert's perfect-
ionism and tended to be slap-dash, his standard slipped.

Wyatt was no Robert Adam, but he was good enough to cash in
on a style his clients wanted. He certainly took from Robert some
patronage and some of the honours. Other architects followed,
Leverton and Holland, for example, but their work, though having
much in common at this date with Robert's, was more individual.

The great Adam adventure of the 1770s was the Adelphi project.
It almost brought the financial fortunes of the family to the brink of
total disaster, and it certainly damaged Robert's reputation as an
architect and a business man. The whole idea arose from Robert's
ambition to build a giant civic scheme. Neither George III nor any
government authority had commissioned him to do this, so he
undertook one of his own which proved so vast a project that it was

unsuitable for private means. Despite the near tragedy, the brothers extricated themselves by their own acumen, their fortune and the help of their many influential friends. The accommodation they built was in great demand from the time it was finished in the early 1770s until its unwarranted demolition by mercenary factions in 1937. The buildings were all continuously occupied during those two centuries as the houses and offices for which they were designed.

In 1768 the firm of Adam Bros. (all four brothers were a party to this venture) took the site of Durham Yard from the Duke of St Albans on a ninety-nine year lease for a yearly ground rent of £1,200. The site bordered the north side of the Thames. The Victoria Embankment, now fronting the Thames at this point, did not then exist, and where the Victoria Embankment Gardens are now laid out there was a pestilential, stinking area of mud, very offensive at low water, forming a bay which filled at high tide. The Durham Yard site lay behind this, extending from the present Savoy Place to

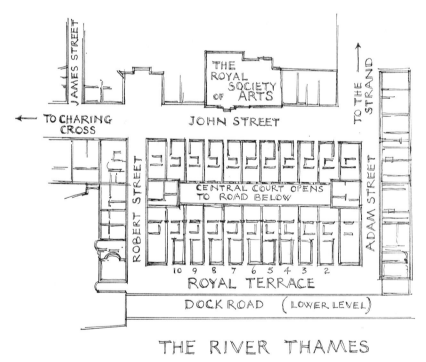

3 *Simplified sketch of the Adelphi as laid out in 1768–74 (upper level)*

the Strand, and from York Buildings on the west to Shell Mex House on the east.

Robert's impressive scheme was to embank or drain the Thames edge, and build up a Royal Terrace above vaulted arches which would be used as warehouse storage. There would be two streets parallel to the Strand in the direction of the river and cross-streets at the ends. The whole was to be designed in the form of palace façades to the river, high up to give a magnificent view over the water and to provide houses and offices all with a high standard of amenity – stabling, water supply, heating, etc. – and of aesthetic beauty inside and out. This was to be a great Roman palace, and the similarity of its theme to the southern colonnaded wall of the Palace of Diocletian on the Adriatic was obvious to everyone, even though the architectural style was quite different.

The entire scheme was carried out between 1768 and 1774. The streets were all named after the Adam brothers; the name Adelphi, chosen by them, is derived from the Greek word ἀδελφοι, 'brothers'. The cost was incredible.

Robert entered into his project with characteristic enthusiasm and impatience. He thought that he had secured government agreement to rent the warehouse accommodation and that this would help to defray expenses. Being an M.P. he thought it would be easy to put through the necessary legislation to enclose the foreshore. He believed that the engineering problems of keeping damp from the warehouses would not be too difficult. He underestimated both the practical problems and the opposition of the City of London, which had allowed a pestilential swamp to exist untreated and neglected for centuries but, now that it was about to be removed from their jurisdiction, fought tooth and nail to keep it. Sir Christopher Wren and Sir Patrick Abercrombie, in the seventeenth and twentieth centuries, had similar experiences with the intractably narrow, prejudiced, mercenary City.

The government decided not to hire the vaulted warehouses, possibly for fear of flooding, which certainly occurred in later years. That decision, however, was not definite till 1772, by which time the Adam brothers were in debt to the amount of £140,000 and David Hume estimated the costs in labour and materials to be running at £100,000 per annum.

To obtain the necessary parliamentary sanction to drain the swampy foreshore several of Adam's friends guided the petition through Parliament. These included Sir George Colebrooke, M.P. for Arundel; Archibald Edmonstone, M.P. for Dunbartonshire; Lord Frederick Campbell, M.P. for Glasgow Burghs; and Jeremiah Dyson, M.P. for Weymouth and Melcombe Regis. Both George III and the Prime Minister, Lord North, supported the petition as did also nearly all the Scottish politicians. But the City of London fought bitterly and debates were stormy. The press, however, lent its aid. A contemporary newspaper, referrring to the Adam brothers, rightly declared: 'These gentlemen have expended £140,000 to raise palaces from an offensive heap of mud and circulated an immense sum to make a palpable nuisance a principal ornament to the metropolis.'

The City's opposition failed. They then appealed to the king, on 3rd May 1771. On the 8th the Royal Assent was given to the Bill. The City tried again. Once more they petitioned the king. Annoyed, he pointed out: 'It is with concern that I see a part of my subjects still so far misled and deluded as to renew, in such reprehensible terms, a request with which I have repeatedly declared I cannot comply.'

That was that. But in 1772 bankruptcy stared the brothers in the face. Having failed to raise a loan on the property, on 25th May 1773 they petitioned Parliament to be allowed to dispose of their assets, except the estate, by lottery. This was not as unusual in eighteenth-century England as it would be now. In 1753, for example, £300,000 was raised in a similar manner to found the first British Museum. After a debate in both Houses the petition was accepted, and the draw in March 1774 raised £218,500. It was enough to save the day. The brothers had come near to financial ruin and had had to mortgage the Blair-Adam estate, sell their collection of sculpture and paintings and dismiss hundreds of workers. With relief Robert writes in late February 1774: 'We have this day paid the half of all our mortgages and whenever the deeds of assignment are ready will pay the whole.' Indeed it was not long before the mortgages were redeemed and they had recovered all their possessions.

It had been a near thing. London was the richer for the Adelphi. Apart from terraces in Bath, architectural designs for houses laid out in terrace manner rather than as individual buildings were unusual at that time. Robert's great Royal Terrace (later the Adelphi Terrace) stood high above the river, giving wonderful, uninterrupted views of London to the nine houses along the façade. Robert himself lived in No. 4 from 1772 until 1786, and David Garrick next door at No. 5 until his death in 1779. His funeral procession extended from his Adelphi house nearly to Westminster Abbey; Robert was in carriage No. 25.

The architecture of the Adelphi was criticized by some at the time for its flat, plain treatment. This was intentional. Adam designed the scheme to be simple and unfussy; Horace Walpole's remarks about prostitutes dressed in regimental braid would appear, in retrospect, to be merely bad taste. Projections were slight, negligible. The Royal Terrace façade had four storeys above the road and two below (basements) descending to the Dock Road at Durham Yard level. John Street is parallel, inland, to the Royal Terrace and south of the Strand. The Royal Society of Arts Building, designed by Robert and built in 1772–4, is still in John Street, its façade intact, but the interior considerably altered. The Royal Terrace had central and end pavilions, very slightly projecting. A continuous entablature ran the full length of the terrace, but the projections had decorative pilasters. These can still be seen in the façade of No. 7 Adam Street, which survives. Two lateral terraces (of which Adam Street was one) extended towards the river where they were finished by pedimented, terminal pavilions (Fig. 3 and Plate 27).

The Adelphi was partly reconstructed in 1872 when a pediment and further ornament were added to the Royal Terrace façade. These were not improvements. Almost the whole scheme was demolished in 1937. This criminal negligence is summed up aptly by Sacheverell Sitwell [1]: 'The Adelphi wilfully, and of cupidity was pulled down. Willing hands did more damage to London than a German landmine'; and by Dr Pevsner [2]: 'In London the principle of the palace facade for a whole row of houses was introduced by Robert Adam in his Adelphi (that magnificent composition of streets with its Thames front known all over Europe, which was destroyed, not by bombs, but by mercenary Londoners just before the war).'

In 1773 the first volume of the *Works* was published. Robert had now, at this middle stage in his career, evolved a number of theories and principles of architectural structure and decoration, and he states them clearly and unequivocally in his preface. He also felt that the firm of Adam Bros. needed some advertisement. The first impetus, caused by the novelty of their designs, was weakening. At the same time their ideas and motifs were being copied by architects and decorators who presented them as their own, a fact that clients did not always realize. Wyatt's Pantheon, opened in the previous year, was one example: its interior decorative theme was Adam, yet the critics who acclaimed it as a new design were unperceiving.

Robert's third purpose in presenting his *Works* was to enunciate clearly and finally what he had developed and created, and to claim it as his own. In doing so his wording was, to say the least, tactless. He made enemies and offended some of his friends and colleagues by his categorical assertions. The fact that his statements were true made them, if anything, more offensive to certain readers. It was felt that it might have been more dignified to have remained silent. King George III, Sir William Chambers and Horace Walpole were among those most incensed, but even some of his clients thought that he had gone too far.

Like the Spalatro volume, the *Works* were finely presented, with excellent engravings of complete exterior and interior views; also a quantity of detail in furniture and furnishings taken from what Robert considered to be his best works. Early designs like Hatchlands and Shardeloes were not used. He felt he had outgrown such treatment. Volume One, which appeared in 1773, includes drawings from Syon, Kenwood, Luton Hoo and public buildings like the Admiralty Screen. After the famous preface the book is divided into five sections, each with a short preface of its own. These are less important and are mainly expressions of Robert's views on the orders and classical form, expounding further his letter to Lord Kames.

Volume Two came out in 1779 and illustrates Derby House, No. 20 St James's Square, Lansdowne House, Syon again, Mistley, the Theatre Royal, Drury Lane, and further detail. Volume Three was published posthumously in 1822. It contains a selection of Robert's work from many different buildings. Some of the plates, engraved by

Zucchi and Piranesi, are excellent; others are of poorer standard. All three volumes have been reprinted, wholly or part, a number of times, especially in the twentieth century.

Volume One is the most important. Its full title is *The Works in Architecture of Robert and James Adam Esquires*. The preface begins:

'Some apology may, perhaps be requisite for giving to the world a book of architecture, after so many works of this kind have been published in Italy, France and England during the two last centuries.

'The novelty and variety of the following designs will, we flatter ourselves, not only excuse, but justify our conduct, in communicating them to the world. We have not trod in the path of others, nor derived aid from their labours. In the works which we have had the honour to execute, we have not only met with the approbation of our employers, but even with the imitation of other artists, to such a degree, as in some measure to have brought about, in this country, a kind of revolution in the whole system of this useful and elegant art.'

Robert goes on to say that the heavy compartmented ceilings and cornices, the three-dimensional stucco wall decoration and carved marble fireplaces designed by the Palladians are now out of fashion, and their limited repertoire has been replaced by his richly improved one. 'We have adopted a beautiful variety of light mouldings, gracefully formed, delicately enriched and arranged with propriety and skill. We have introduced a great variety of ceilings, freezes and decorated pilasters, and have added grace and beauty to the whole by a mixture of grotesque stucco, and painted ornaments together with the flowing rainçeau, with its fanciful figures and winding foliage.' He explains in footnotes that by 'grotesque' he is referring to ancient Roman stucco decoration in villas and palaces, and that rainçeau is a French word describing acanthus scrolls intertwined with flowers, birds and human figures (Glossary).

One of the important principles which he enunciates in the preface is his theory of 'movement' which, as mentioned earlier, is simply the basis of Baroque architecture and decoration. In Italy or Germany it would have needed no defining; it would have been obvious. Baroque principles were so little used or understood in England that Robert's enunciation was regarded as something new.

He defines it: 'Movement is meant to express the rise and fall, the advance and recess, with other diversity of form, in the different parts of a building, so as to add greatly to the picturesque of the composition. For the rising and falling, advancing and receding, with the convexity and concavity, and other forms of the great parts, have the same effect in architecture, that hill and dale, foreground and distance, swelling and sinking have in landscape.'

He develops the theme, then quotes St Peter's and others as ideal examples. 'The effect of the height and convexity of the dome of S. Peter's, contrasted with the lower square front, and the concavity of its court is a striking instance of this sort of composition. The college and church des quatres nations at Paris [now the Institut de France] is, though small, another of the same kind.'

He goes on to cite his own contribution to 'movement': 'We really do not recollect any example of so much movement and contrast as in the south front of Kedleston house in Derbyshire.' Here Robert is referring of course to the complete design with wings, which he was still hoping to implement.

He then pays his tribute to Vanbrugh, the English architect of the Baroque whose reputation, like that of Adam himself, suffered so much from misinterpretation and prejudiced criticism after his death. He says: 'Sir John Vanbrugh's genius was of the first class; and, in point of movement, novelty and ingenuity, his works have not been exceeded by anything in modern times.'

Typically, though, Robert had to qualify his praise. 'We should certainly have quoted Blenheim and Castle Howard as great examples of these perfections, in preference to any work of our own, or of any other modern architect; but unluckily for the reputation of this excellent artist, his taste kept no pace with his genius and his works are so crowded with barbarisms and absurdities and so borne down by their preposterous weight, that none but the discerning can separate their merits from their defects.' Robert no doubt thought himself one of the 'discerning', but it does not seem to have occurred to him that Vanbrugh's genius intentionally created both 'movement' and handling.

Much of the rest of the preface is a survey of classical architecture, its forms and development, of the orders and ornament. Robert criticizes much of the Renaissance interpretation of the ancient classicism, calling it sterile and monotonous. He holds the Italians responsible for reviving the style incorrectly and with so many mis-conceptions, the French for continuing and worsening the tradition, and the English Palladians for their slavish copying of a worn-out theme, though he excepts most of the great architects from these strictures.

Referring to the Palladian practice of following literally the rules of Vitruvius and Palladio he writes: 'Among architects destitute of genius and incapable of venturing into the great line of their art, the attention paid to these rules and proportions is frequently minute and frivolous. The great masters of antiquity were not so rigidly scrupulous, they varied the proportions as the general spirit of their composition required, clearly perceiving that, however necessary these rules may be to form the taste and to correct the licentiousness of the scholar, they often cramp the genius, and circumscribe the ideas of the master.'

He concludes: 'Whether our works have not contributed to diffuse these improvements in architecture, through this country, we shall leave to the impartial public. We, by no means, presume to find fault with the compositions, or to decry the labours of other authors; many of whom have much merit and deserve great praise. Our ambition is to share with others, not to appropriate to our-selves the applause of the public; and, if we have any claim to approbation, we found it on this alone: That we flatter ourselves, we have been able to seize, with some degree of success, the beautiful spirit of antiquity, and to transfuse it with novelty and variety, through all our numerous works.'

At the end of Volume One Robert echoes a cry from the heart which has been expressed by many a great English artist through the ages down to Sir Edward Elgar. Referring to the varied pattern of the expression of ability in different nations during their history he says of the Italian Renaissance: 'National genius awakened at once, and exerted itself with vigour, in every direction. The sixteenth century is the splendid age of that country; and during the course of it, flourished the great poets, historians, painters, sculptors, architects and musicians.'

He refers to England and its different heritage, of how the English genius, equally vigorous, ran in different channels – literature, science, exploration. He concludes: 'But whilst England led the way in these important investigations [he is thinking here of Sir Isaac Newton] she could not boast of the same pre-eminence in the fine arts. In painting, sculpture, architecture and music, her progress was extremely slow, and in all of them she has been far excelled by other nations of modern Europe.'

Much of Robert's work in the 1770s took the form of street architecture, particularly in London. The Adelphi was his first and greatest venture. He also embarked on other speculative building, designing whole streets of houses for sale. Portland Place was one of these, but, due to the American War of Independence and the consequent withdrawal of capital and confidence by wealthy English landowners, it was delayed till the 1780s, by which time Robert had lost interest and James was largely responsible for the emasculated scheme (Chapter 6).

Mansfield Street, W.1, retains more of its original form. The street was laid out from 1770; many of the clients were Robert's country-house patrons who wanted *pieds-à-terre* in town: Lord Scarsdale, for example, at No. 5. These are typical examples of Adam's speculative building. Only those on the west side, Nos. 5–15 survive. They are in a four-storey terrace block, simply built in brick, without orders and with very little decoration. The doorways are characteristic, all Ionic in three-part style with decorative semi-circular iron fanlights. There is a plaque on No. 13 to show that J. L. Pearson and Sir Edwin Lutyens lived here, and died here in 1897 and 1944 respectively. The interiors are greatly altered. They were, like most Adam speculative building, of less careful standard than his commissioned work, with ceilings and fireplace designs repeated along the row. The stucco decoration was typical, with arabesques and griffins and, though a business venture, was by today's standards of quality design.

A number of speculative schemes were laid out in emulation of Adam's at this time and were, in the earlier twentieth century, credited to him. Stratford Place, W.1, is among them. A brick, stuccoed façade terrace with low relief Ionic pilasters, it is in the classic Adam pattern, but certainly of lower standard in proportion and execution. The street was promoted by the Earl of Stratford in 1771 and designed by Richard Edwin.

At the end of the street, which is a cul-de-sac, is Stratford House,

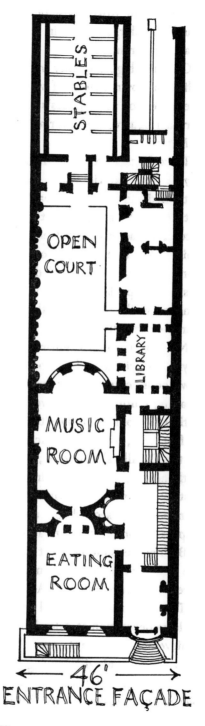

4 Plan of ground floor of 20 St James's Square as Adam designed it. Typical of his town house pattern and having close affinities with Pompeian town houses

which was the town house of the Earl of Derby and is now a club. This has undergone certain alterations, but a quantity of genuine Adam work remains.

Of much higher quality in London at this time were the Adam individual town houses of which three outstanding ones survive. These are No. 20 St James's Square, the Distillers' House; No. 20 Portman Square, the Courtauld Institute; and Chandos House, all in Mayfair.

These houses are all characteristic of the London Adam in the 1770s. The exteriors are simple, mostly astylar, the windows restrained and barely noticeable and the porch the focal decorative feature. Inside, all of Robert's ingenuity went to create the appearance of a spacious elegant house several storeys in height on a site which, due to the high cost of land, had an extremely narrow frontage, but which extended back a long way. His inventive genius is shown especially in the varied and beautiful staircases within confined wells, which give the impression of having far more space than they actually possess.

No. 20 St James's Square was built for Sir Watkin Williams-Wynn, a friend and a good patron of Adam. This was the town house equivalent of Syon or Kedleston, where the client was wealthy, cultured and a lover of the arts. Robert had a free hand within the confines of the site. The original façade was narrow, only 46 feet wide, but is now twice that. Both Nos. 20 and 21 are owned by the Distillers' Company, who duplicated Adam's façade across both houses, forming an impressive front. The lower storey is rusticated, broken by windows and two beautiful doorways. The *piano nobile* and second floor are spanned by a giant Corinthian order in pilaster form; above are attic and dormers (Fig. 4).

Both houses suffered great damage in the Second World War, but the structure remained sound, and No. 20 has now been restored carefully and accurately to Adam's designs in the Soane Museum.

There are many beautiful rooms, typical of the low-relief, very delicate decoration of Adam's middle period. The two outstanding achievements are the staircase with its hall and well and, on the first floor, the second withdrawing-room.

The staircase and well was an Adam prototype and is a masterpiece. The hall rises to the full height of the house and the single staircase ascends, as is customary with Adam, only to the first floor, where it ends in a balustraded landing with a fine stuccoed niche opposite to a large painting (*see* notes on page 196). The secondary staircase then continued upwards (though a lift has now been installed here). The ground-floor hall is plain; the focus is on the beautiful staircase, which had a delicate iron balustrade and mahogany handrail (Plate *42*). The well is lit at the top by an oval fanlight, having convexly curved ribs, and drum decorated with paterae and swags. The whole staircase well is enriched sparingly with quality low relief stucco in typical Adam motifs: anthemion, figure panels, arabesques, winged lions and vases.

The first-floor withdrawing-room at the rear of the house is the *pièce de résistance* among a series of fine interiors. It is one of Robert's best, though the stucco decoration is linear, so low and delicate is the relief design. The great ceiling is a segmental barrel vault in form, terminating at both ends in shallow semi-domes. The whole is compartmented by bands of decoration into ovals, squares and circles, much like the library at Kenwood. There are two schemes in the Soane Museum showing the favoured Adam colours with backgrounds in pale yellow, greens and pale and deep pinks, white stucco decoration, then touches of strong caerulean blue in the painted roundels (Plate *13*).

The room is now used as a board-room and the furniture is all modern, but the exquisite doors and doorcases and the white marble mantelpiece remain. This is a superb state room still.

No 20 Portman Square, built for the wealthy Countess of Home, has much in common with the house in St James's Square. The façade though is much wider, so Robert had more room to play with. His brick exterior to the square is still plain and, this time, astylar. The windows are simple, there are decorative panels between and the main interest is the pedimented Doric porch (Plate *35*). At the rear there is a pleasant, square garden. The façade on this side has a central semicircular Ionic portico and, above on the second floor, three Venetian windows in the Corinthian order, while those below are Ionic.

The room interiors show a more superb quality of craftsmanship and design even than those in St James's Square, but their linear characteristics are typical of this period of Adam's life. Also, despite the perfection of proportion, form and colouring, one senses a stereotyped approach. Robert had now done many such fine interiors, and he seems to be resting on his laurels. There is nothing shoddy or, indeed, anything which is not just right, but one feels that one has been here before: a carping criticism no doubt.

Among the many beautiful rooms two features stand out in their originality and perfection: again, as at St James's Square, the handling of the staircase well and the first-floor music-room.

The staircase is remarkable for its unusual design, to which Adam returned later at Culzean. The decoration of the lower part of the well is simple; the focal centre is the staircase, which here also extends only to first-floor level, being carried upwards by a secondary stair. The originality here is in the shape of the well, which is circular. The stairway ascends from the ground floor in one central flight, and divides at the half-landing into two branches which sweep round the well to the first-floor landing. The balustrade and stairs are similar to those at St James's Square. On the first floor the wall is decorated with panelled gravure paintings in monochrome; below are sculpture-filled niches, and doors leading into the rooms. Above is an Ionic colonnade, extending to a stucco decorated drum and then a low-domed, delicate, circular lantern with graceful iron-work decoration. The staircase well is tall and not extensive, but the Adam design makes utmost use of the available area, giving an impression of a much greater spaciousness than actually exists.

The first-floor music-room is Robert's finest in this linear tradition. The ceiling particularly is exquisitely modelled and painted. Mr Sacheverell Sitwell [1] describes it 'as complex and fine drawn as a spider's web upon a frosty morning'. An apt description, but one which conveys no feeling of the rich colour and fine painting. The rest of the room is in keeping: walls, door-cases, fireplace. These are obscured at the moment by the necessary but not beautiful bookcases (Plate 32).

Of special interest next door is the redecorated little Etruscan room, which shows us an example of this now rare Adam decorative method. The enrichment is mainly painted, not in relief, and in Robert's 'Etruscan colours' of black, cream and Pompeian red. Ceiling, doorcases and walls are treated in one scheme; the white marble mantelpiece is painted and inlaid with marbles and terra-cotta in the same motifs.

Chandos House, on the corner of Queen Anne Street, has a plain, attractive exterior with one superb feature – the porch. This has fluted columns with characteristically Adam capitals, boasting low-relief anthemion decoration instead of volutes and acanthus leaves. The entablature has no architrave, but a frieze enriched with rams' heads, swags and paterae. The door, fanlight and railings are in keeping. The house was built for the Duke of Chandos. The interior has been slightly altered, but was not of the superb standard of Portman Square, though elegant and tasteful throughout (Plate 33).

A number of Robert's London houses of this decade have been totally destroyed or drastically altered. Derby House in Grosvenor Square, which he altered and decorated in 1773 for Lord Derby's heir, Lord Stanley, must have been one of his finest achievements; it is now demolished. Here there were one of his outstanding Etruscan rooms and some fine apartments decorated in his best-quality style.

Lansdowne House in Berkeley Square has fared a little better in that part of it still exists. It had an unusual history. Robert designed it in 1762 for Lord Bute, who in 1765, when it was partly built, sold it to Lord Shelburne (later Marquess of Lansdowne) for £22,500. This sum was inclusive of Robert's fees and costs for completion, which was carried out by 1768. Lansdowne House was another of Robert's best works, with a notable Doric hall, an ante-room on his classic pattern, a fine staircase and suites of rooms. In 1929 most of the building was demolished. The Portland stone façade was largely used to face a modern shell, so that the present building, now No. 9 Fitzmaurice Place, still retains its pediment over a four-column Ionic feature with decorative Adam frieze.

The building is now an exclusive club, whose rooms include a circular interior (now called the Adam Room), which was originally the drawing-room. The two-feet-deep monochrome gravure figure composition frieze still encircles the upper part of the room.

The British Coffee House in Cockspur Street was demolished in 1886. No. 1 Whitehall suffered a similar fate. Roxburghe House, built for the duke in 1776 in Harewood Place, off Oxford Street, disappeared in 1908. London perpetually renews itself. This is an inevitable process in a wealthy, thriving capital city. It is probable and, we hope, certain nowadays that works of art of this calibre will not be so casually disposed of as they were by our Victorian and Edwardian predecessors. We can much less afford to lose them.

Barely had the dust settled from the Adelphi dispute than Robert was once more involved in difficulties which led, this time, to litigation and caused further harm to the business reputation of the firm of Adam Bros. This was the matter which culminated in the Liardet v. Johnson trial.

The whole subject turned on the patent rights of stucco compositions. From early days in the eighteenth century different types of *stucco duro*, or hard composition, had been made by various firms for use by craftsmen in applying decoration to ceilings and walls. Robert, as we know, used such compositions extensively, and in order to achieve his delicate form of ornament, much finer and lower in relief than earlier eighteenth-century designs, the high quality of the composition was vital, as was also facility of handling.

Though the earlier compositions were hard and lasting, they took time to set and were not easy to handle. New products which came on to the market included one by Mr David Wark, patented in 1765, and another by M. Liardet, a Swiss clergyman, in 1773. The Adam firm bought both patents and obtained an Act of Parliament in 1776 authorizing them to be the sole makers and vendors of this material. Their manufacture was called 'Adam's new invented patent stucco'.

More new versions appeared, among which was one by Mr. Johnson, who claimed it to be an improvement. The Adam brothers, having paid highly for their rights, took him to court. The case was decided in 1778 by Lord Mansfield, fellow Scot and patron (at Kenwood). He gave judgment in favour of the Adams.

As in the Adelphi affair and the publication of the *Works*, Robert's actions were in the normal way of business, legally correct and in no way underhand. But in all these matters his professional colleagues, and a number of potential clients, felt that his attitude savoured too much of business and too little of professional etiquette. In the specific case of the stucco composition architects thought that, concerning a material being so constantly altered and improved, it was not professionally just that one architect should possess sole legal rights to its use.

The immediate effect was to harm Robert's business and professional reputation. The long-term result was to devalue his decorative designs. He himself was partly responsible for this, in that the new stucco was more plastic and therefore easier to handle. The designs were thus mass-produced and became stereotyped. Even worse, the malleability of the substance encouraged others, of far less ability and possessing less scrupulously high standards of execution, to imitate Robert's designs. It was this wide-scale copying of his work which led to its condemnation by nineteenth-century critics, who erronously believed it to be genuine Adam.

The village of Mistley in Essex, on the River Stour, is still a quiet backwater, and though many of its buildings have disappeared, one can visualize the pleasant eighteenth-century watering-place of which David Garrick wrote when he stayed at Mistley Hall: 'While I am writing this in my dressing room, I see no less than 50 vessels under sail.'

The River Stour does not look quite like that now. At low tide the channel, though deep, is narrow and winds round the mud of the estuary; a haven for an immense colony of white swans.

In 1776 Mr Rigby, whose seat was Mistley Hall, asked Robert to remodel and enlarge his house. Robert also redesigned and completed the building of the church and prepared designs for the lodges, gates, an inn, bathing pavilion, fountains and pools. The bathing centre was to be where the present wharf stands, but, possibly due to the climate on a north-facing coast, little of this was finally constructed.

Robert did, however, build the church, and it is the only church of his to survive, even in part. An unusual design, it had twin classical towers, one at each end and, between, a rectangular nave with porticoes on either side. The building was of brick, stucco-covered, and with stone towers topped with lead cupolas (Fig. 5).

Not a great deal of Robert's work survives here. The hall was demolished when the Great Eastern Railway to Harwich was constructed across the park, and in 1870 the church fell victim to the enthusiasm and prejudice of the Gothic Revival. The centre part was demolished, but the towers were retained as navigation landmarks.

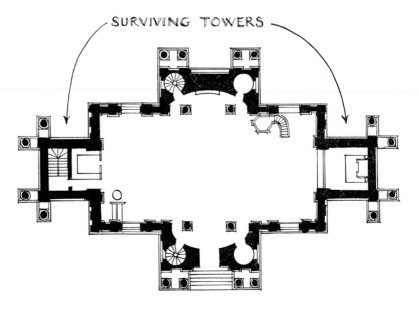

5   Ground plan of Mistley Church, Essex

Fortunately the Ministry of Works now looks after them and they are in excellent condition. It is interesting to compare them with the complete illustration by Robert in the *Works*.

Though he was principally occupied in this decade, up to 1780, with the building of town houses and terraces, as well as with the completion of his houses begun in the 1760s, he worked on at least three major new country-house schemes. At Audley End, in Essex, he redesigned and decorated a suite of rooms on the ground floor of the south wing for Lord Braybrooke. Unfortunately they have been considerably altered. But the grounds, laid out by Capability Brown, possess some interesting and, in places, charming Adam works. These include the Lion Gate entrance, the circular temple and the two bridges over the stream dammed by Brown to form a lake. The temple is in a field now under cultivation and thus inaccessible to public inspection. The *pièce de résistance* here is the elegant Ionic bridge temple, now called the Tea House Bridge, which he designed in 1783.

Robert's quality country-house work of this decade is in two widely separated places: Saltram in Devonshire and Mellerstain in

Berwick. Saltram Park was in the news on 26th November 1968 as being the first example of land designated as 'inalienable' lost by the National Trust to a developer, in this case the Ministry of Transport. Fortunately, though the loss of the land will spoil some of the amenity of the park and creates a disturbing precedent, the house itself remains inviolate.

Robert prepared designs for Saltram in 1779 for John Parker, later Lord Boringdon, ancestor of the present owner Lord Morley. The large mansion is finely situated in a wooded park overlooking Plymouth and the Catwater. Robert designed alterations which would have created a magnificent circular dining-room of 32 feet in diameter, extended to an oval by semicircular apses on two sides, and a great gallery to connect his dining-room to the drawing-room. None of this was built.

What was carried out was the redecoration of the existing east range, of which two rooms in particular remain: the adjoining saloon and dining-room. Notable in these rooms are the original carpets, both designed by Adam. They both reflect closely the respective ceiling designs.

The saloon is a double cube, 50 by 25 by 25 feet, and has a deeply coved ceiling in classic Adam pattern. Robert redesigned the great Venetian window, provided the pier glasses and frames for the paintings, the doorcases, doors and much of the furniture (Plate 22).

The dining-room is simpler Adam with a superb ceiling, patterned with central circle and painted lunettes surrounded by stucco roundels and arabesques. Below is a restrained entablature with low relief patera and swag frieze; a motif repeated in the doorcase friezes. The room is a decorative whole: white marble fireplace, stucco decorative frames to the pictures and roundels, and pedestals with urns above flanking the beautiful sideboard, which has a polished, inlaid wood top and legs decorated in green, cream and white (Plate 36).

The new house at Mellerstain had been begun in 1725 by William Adam (Chapter 1, page 29), who completed the two wings. These remained separate for forty years, until George Baillie asked Robert to complete the work. The exterior is castellated stonework with little of Robert's influence visible, though the projecting entrance block shows something of his 'movement'. Inside, the main central portion is typically Adam, particularly the library, dining-room, drawing-room and hall.

An original surviving feature on the lower floor is the Adam bath-room, with stucco dolphins spouting water over the entrance arch. The actual bath has now been filled in. It was square or rectangular and is tiled over. Brass vessels for filling the bath with hot water are still there; also heating stoves.

Some of the medieval, castellar approach has pervaded the interior in, for example, the undercroft appearance of the vaulted ground floor, the medieval corridor ceilings and the small room next to the library, which has a ceiling decorated all over with interlaced, cusped circles in ribbed plaster.

The house itself is in magnificent condition; nearly all the Adam ceilings and walls are in his original colour designs, and there is a fine variety of mantelpieces, all different but all good.

The library is the finest room, with wooden bookcases all round the walls in applied wood decoration, painted white, very much like those at Osterley. The walls above the bookcases are decorated with panels in Wedgwood-type design and white stucco figures on blue-grey backgrounds. The ceiling is particularly fine. It is designed in three compartments, each with a painted roundel centre-piece and stucco arabesque and reeded decoration around it. It is one of Robert's excellent and least publicized interiors (Plates 37, 38).

NOTES

1 Sacheverell Sitwell, *British Architects and Craftsmen*, pp. 152 and 154, B. T. Batsford, 1948.

2 Nikolaus Pevsner. *An Outline of European Architecture*, pp. 582–3, Penguin Books, 1961.

6. FRUSTRATION

In THE last decade of his life all Robert's enthusiasm and originality returned. The linear, sometimes fussy, decoration of the 1770s, together with the flat, low-relief exterior façades disappeared. Instead Robert rediscovered his zest for architectural plasticity. His exteriors once more displayed 'movement'; they were characterized by the vitality of their monumental design. Interior schemes were simpler and plainer, but also more coherent. There was less of the 'spider's web' tracery and more of the rich interplay of colour and form that had been seen in the 1760s.

Both for Robert and for posterity it was a great loss that so many of the extensive schemes of the 1780s, which he designed with utmost care and down to the smallest of details, should have come to naught. Partly this was due to their sheer size; the money was not forthcoming when the designs had been made. Partly it was just bad luck.

These circumstances have been the lot of most of the world's great architects throughout history. It is only occasionally that the power, the money and the will to build some large, single building or comprehensive scheme are all present at the same time.

The vision, knowledge and taste of a great patron are necessary, together with the autocratic power to thrust aside objections and overrule interested factions; and of course financial backing must be available. Classic examples of the successful combining of these circumstances with the availability of the services of a great architect or planner come to mind: the *grands boulevards* of Paris under the Emperor Napoleon III and Baron Haussmann; St Peter's in Rome with three different popes and a succession of architects of genius,

Bramante, Michelangelo, Bernini; the palaces of the Nile under powerful Pharaohs.

In England two architects were fortunate in being available for such a combination of circumstances: Sir Christopher Wren, at the time of the Great Fire of London, and John Nash, who was supported by the Prince Regent in building Regent Street and the famous Park terraces.

Robert Adam, like Inigo Jones before him, was unlucky. Both these architects expended tremendous time and effort designing comprehensive schemes, Jones on Whitehall Palace and Adam in Edinburgh, Bath and Cambridge. Neither accomplished their life-long ambition, to build one great scheme. Apart from some country houses, mainly in Scotland, all Robert's work of the 1780s (and he designed a vast quantity) was either still-born or built only as fragments of his conception. Most of those fragments were erected after his death and with alterations.

In London there were two projects: Portland Place and Fitzroy Square. Robert had made his designs for Portland Place in the early 1770s. He did not envisage it as a thoroughfare. It was to be a *Grande Place* on the continental pattern, surrounded by individual town palaces, each different and specially designed for wealthy patrons. The southern end of the *Place* was already occupied by Foley House, which stood on the site now, unfortunately, filled by the Langham Hotel. The northern end was open, ending in fields and a vista over Marylebone Farm. Lord Findlater and Lord Kerry were two of the patrons early interested in the scheme, and others followed; but the American War of Independence, which began in 1775, curtailed desire for financial speculation. The noble lords retired to their country estates to sit it out.

In the 1780s interest revived, but Robert was busy elsewhere and had lost enthusiasm, especially as it appeared that money would not be forthcoming for such palaces as he envisaged. He handed over to James, who eventually built a long, low, three-storeyed terrace block on each side of the wide thoroughfare. Like the later examples on the sea-front at Hove, these were too long for the interest of the designs and became monotonous in their repetition. The builders were inadequately supervised, and the Portland Place houses came as near as Adam's work ever did to slap-dash standards.

Portland Place is still a stately thoroughfare. Its broad dimensions are unaltered, and Nash's early nineteenth-century additions of All Souls' Church at the southern end and Park Crescent at the northern were undoubted assets to the street. Wide-scale demolition in the 1930s, and war-time damage in the following decade, with consequent free-for-all in rebuilding, have between them totally destroyed the homogeneity of the original.

There are two instances of town squares laid out to Robert's designs, one in London and one in Edinburgh. Both were barely started when he died, and neither was completed to his scheme. In Fitzroy Square, London, two of the four sides are more or less as he planned; the other two are in keeping, though later, on Greek Revival pattern.

Work in Fitzroy Square was begun in 1790. The south and east sides were built in Portland stone with decoration in the patented Liardet stucco. They are much more three-dimensional than was the Adelphi. The architectural quality can be seen in the bold massing of the central block and end pavilions. Both the Ionic order and the fenestration are well and interestingly handled. Much of the interior has been altered, but what remains is plain and almost severe. Certainly it was all carried out after Robert's death (Plate 39).

Adam was consulted by Sir William Johnstone-Pulteney in the design of the layout of a new town at Bathwick. His wife had inherited this land and he wished to develop it as a suburb of Bath. At the time it was divided from the city by the River Avon and the only transport connection was a ferry.

Robert designed a bridge to replace the ferry and drew up plans for a complete town. The bridge was built soon after 1770. The Pulteney Bridge – it still stands – is based on the pattern of the Ponte Vecchio in Florence, with a roadway lined by shops on either side. It has been altered and truncated by road-widening schemes, but it is still a delightful bridge and an asset to Bath (Plate 40).

Of the remainder of the scheme virtually nothing was built till much later, except that Robert's intended main artery, a street 100 feet wide, was laid out. This is the existing Pulteney Street, which continues on from the bridge.

Since he left Scotland in 1754 Robert's ideas on architecture had moved further and further away from the dour solemnity of Scottish Palladianism. After twenty years of practice in London he had become completely southern in his architectural design. In the decade of the 1780s, apart from the London building just described, the bulk of his work was done in Scotland, in country houses and, especially, in Edinburgh.

He returned to Edinburgh to help solve the problems which had beset the city in his youth, the draining of the North-loch and the spanning of this and the Cowgate by bridges, so that expansion could take place in a new town north of the city.

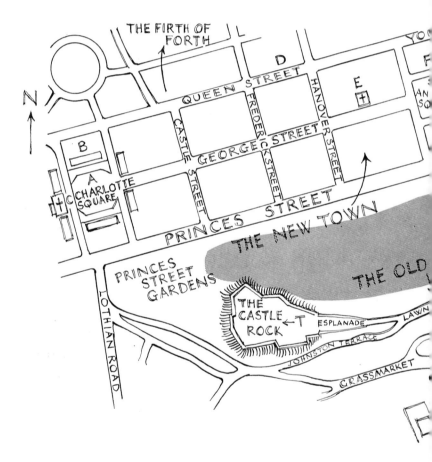

6.*Simplified plan of Edinburgh as planned c. 1790 (wynds and closes omitted). Note the straight lines of New Town streets and winding ones in the Old Town. Shaded area represents the low ground originally covered by the North-loch water and marshlands: now the site of*

Robert carried out countless surveys and designs for Edinburgh between 1780 and his death in 1792, for the university, the Register House, the South Bridge and the New Town. It was his groundwork that led to their final success, though only a small percentage of what he planned was carried out to his designs. The extent of the tragedy that this loss is to Edinburgh can be judged by comparing the fragments of genuine Adam – in the university façade, the Register House, Charlotte Square – with the much more typical work of such architects as Robert Reid and William Playfair who finally created the 'Athens of the North' (Fig. 6).

KEY

A   Charlotte Square
B   north side built to Adam's designs
C   St George's Church
D   Adam houses in Queen Street
E   St Andrew's Church
F   St Andrew's Square
G   Dundas House (now the Royal Bank of Scotland)
H   H.M. General Register House
I   Old Calton Burial Ground (David Hume's mausoleum)
J   the Exchange (now City Chambers)
K   North Bridge
L   the Tron Church (near Mrs Adam's house in Niddry's Wynd)
M   St Giles' Cathedral
N   South Bridge
O   the University
P   site of the old High School
Q   William Adam's mausoleum
R   Greyfriar's Church
S   Heriot's Hospital (later school)
T   the Castle

the Waverley Station, the railway, the Princes Street Gardens and the Mound and art galleries. The Mound was created from the earth excavated from the New Town

Modern Edinburgh is a beautiful city, but this quality springs chiefly from the magnificent landscaping in hills, rocks and valleys, and from its medieval heritage: Holyrood, the Royal Mile, the Castle Hill. Its classical buildings, mostly nineteenth-century, are sound and well designed, but, in comparison with Adam, heavy, dour, grim.

Even Robert seemed to be affected by this atmosphere of the north. His work contrasts with the rest by its elegance and vivacity, but, compared with his buildings in London or English country houses, it has a weighty, humourless look. The nearest that Robert ever got to producing his 'monumental work' was in Edinburgh, at the university and the Register House. These, though infinitely better than what followed them, do not represent Robert at his best.

As mentioned in Chapter 1 (page 40) John Adam, who had continued to practice in Edinburgh, was largely responsible for the new Exchange building in the High Street and was intimately concerned with the construction of the North Bridge.

Work on draining the North-loch had finally begun in 1759, and by 1763 was sufficiently advanced to start the North Bridge project which would span the dried-out valley. Public subscriptions were organized and the foundation stone was laid in October. The scheme was for a three-arched stone bridge, 1,000 feet long, 40 feet wide and 70 feet above the valley. It was designed by William Mylne in co-operation with John Adam, and was to cost ten thousand pounds.

Like many new projects, it ran into difficulties. Due to partial collapse and consequent redesigning, it eventually cost over sixteen thousand pounds and was not completed until 1772. Edinburgh's present North Bridge is a much less attractive one aesthetically. It is of iron and a product of the railway age, built in 1896–7. The valley below the bridge, which in 1772 was covered with market stalls, is now the Waverley station. A century of trains has blackened the face of this part of Edinburgh, though with the advent of diesel the buildings are being gradually cleaned.

The next step was to continue the bridge southwards. The northern area of the town was now connected to the ridge of the Royal Mile. If the Cowgate also were spanned the Royal Mile would be linked to the now developing, fashionable area south of it. This was where Robert came into the picture. He had already built some houses near the university, in George Square, and was asked to design the South Bridge to link up all this work.

It was on this North and South Bridge unification scheme that Robert first came up against the intractable bureaucratic difficulties which bedevilled his work in Edinburgh for the whole decade. The letters written to and fro between Robert, the Lord Provost, the Bridge Trustees and other interested parties and municipal authorities show his masterly and tactful handling of prickly, pompous clients. His design also was masterly and incredibly detailed, comprising the two bridges with the great viaduct over the Cowgate, the fine approaches and the houses on the top level of the bridge between Nicholson Street and the Tron Church.

Delaying tactics went on for months in 1786 on the alignment of the North and South Bridges between the Register House (on Princes Street) and the Tron Church (High Street). The Edinburgh worthies found objection after objection; as Robert dealt efficiently with each one, so they produced another.

Finally, the public took a hand. Indignant letters were sent to the newspapers, like one published in the *Morning Chronicle* on 30th July, signed 'A native of Edinburgh' and addressed to Sir James Hunter Blair, Barnt, Lord Provost of Edinburgh. The writer complains that, despite Mr Adam's detailed plans for sewers, bridge, alignment and buildings of elegant ornamental elevations, the Provost was prevaricating, economizing and generally doing down the citizens of Edinburgh, who needed their bridge, had helped to pay for it and wanted to see Mr Adam's beautiful scheme built.

Typical of Robert's efforts to get the work done at a high level of design and building is a letter he writes to the Lord Provost on 24th March. He deals with all the objections and difficulties and says, with reference to one of the typical suggestions from the Trustees, that one house design should be repeated and mass produced throughout the terraces, that it would be a pity to waste this opportunity to build such a fine undertaking. He ends: 'I have troubl'd your Lordship with a very long Letter in which I have given you my sentiments freely. I am sorry to find that they differ so much from those of your Lordship and of the Trustees, but I cannot help feeling, as others do, extremely disappointed on thinking that so uncommon and so fine an opportunity, which does not occur once in a Century, should be lost both to your Lordship, to myself and to the Public.'

The South Bridge was opened in 1788. It was nineteen arches and over 1,000 feet long, 55 feet wide, and extended to the university. The final work was less fine than Adam's original plans. What remains of it now is fundamentally an engineering project. None of his architecture is visible and the street façades are all modern.

Soon after building started on the North Bridge, to span the valley of the North-loch, the scheme for the New Town of Edinburgh was drawn up (Fig. 6). It was to be laid out on grid-iron, classical pattern within a rectangle about 4,000 by 1,100 feet. Its main thoroughfare, George Street, was to run east–west along the high ground of the ridge parallel to and north of the Royal Mile and Princes Street. It would be terminated at each end by a square: Charlotte Square at the west and St Andrew's at the east. St Andrew's Square was built 1778–84. Its best building was (and still is) Dundas House, facing the George Street axis, designed by Sir William Chambers and now the Royal Bank of Scotland. Robert was responsible for Mr Crosbie's house next door. At the other end of the axis is St George's Church in Charlotte Square. It had been intended to build St Andrew's Church in the corresponding position in the square of this name, but Sir Lawrence Dundas got in first with his house. St Andrew's Church was erected by Fraser in George Street in 1785.

Most of the New Town was laid out after Robert's death, but he had a good deal to do with the original plans, particularly for Charlotte Square and Queen Street. This thoroughfare runs parallel to George Street on the north, nearer to the Firth of Forth and lower down the hillside. Adam work remains in some of the houses here and in Castle Street, particularly the porches and doorways.

Robert designed the whole of Charlotte Square in 1791. He planned St George's Church to dominate the centre of the west side, facing up the vista of George Street. It was an elegant design: a slender domed church, beautifully scaled, with the two identical blocks of houses flanking it on either side. It had a portico fronted by eight coupled Corinthian columns. He planned the whole square as a classical ornament to the city, took immense pains as always with the detailed designs, but died before work began (Plate 34).

Then came the French Revolution, and it was not until 1800 that building began. The north side of the square was carefully erected to his designs, but after that economy measures were instituted; the whole town was costing too much. The south side was built similarly, but to a lower standard of finish and workmanship. The east and west sides are similar to one another, but inferior to Robert's plans. The church was finally built in 1811–14 by Sir Robert Reid. It is an ugly, heavy building, badly proportioned and scaled, as different from Robert's design as possible within the same constituent elements.

H.M. General Register House in Edinburgh is Robert's most complete public building. He designed it in 1772 and it was almost finished when he died twenty years later, so that he was able to supervise every stage of its building. John, based in Edinburgh, exercised close surveillance while Robert was in London.

The building was designed for its present purpose: to house the nation's (Scotland's) records. It is in Princes Street opposite the entrance to the North Bridge. Before the G.P.O. building on one corner of the bridge and the North British Hotel on the other were built over a century later, there was a fine view (as Robert intended) of the Register House from the South Bridge, where it terminated the vista. It is from here that the low, subtly curving dome rises to form an ideal composition with the contrastingly severe façade. Now, from the bridge, the dome is visible, but the ends of the façade are cut off from view (Fig. 6).

The 200-foot-long Princes Street elevation is much as Robert designed it. It has a rusticated lower storey. There is a central block with Corinthian order which is echoed in end pavilions, themselves surmounted by lanterns. It is a plain, monumental, almost Palladian elevation, of quality masonry, but not Robert at his most vital. When Princes Street was widened later the semicircular front steps were replaced by the present ones and a containing wall built. The large equestrian statue of Wellington was set in front.

Inside, the rotunda retains its Adam decoration. It is a circular dome with central oculus. There is a light balcony encircling the walls at first-floor level, which is supported on corbels so as not to impede the working space on the ground floor below. The circular walls on both floors are covered with bookcases.

By the later eighteenth century the university buildings in Edinburgh were in a ruinous condition and, after many years of discussion, it was agreed in 1785 to raise money by public subscription and to commission Adam to design new buildings.

It was not an easy site. The façade and main entrance are on South Bridge which then, as now, was a narrow thoroughfare (Fig. 6). This part of Robert's work still stands, with its monumental Doric portico with coupled columns, its fine archway entrance and plain, almost severely Roman façade. Robert planned a tall, elegant dome above. The whole college was to be built round two quadrangles. The front one of these was to be a horizontal rectangle of 178 feet by 38 feet, opening at the back into the grand court, approximately 145 feet square (Fig. 7).

The foundation stone of the New College, as it was called, was laid on 16th November 1789. Work progressed slowly. As in the South Bridge scheme there were countless frustrations and difficulties. Money supplies were inadequate. Professors wanted plans for their individual accommodation altered after work was begun and long after they were supposed to have approved the design. Objections were raised by the Trustees to Robert's insistence on overseeing every stage of the work and to his choosing his own craftsmen and workmen. Clerical and administrative officers dogged his every step, full of suspicion and hostility towards this renegade Scot who had made fame and fortune in England and was now brought back to Edinburgh to dictate to them. Only Robert's endless tact and pleasant persuasion, combined with the loyal, firm backing from the principal, Dr William Robertson, Robert's cousin, steadily got things done.

But three years after its beginning Robert died. James carried on. In 1793 Dr Robertson died, and in 1794 James also. Work ceased. The façade had been built, and part of the smaller, inner court.

For twenty years the buildings gradually deteriorated and nothing was done. Eventually, at the end of the Napoleonic Wars in 1815, work on the university started again, to a cheaper design of one large court only, on the advice of Sir Robert Reid and under W. H. Playfair. It was finished in 1834, but the dome was not finally added till 1887. It is quite different from Adam's design, much larger and heavier and certainly less graceful; a typical product of its date.

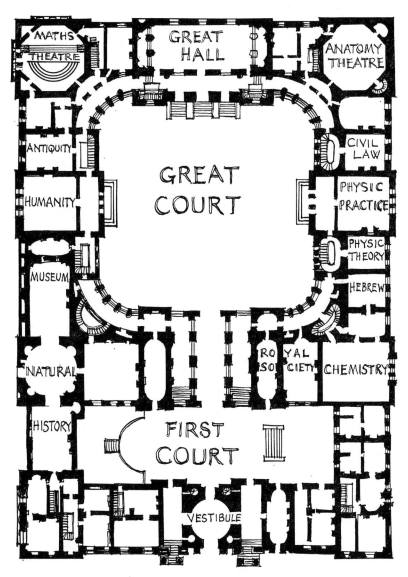

N

MATHS THEATRE

GREAT HALL

ANATOMY THEATRE

ANTIQUITY

CIVIL LAW

HUMANITY

GREAT COURT

PHYSIC PRACTICE

PHYSIC THEORY

MUSEUM

HEBREW

NATURAL

ROYAL SOCIETY

CHEMISTRY

HISTORY

FIRST COURT

VESTIBULE

SOUTH BRIDGE

7   *Adam's design for the ground floor of Edinburgh University. On the first floor were
several libraries and a chapel. The existing layout is not dissimilar, but there is only one
large court. The façade on South Bridge is the one built to Adam's designs*

Robert really did have his great chance here. If he had lived longer, and Dr Robertson also, the university would probably have been built to his designs. It was a fine scheme architecturally and functionally, taking full advantage of a difficult site to create a monumental, aesthetically satisfying building, comparable with some of the great colleges at Oxford and Cambridge (Plate *43*).

On a large stone tablet over the South Bridge entrance façade Robert and his cousin are remembered. It reads:

ACADEMIA JACOBI VI SCOTORVM REGIS
ANNO POST CHRISTVM NATVM MDLXXXII
INSTITVTA
ANNOQVE MDCCLXXXIX RENOVARI COEPTA
REGNANTE GEORGIO III PRINCIPE
MVNIFICENTISSIMO
VRBIS EDINENSIS PRAEFECTO THOMA ELDER
ACADEMIAE PRIMARIO GVLIELMO ROBERTSON
ARCHITECTO ROBERTO ADAM

Much of Robert's work in the 1780s was in Scotland, as far north as the Highlands, yet his office was still in London, as also were all his contacts and a number of his commissions. He became a commuter, maintaining as high a standard as ever for surveillance of work done to his designs, however far away. Commuting between London and Scotland was not easy or cheap. The journey by coach still took three days of continuous travelling from London to Edinburgh, and its cost was over £7. Robert had then to go still farther.

He was now a man of sixty, still energetic and still fit, but such tremendous pressure of work, added to such conditions of travel, especially in autumn or winter, must have taken its toll. Some writers have attributed his sudden and comparatively early death to overwork. There is a possible connection here, but this presumption does not appear to be probable.

Elsewhere than Edinburgh, Robert was working on classical designs and alterations for Yester House at Gifford, East Lothian, for the Marquess of Tweeddale, Gosford House on the coast near North Berwick for the Earl of Wemyss and March, a new house at Newliston in West Lothian and several projects in Glasgow, particularly the Assembly Rooms and the Royal Infirmary.

32   *Ceiling detail, music room, 20 Portman Square, London*

Above, left to right

33 *Entrance porch, Chandos House, London*

34 *Doorway, Charlotte Square, Edinburgh*

Left

35 *Entrance porch, 20 Portman Square*

Opposite

36 *The Dining-room, Saltram, Devon*

37   *Ceiling detail, music room, Mellerstain, Berwickshire*

38   *Wall panel, library, Mellerstain*

39 *Fitzroy Square, London*

40   *Pulteney Bridge, Bath*

41 The stair-
case, first floor,
Culzean Castle,
Ayrshire

42 The stair-
case, 20 St
James's Square,
London

43 *Façade on South Bridge, the University, Edinburgh*

He was also designing in a sort of castellar Medieval. The Gothic Revival in its literary form had been growing step by step since the middle of the century in Britain. Most architects designed one or two buildings in the Gothic style as they saw it, or, possibly only a detail, like a gateway or a tower. None of them possessed the experience and knowledge to build properly in Gothic. Their understanding was limited and fallacious. It was a romantic theme and they treated it in a romantic way, as they did the 'ruins' which they scattered around the great country estates.

Robert was likewise affected.[1] He had always been a romantic, and the castle-ruin approach appealed to him, he played with the idea, and in the 1780s designed a number of buildings with castellar exteriors, but for the interior firmly kept to his classical pattern. Robert did not comprehend Gothic architecture any better than other architects of his day, but his castellar houses are interesting, well built and have a Walter Scott atmosphere. They are not in any sense medieval, only classicism in Gothic fancy dress.

Robert had carried out the interiors of Alnwick Castle for the Duke of Northumberland in the 1760s in Gothic style, but only because asked to do so by the duchess. His heart was not in it, and the work was redecorated in the nineteenth century. He designed a castle at Lauder which was not built, and even worked out a ceiling for Horace Walpole's famous Gothic villa, 'Strawberry Hill', at Twickenham. The drawing is in the Soane Museum. It resembles a medieval rose window with curvilinear tracery. He also designed two chimney-pieces to go with it.

It is clear that Robert really felt Gothic architecture to be an ecclesiastical style, though it might be adapted in castellar form for houses. For the rest, classicism was the only mode. He did design one Gothic church in Edinburgh: St George's in York Place, which is a continuation of Queen Street. The church was octagonal, low and simple, built in stone with traceried windows. In typical manner of the time he appended a beautiful but incongruous classical porch. Eighteenth-century architects saw no strangeness in this type of thinking. There is a Gothic church on the site. It is not Adam's, but a commonplace nineteenth-century Tudor Gothic building.

Next door Robert built the Manse. This was in his castellated style with battlemented parapet above machicolations, then severe classical windows and a porch. A modern garage now stands in its place.

It was at Culzean Castle, on the Ayrshire coast, that Robert had an opportunity to indulge his leanings towards romanticism, create architectural 'movement' and, as well, some of his most beautiful and spectacular interiors. In 1776 he was commissioned by the tenth Earl of Cassilis, who had recently succeeded to the title, to enlarge and modernize the existing castle, which was of the traditional Scottish keep design. Robert worked here till after 1790, gradually turning the old square castle into a fine stately home, romantic medieval outside, classical Adam within (Fig. 8).

Culzean has a truly magnificent situation, built on the edge of a bluff, overlooking the sea which washes the foot of the precipitous basalt cliffs 150 feet below. The Scottish baronial pile stands four-square, medieval in its round, battlemented towers and machicolations, but classical in much of its detail and fenestration. On the landward side are beautiful terraced gardens, laid out over the old fortifications and, at the approach to the glen, Adam's turreted forecourt and great gateway entrance.

While the outside of the house is dramatic and a good skyline composition, the interior is a masterpiece, both in its planning and disposition of rooms and levels and in its treatment and decorative handling. The various drawing-rooms, dining-room, library and ante-rooms are good quality Adam, but, unique and of superb standard, are his circular saloon and oval staircase well.

The shape of this saloon was not dictated by that of the round tower. Robert himself designed and built the great drum tower in 1785 on the north, seaward side as a classic instance of 'movement' in architecture, and then took advantage of its form to make his unusual room. It is a complete circle; its six tall windows, set on the seaward side, give a breath-taking view of unlimited sea and sky with a backcloth of the mountains of the Western Isles. Since the windows are placed at regular intervals in one half of the circle, the north-facing room is lit by both morning and evening sunshine. In the other semicircle are three entrance doorways, white marble fireplace and plain niches.

Both ceiling and carpet design are Robert's, not identical but a part of one theme. The ceiling is patterned in concentric circles, one of his best and very typical, ornamented with vases, rams' heads, sphinxes, arabesques, paterae and swags. The specially designed carpet was probably, though not certainly, woven locally. Much of the furniture also was designed by Robert for the room. An example of his attention to detail is seen in the two semicircular side-tables in front of the niches, whose inlaid satinwood tops have their 'straight' sides subtly fitted to the curve of the walls.

All Adam enthusiasts have their favourite staircases: the circular one at Portman Square; the elegant, single design in St James's Square; the double ascent at Harewood; or his more traditional patterns at Osterley or Newby. Whatever the preference, Culzean must rank near the top. It is structurally and functionally ideal, linking as it does the older house with the new. Aesthetically it is perfect.

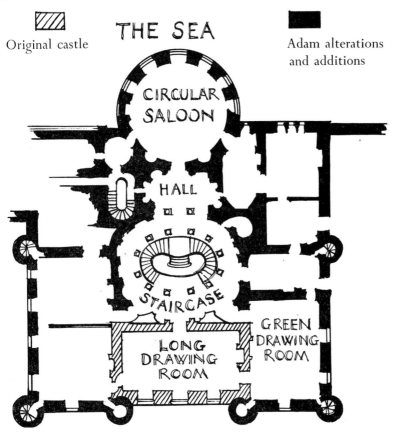

8   *Sketch plan of first floor of Culzean Castle*

The form is oval. Three orders are used, but not in the traditional manner of selection. Here the usual Doric is on the ground floor as rectangular pilasters, but Corinthian columns surround the first-floor landing and Ionic the top. The whole scheme is in white, with restrained gilding of enrichments and pale shades for the oval lantern and delicately stuccoed walls. The whole stairwell is Italian in conception, of the later Renaissance villa theme, but the cantilevered stairs and staircase balustrade curving round the well and landings are typical Adam, with gilded metal and polished mahogany handrail (Plate *41*).

One scheme to which Robert devoted much time and effort in the 1780s was at King's College, Cambridge; but it all came to naught – an irreparable loss to the university and to posterity.

Cambridge University let slip two opportunities for extensive fine quality schemes by eighteenth-century classical architects at this college: James Gibbs and, half a century later, Robert Adam.

The authorities handed out a shabby deal to both. They commissioned them to spend a great deal of time on planning and designing comprehensive schemes for the great quadrangle and the university library complex. In Gibbs' case one classical block was built – now called the Fellows' Building – and the Senate House. Both of these are exceptionally fine. Both were mere fragments only of complete projects; yet, due to endless university wrangling, Gibbs recovered only £100 in lieu of his fees on one building (the Senate House) which cost £13,000. By any standards this is poor dealing with one of the great architects of his day (1730). In Robert's case, nothing at all was ever built. He was paid for his drawings, but not fully recompensed for his time and trouble.

The university was the greatest loser. It ended with William Wilkins's indifferent Gothic Revival scheme, cheaper admittedly, in place of one of two architectural masterpieces. Perhaps Cambridge has enough of these. It is doubtful if architectural historians would agree, let alone the discerning public.

The two problems which confronted both Gibbs and Adam were firstly to complete the large quadrangle, measuring about 280 feet by 240 feet, which had been dominated since the Middle Ages by King's College Chapel, and to build a university library and administrative centre. Two different schemes but, since the sites were close together, it would be better for the architectural layouts to be homogeneous.

For both architects the great chapel posed a difficulty. Though medieval architecture was out of fashion in the eighteenth century, especially in Gibbs' time, the unique, fifteenth-century building was regarded as sacrosanct, not only by the university authorities, but by the architects as well. But how to marry this with a classical scheme, and how to adapt a classical layout to such a large medieval building?

Gibbs' solution was for one block on each side of the quadrangle. The chapel is on the north side. He designed the hall opposite, on the south, with a great portico to face the chapel. East and west were two classical, plainer blocks, of which only the west (the present Fellows' Building) was constructed. His library and administrative layout comprised three blocks round an open court, of which the northern one, the present Senate House, was built.

Robert therefore in 1784 inherited a quadrangle with two sides occupied by the chapel and the Fellows' Building, one medieval, one classical and, on the other site, the Senate House. His scheme for the quadrangle was livelier and more original than Gibbs'. He proposed to build a larger, more imposing hall block opposite to and commensurate with the chapel. This would contain a unique, circular college hall in the centre, 46 feet in diameter, and a dome above. In front was the rectangular vestibule and portico with entrance steps. The building was to contain also the provost's lodge and students' room for study and sleeping. The façade was rusticated like a great fifteenth-century Florentine palace on the lower part. Above was a giant Corinthian order in columns and pilasters, spanning the *piano nobile* and the second floor, with balustrade overall. The centre front was colonnaded, and there were four projecting masses (two at the ends and one on either side of the centrepiece). These were pedimented with sculptured finials above. The Venetian windows had Ionic columns.

Robert proposed to keep Gibbs' block inviolate, apart from a touch of alteration here and there, and to have a great open space in front, on the east side. This is where now stands Wilkins's pseudo-Gothic screen and entrance gateway, and the hall was also built in Gothic design, leaving Gibbs' Fellows' Building a lonely classical island in a sea of genuine and neo-Gothic.

Robert's plans for the library and administrative block again intended to utilize Gibbs' Senate House as it stood. He planned a replica block to continue beyond it westwards and, in the centre between the two, the library, which would have a central Corinthian portico and, above it, a tower and small cupola. The side ranges would also have small domes and be articulated with Corinthian columns and pilasters.

Adam's drawings for the university layouts are in the Soane Museum. There are a number of them, showing the whole scheme for various elevations, with suggested alterations and extensions to comply with the university's criticisms. They show the infinite care he bestowed on such themes, with every item carefully thought out and drawn in detail.

In the last years of his life the pace of Robert's work was stepped up even more. He was engaged, not only in Scotland but in London also, on a number of projects, several of which he did not live to see carried out. As one obituary stated in 1792, 'at the time of his death he had on hand 8 public works and 25 private buildings, mainly in Scotland'.

On 20th July 1789 he was one of a group of architects who presented a report to the House of Commons on the question of fire danger to the Palace of Westminster and Westminster Hall from nearby buildings. The House of Commons had requested the report, being concerned at such possibilities. How right they were to be concerned was proved on that fatal night in 1834 when the Palace was so seriously damaged by fire that Sir Charles Barry was commissioned to rebuild it (as it now stands) after winning the competition held for the purpose.

The signatories to the 1789 report represent an interesting example of the co-operation between such differing architects. They read: Robert Adam, George Dance, S. P. Cockerell, H. Holland, John Yenn, John Soane, Robt. Browne, Tho. Tildesley, John Woolfe Jun., R. Adam for R. Mylne, Thos. Fulling, Chas. Alex. Craig, James Wyatt.

Between 1780 and 1788 Robert designed alterations to the Duke of Cumberland's Pall Mall house; also many of the fittings and furnishings. This work has unfortunately been lost.

In 1781 he was elected Honorary Member of the Society of

Antiquaries of Scotland, being already a member of the London society. In 1788 he was elected a Fellow by the Royal Society of Edinburgh.

In 1791 the Architects' Club was formed. The first meeting took place on 20th October in the Thatched House Tavern, in St James's Street. (The Conservative Club now stands upon the site.) It was agreed that the members should meet there for dinner on the first Thursday of every month and that the annual subscription would be five guineas. The founder members were: James Wyatt, George Dance, Henry Holland, Samuel Pepys Cockerell, Sir William Chambers, Robert Adam, Robert Mylne, John Soane, John Yenn, James Paine, Richard Norris and Richard Jupp. Honorary members included John Carr, Thomas Sandby and James Gandon.

That the club prospered can be judged by the building in Portland Place belonging to the society which grew out of it: the Royal Institute of British Architects.

Robert had moved from the Adelphi with his family and *entourage* in 1786. He went to No. 13 Albemarle Street [2] where, on the evening of 1st March 1792, he suddenly suffered a fatal haemorrhage from the stomach.

Robert was living here with his two sisters and James and William. William, writing on the day Robert died, 3rd March, to his sister Susy, describes his illness and death.

'As I had not time before the post went off yesterday, I desired my Sister Mary to communicate to you the very unlooked for illness that Bob had been suddenly seized with in so alarming a manner, of which however, we at that time, entertained sanguine hopes that this danger was over and it continued for 20 hours, he sleeped very composedly the first part of the night but all at once the vein open'd again at 4 o'clock this morning when he threw up a vast quantity of blood that weakened him to that degree that he appeared then to be quite gone, his pulse being totally gone, he however revived again but in so low and exhausted a state that he only struggled for life in very great Pain, till 2 o'clock when he became quiet and went off very easily.'

Robert's will, signed only when he knew what was coming, on 2nd March, left his possessions to the two sisters who had devotedly run his household for him for over thirty years, Elizabeth and

Margaret Adam. James and William were his executors. Robert never married. His work had been his whole life, and the family circle, close since the Scottish days, remained indissoluble to the end.

John, in Edinburgh, died in June of the same year, and James, who tried unsuccessfully to carry on the great Adam practice, succumbed to apoplexy on 20th October 1794. William, the youngest of the family, was one of the few who lived to old age. He stayed on in the Albemarle Street house till 1821, looked after by his niece, Susannah Clerk. Then, almost destitute, the once prosperous Adam firm being reduced to nothing, he sold the house.

Robert's magnificent library, his furniture, prints, antique sculpture and paintings were auctioned at Christie's in several sales between 20th May 1818 and 1821. William had carefully and lovingly tended them all till he had nothing else. Robert's work and his collection were a sacred trust to him. He then moved to a house in Welbeck Street, where he died at the age of eighty-four in 1822.

He left what he possessed, which was little, to Susannah, who attempted to sell Robert's drawings (nine thousand of them) to Sir John Soane, who eventually bought them for little over two hundred pounds in 1833. His house in Lincoln's Inn Fields, now the Sir John Soane Museum, houses these drawings, carefully documented for study.

Robert was buried in Westminster Abbey on 10th March 1792. His grave lies in the floor of the south transept, with those of other architects, on the opposite side to Poets' Corner. Near to James Wyatt and Sir Robert Taylor, Robert lies, ironically, next to his old enemy and rival, Sir William Chambers. The simple stone is placed in direct line of tread up the transept. Consequently the lettering is worn but still decipherable. It reads:

ROBERT ADAM Efquire
ARCHITECT
born at Kirkcaldie
3rd July 1728
died in London
3rd March 1792

There were not many obituaries. Typical perhaps are Dr Robertson's remarks: 'I have lived long and much with many of the most distinguished men in my own times, but for genius, for worth, and for agreable manners, I know none whom I should rank above the friend we have lost.' A long obituary appeared in the *Gentlemen's Magazine*, which commented sadly on the loss 'to the Arts of two of their greatest ornaments, Sir Joshua Reynolds and Robert Adam; and it would be difficult to say, which of them excelled most in his particular profession'.

Much has been written of Robert's reputation and of his critics' comments after his death. This is not the place to repeat them, but what should be noted is the widespread influence which his work achieved overseas, particularly in the U.S.A. and Russia. This is surprising in view of the essential Englishness of Robert's work.[3] He based his ideas on the antique, but made the 'Adam style' into something so personally 'England' and 'Robert Adam'.

In many countries there were architects who modelled their work closely on Adam. Charles Cameron, a fellow Scot, was one of these. Like Robert, he studied in Italy, but then went to Russia in the employ of the Tsaritsa Catherine and spent most of his life there. At the royal summer palace of Tsarskoe Selo in particular, one felt, before the severe damage caused in the Second World War, that one had entered one of Adam's most sumptuous apartments. Here, on the Gulf of Finland, richer materials were at this architect's disposal, and, where Robert had used stucco, marble and ormolu, Cameron used as well porphyry, porcelain and agate.

Cameron was also influenced by Clérisseau, who spent many of the later years of his immensely long life also in Catherine's service. As a result, many of his drawings, including some of those done with Robert in Italy, are in the Hermitage Museum in Leningrad.

In the early 1790s the popularity of Robert's work spread to the U.S.A. Charles Bulfinch took it to New England, where he built a number of houses, especially in Boston. Others followed, and the 'Adam style' continued, though in watered-down form, well into the nineteenth century; more popular on that side of the Atlantic than in contemporary Britain.

Nearer home there were French and Swedish enthusiasts for the style and, even more so, Irish. In this case the influence was more direct; some wealthy landowners actually saw Adam houses in England or Scotland, then returned home to commission equivalents. Robert himself designed houses for Irish clients but, as far as is known, never went there to supervise the building of them.

It is still a mystery why the death of a man so pleasant and gifted, a close friend of figures like Reynolds, Garrick, Lord Bute and Robertson, should have caused so little sensation.

That his reputation should sink in the decades after his death is normal, but the condemnation or total silence with which his work was treated, not only in the early nineteenth century but also throughout the Gothic Revival, was more excessive and lasting than would have been expected. Sir John Soane's remarks in his defence and praise [4] represented one lone voice crying in the wilderness.

The late nineteenth century reversed the whole adjudication and became fulsome in its praise. Everything remotely like Adam, all the copies and imitations, were adjudged as by the master, and consequently revered.

We are fortunate today to have so much work by Robert Adam extant. It is deeply valued for its elegance and beauty. We salute him as the leader of the Classic Revival in Britain and the revolutionary who changed the whole basis of our interior decorative schemes, as well as being one of our finest architects.

NOTES

1 Adam produced a number of designs for castles, mainly in the last decade of his life. The work consisted mostly of additions and alterations to existing buildings, and the bulk of it was carried out after his death. Examples include Rudding Hall, Maudsley Castle and Thirlstane Castle. None of his work in this field would be considered of special interest or quality.

2 No, 13 Albemarle Street is now a fairly modern building occupied by Gieves the tailors. No G.L.C. plaque appears upon its walls.

3 As far as the U.S.A. was concerned, both Wren and Gibbs enjoyed a similar widespread popularity and imitation.

4 Remarks on the contribution of Robert Adam to architecture and decoration in a series of twelve lectures given by Sir John Soane to the students of the Royal Academy of Arts between 1809 and 1836 (Royal Academy Library Records).

APPENDIX

SURVIVING WORKS OF ROBERT ADAM

A description of existing buildings as they stood at the time of writing. Minor buildings and those where only fragments remain have been omitted. Some buildings where little now exists are included in order to bring up to date existing information.

ENGLAND

BUCKINGHAMSHIRE

Little Market Hall, High Wycombe

Designed and built as the 'New Shambles' for the butchers. Still stands across the High Street from the Guildhall. Altered *c.* 1900, when dome was raised three feet; also gable pitch to match. Due to this unfortunate alteration, it has since been known by the popular name of the 'Pepperpot'. Now provides office accommodation for local planning authorities.

Shardeloes (near Amersham)

House completed and decorated by Adam for William Drake, 1758–63.
Present owner: Landstone Investments Ltd. Agents: William Willett Ltd.
  House and coach and stable block now converted into twenty flats and maisonettes. Adam *décor* and fireplaces preserved.
  Hall (later saloon). 30 feet square. Entered from great portico in centre of east front. Doric order used throughout. Compartmented early Adam *ceiling* with central coved octagon.
  Dining-room ceiling has oval centre-piece with foliage garlanded over and under the rib mouldings. Rococo handling. *Walls* panelled with stucco decoration in high relief. Arabesque motifs, also figure composition panels. White marble *fireplace* of console type with central panel in high relief depicting boys at play. Frieze decoration by anthemion pattern. White marble on deep red marble ground.
  Drawing-room. Simple, low relief *ceiling*, with circular centre-piece, surrounded by swags and drops. Outside this, arabesques and

paterae with four fans. White marble *fireplace* in Ionic order. Swag and paterae frieze with high relief centre panel.

Library. In centre of south front. Room lined with bookcases, with panels above. These are filled with chiaroscuro paintings of figure compositions. (This wall *décor* was possibly altered *c.* 1775 by the Wyatts, the panels by Rebecca replacing Adam's original designs.) Simple, white marble console type *fireplace* with Siena marble inlay. Good quality woodcarving throughout, especially mahogany doors.

DERBYSHIRE

Kedleston Hall (near Derby)

House built for Sir Nathaniel Curzon (created Baron Scarsdale 1761) by Matthew Brettingham, James Paine and Robert Adam 1758–68.

Present owner: Viscount Scarsdale. *House open to public.*

Exterior Adam work:
South (garden) front (Plate *17*). Three-arched bridge over Cutler Brook (Plate *18*). Fishing-house. Orangery. Entrance screen; the main gate to the park (Fig. 2).

Interior:
The Hall 67 by 42 feet, 40 feet high. Sixteen columns and four half-columns in Corinthian Order. Fluted shafts and bases of local veined alabaster, warm reddish-brown and cream. Capitals white marble. *Floor* of Derbyshire Hopton Wood stone with pattern of Italian marble. *Ceiling* deeply coved with three oval skylights. Stucco by Joseph Rose to designs by George Richardson. Motifs mainly arabesques and putti with circular panels of figure compositions. *Entablature* has richly modelled frieze of winged lions, putti, anthemion and vases. White stucco on grey/green background. Two superb *fireplaces* in white marble by Spang or possibly Wilton. The plaster figure designs above are by Joseph Rose with painted panels by Gravelot and Domenichino respectively. Magnificent gryphon grates, fenders and fireirons of burnished brass and steel (Plate *19*). *Walls* decorated in panels in monochrome with Homeric scenes. Below are niches containing statuary classical figures. Under these are Adam-designed sarcophagus benches with plush seats. Statuesque astylar *doorways*. Door panels covered with paper composition, painted and varnished. Now dark and discoloured. Originally painted by Angelica Kauffmann.

Saloon. Magnificent rotunda, 42 feet in diameter, with central oculus of coffered dome 62 feet above ground level. Whole room in cream with gilt enrichment. Gilding on rosettes in dome lacunae, also on richly decorated frieze of entablature. *Walls* have framed paintings of ruins by William Hamilton over the doorways alternating with chiaroscuro paintings by Biagio Rebecca over the alcoves, illustrating scenes from British history. The *doorways* (shaped to the curve of the walls) are pedimented and flanked by Ionic grey/green scagliola pilasters (by Bartoli). The six-panelled doors have gilded mouldings. The two most striking features of the apartment are the cast-iron stoves (Plate *21*), designed by Adam and made by the Carron Works, and the decorative tablet candelabra on the walls. These have white, polished amorini figures on a dark red, painted background, surrounded by a gilded frame with dependent swags. The green and gilt chairs are to Adam's designs.

Drawing-room. Earlier Adam work. Fine Derbyshire alabaster *doorways* and Venetian *window* in warm reddish-brown markings on cream. Corinthian order used on all of these. Polished mahogany six-panelled *doors*. Panels reeded with paterae at the corners (the classic Adam pattern). Deeply coved *ceiling* in a free design of large-scale anthemion and arabesques with oval panels containing high-relief figure compositions. *Walls* originally hung with blue damask, but now a golden one. White marble *fireplace*, flanked by large, sculptured, draped female figures. Central high relief panels of figures by Michael Spang.

Most of the *chairs* are by Adam. The four large, exuberant sofas were made by John Linnell: it is not certain whether or not to Adam's design. They have merfolk terminations and dolphin feet. They are more reminiscent of Bernini in their rumbustiousness than of Adam (Plate *20*).

Dining-room. Ceiling traditional good quality Adam pattern, now redecorated in unfortunate colouring. Contains roundels and panels of landscape compositions, painted by Zucchi and Zuccarelli. *Walls* display many fine paintings. Many were originally intended for this room. The artists include Claude Lorraine, Romanelli, Zucchi, Snyders and Zuccarelli. The finest part of the room is the *alcove* with relief work by Collins and furniture and silverware designed especially for display here by Adam. The alcove composition is completed by two beautiful doorways. A typical Adam white marble *fireplace* with its flanking figures and central plaque by Spang. Between the *windows* are two Adam *pier glasses* above *side-tables*.

Music-room. Early Adam *ceiling* design with large motif anthemion decoration and circular centre-piece. Interesting white marble *fireplace* in Ionic order. Central plaque by Spang. Inlay ornamentation in bluejohn. *Walls* covered with paintings.

Library. Also early Adam. *Ceiling* design of octagons and circles in high relief. *Doorcases* and *fireplaces* have Doric fluted columns.

DEVONSHIRE

Saltram (near Plymouth)

Adam interior remodelling from 1779 for Mr John Parker, later Lord Boringdon.
Present owner: The National Trust. *House open to the public.*
No exterior work.

Saloon. A very fine room. Double cube proportions: 50 by 25 by 25 feet. *Ceiling* deeply coved. White stucco decoration. Grounds in cream and blue with painted roundels. Ornamentation on the coved part includes griffins with roundels between them. *Carpet* made at Moorfields to Adam's design. Reflects ceiling pattern, but not a replica. *Walls* silk covered in blue floral material. *Door-* and *window-frames* beautifully carved in low relief. Painted white. Composite order used in column form on Venetian window and as pilasters on bookcases. Capital specific Adam type without volutes, one row of acanthus and one of water-leaves. *Pier glasses*, picture frames and furniture all in keeping, mostly Adam, gilded and carved. White and coloured marble *fireplace* in Doric order. Burnished metal *grate* and fender (Plate 22).

Dining-room (intended as the library). Original *carpet*, Axminster, designed by Adam. An almost exact replica of the ceiling except that where the ceiling lunettes have figure compositions representing learning, the carpet ones are in floral design. Whole room is remarkably homogeneous in the unpretentious Adam manner. *Walls* and *ceiling* all stucco decorated. Ornamentation in white on pale green for the walls, and green and cream for the ceiling, broken by wall paintings by Zucchi and an ornamental picture by Zuccarelli. *Fireplace* in white marble with simple fluted pilasters and restrained centre plaque of anthemion and putti. Fine grate and fender. *Doorcases* astylar with decoration of paterae and swags to match the room frieze. Quality Adam-style mahogany doors. *Furniture* all Adam except for table and chairs. Particularly good are the pedestal urns and sideboard, designed to match the room (Plate 36).

ESSEX

Audley End (near Saffron Walden)

Adam redecoration of a suite of rooms and buildings in the grounds, 1763–85, for Lord Braybrooke.
Present owner: Ministry of Public Building and Works. *House open to the public.*

Exterior Building:

The Lion Gate (remodelled only). The bridge over the lake. Palladian Bridge (Tea House Bridge) over the stream. Ring Hill Temple.

Interior:

Great Drawing-room. Adam ceiling of Syon gallery type and marble fireplace in two colours. Much of the furniture designed by Lim, but not the carpet. Doors and doorcases very fine, in white with gilt enrichment.

Painted Drawing-room. Striking example of painted and gesso decoration in Adam style. Ceiling, walls and doors all painted in Pompeian type of decoration, mainly by Biagio Rebecca.

Mistley Church

Built by Robert Adam 1776–7. Under care of the Ministry of Works. The two towers and cupolas remain (Fig. 5).

HERTFORDSHIRE

Moor Park (near Rickmansworth)

Now a golf club.

Tea Pavilion. Near the river bank, exists as a building but only in its octagonal form. Nothing now remains of the interior *décor* or furnishings, and the exterior has been renovated.

Present owners: Mr and Mrs J. W. Gray.

HUNTINGDONSHIRE

Kimbolton Castle

The Doric screen and gatehouse built 1762. The castle is now Kimbolton School. Screen and gateway in perfect condition, accessible and clearly visible from the town.

KENT

Brasted Place (near Westerham)

Built by Adam for Dr Turton in 1784.

Present owner: Four Trustees. Senior is the Archdeacon of Bromley. House used as a Pre-theological College for Anglican ordinands.

Exterior :

A simple square house with an Ionic, pedimented portico on the garden façade. The entrance porch is Doric. Considerable alterations and additions made in the nineteenth century. The roofline was raised and a further block added to the house. Since 1953, two new wings have been added, and a chapel.

Interior :

A number of alterations made, including moving the staircase, but much of Adam's stucco decoration remains in the drawing-room.

Mersham-le-Hatch (near Ashford)

Built for Sir Wyndham Knatchbull, 1762–72.

Present owner: Lord Brabourne. House occupied by the Caldecott Community.

One of the very few houses which are entirely Adam.

Exterior :

Remains largely as he built it.

Interior :

Alterations were made in the early nineteenth century and again in the 1870s. Now almost nothing of the furniture and furnishings exists here.

Entrance Hall. One of the best rooms extant. Rectangular, with two main *doorways* and two stone *fireplaces* opposite to one another (by Thomas Carter). Doric order used throughout; in pilasters on the principal doorways and as an entablature round the room. All now decorated in white.

Dining-room. There are four *doorways* and *windows* along two sides. These are of good design with rectangular panes and the usual Adam reeded, panelled shutters. *Fireplace*, ceiling and frieze typical and not outstanding Adam.

Drawing-room. A beautiful *ceiling* to a rectangular room, panelled in low relief, with circular centre-piece and arabesque and reeded decoration. Simple yet varied. The room has a large, semicircular bay with matching ceiling. The frieze decoration is of griffins, anthemion and vases, with a magnificent cornice above. The effective, existing colour scheme is in white, gold and cream. Below are three large windows. The room has four doorways, also with griffin friezes. The *chimneypiece* is typically Adam. The fireplace below is in white marble (by Thomas Carter). It has Ionic columns and an anthemion frieze. Above is an Adam mirror with a cresting of scrolls and central panel with griffins flanking a vase. On the wall above is the portrait plaque of Robert (an idealized version).

LONDON
The Adelphi (Strand)

Still existing are the Royal Society of Arts façade in John Street and one or two isolated fragments and houses in Robert Street at the west end and Adam Street at the east (Fig. 3, Plate 27).

The Admiralty Screen, Whitehall

Exists almost as built. Dolphin panels on entrance archway by Michael Spang (Plate 8).

Chandos House, Queen Anne Street, W.1

Built 1769–75 for the Duke of Chandos.
Present owner: The Royal Society of Medicine.
The simple façade and elegant porch exist in excellent condition (Plate 33).
Interior:
The standard of Adam decoration is good, but less fine than in Portman or St James's Squares. A number of alterations have been made, notably in the early nineteenth century. Interior now in excellent decorative condition, with typical Adam coloured grounds, though the ornament too is picked out in vivid colours.

Hall and staircase. Finest feature here. Very plain, simple, spacious and light. An unpretentious staircase round a rectangular well. Plain walls now except at the top where there is a Doric entablature under the decorative ceiling and circular lantern. There is an Ionic screen at the second floor. Staircase ends at first floor, as in usual in Adam town houses.

Ground floor. All the *doors* on this floor are original Adam mahogany with reeded and paterae panels. Painted astylar *doorcases*.

Three rooms. Best is the large front apartment which has a colonnaded screen in the Bowood type Composite order, with two columns and two pilasters. There is a bar entablature above with fan decoration which is repeated round the whole room and on the doorcases.

At the rear, one room (now a snack-bar) has a large semicircular bay window.

Next to it is a long apartment, 45 feet long, now used for lectures. It was originally the library and appears to have had Adam's usual screen of columns at the far end to cut the apparent length of the room. The bar entablature and side pilasters remain of this but the columns have gone. The ceilings of all three rooms are pleasant and typical but not outstanding Adam.

First floor.

Three rooms again. A small ante-room with a good ceiling and Adam window shutters.

The two *reception-rooms* are now opened out into one large ball-room though probably they were originally separate or, at least, divided by a screen of columns. The wall decoration and doorways and doors are all later on this floor, as are also the pier glasses.

The *front room* has a good Adam marble fireplace with Ionic pilasters and a central panel of griffins, vases and arabesques. There is a good steel grate and fender.

Fitzroy Square

Façades of east and south sides are still almost unaltered (Plate 39).

Kenwood

Remodelled by Adam for Lord Mansfield, 1767–8.

Present owner: Greater London Council under the Iveagh Bequest.

House open to the public.

Exterior:

The central part of the main entrance front with doorway based on that of the Erechtheion in Athens.

On south, garden side, Adam refaced the main house in the centre and added two lower wings. The western one is designed as an orangery and the eastern as the library. Ionic order throughout.

Interior:

Good, typical Adam *staircase* of polished oak, with wide treads and low risers. Wooden handrail, metal balustrade (now painted) of anthemion pattern.

Library. The important Adam room of the house. Rectangular, with a screen of Corinthian columns and bar entablature at each end with semi-domed *apse* behind. Particularly fine ornamental stucco in low relief in these domes. A remarkable *ceiling*, barrel vaulted, then panelled and decorated with lunettes and ovals which have central paintings and surrounding stucco designs of delicate Adam motifs. The paintings are by Zucchi and the plasterwork by Rose. Below the panelling is an anthemion border and, under this, the entablature with lion and stag's head frieze. *Bookcases* line the walls of the apses, with painted panels above them and, on either side of the white marble *fireplace*, are more bookcases, with stucco decorated arched recesses over them. Originally there was a painting over the fireplace in an Adam frame. There is now a mirror in its place. *Doors* are of fine-quality Adam, reeded panel design. This room is one of the three or four best Adam interiors and is remarkably complete (Plate *28*).

Lansdowne House (Berkeley Square)

Begun in 1762 for Lord Bute. Completed 1768 for Lord Shelburne, later Marquess of Lansdowne. House largely demolished 1929 but rebuilt on a smaller scale using original facing of Portland stone. Now a club, No. 9 Fitzmaurice Place, just off Berkeley Square. Central feature, of Ionic colonnade with pediment above, survives, with Adam frieze decoration.

Interior:

Circular *drawing-room* (called the Adam Room) exists, on similar design to the original, with the two-feet-deep frieze of gravure monochrome figures all round the room.

Ballroom has features similar to Adam's dining-room, particularly the stucco panelling.

Mansfield Street, W.1

Laid out from 1770 as town houses for sale. Half of the west side of the street survives, numbers 5–15. Brick astylar façades of four storeys. Ionic doorways with metal lunette fanlights.

Portland Place, W.1

General layout of street survives, but little of the Adam scheme. The character of some of the houses in the centre part of both sides has been maintained.

20 Portman Square, W.1

Built for the Countess of Home, 1777.

Present owner: The Courtauld Institute of Art.

Exterior:

The façade on the north-west corner of the square is almost as it was built, though the top storey and balcony were added later. The simple porch has ox skulls in the corners of the frieze over the Doric columns (Plate *35*). At the rear, the façade facing the pleasant garden has a semicircular, balustraded, Ionic portico in the centre and Venetian windows to ground and first floors. The lower ones have Ionic columns, the upper, Corinthian. The whole house is of brick with Coade stone decorative panels and paterae.

Interior :

Also remarkably unaltered. The unusual circular *staircase* is the unique feature of the house. It begins in the hall as a single flight of stone steps, branches into two at the half-landing and sweeps round the walls to a complete circle at the first-floor landing. The iron balustrade is typical Adam design, more delicate than the Kenwood or Osterley type and nearer to the St James's Square pattern. The circular *stairwell* ascends to the round lantern above. At the first floor it is decorated with chiaroscuro paintings and, above, Ionic columns and pilasters are grouped round the well. The top storey drum is ornamented in low relief stucco in cream and blue up to the delicate ironwork of the lantern.

There are two rooms on the *ground floor*. The larger, the *dining-room*, has a simple, low relief *ceiling* with painted panels and delicate stucco, white on blue ground, of arabesques and vases with anthemion and guilloche banding, based on an oval overall design. The white marble chimneypiece has a superstructure. Fine mahogany *doors*. An unusual element is the placing of the four Corinthian-type columns, one at each corner of the room.

The outstanding rooms are on the *first floor*.

The front *drawing-room* is a large rectangle, its windows overlooking the square on one long side. Two of the *doors* are set in the deep alcoves opposite. They are mahogany, double, with ormolu door furniture. The alcoves and semi-domes are richly ornamented with swag and paterae stucco decoration (at present gilded on a green ground) and with arabesque panels above the doors. The *ceiling* is covered all over in circles and lunettes. Some of these have stucco decorated centres, others painted roundels. At the rear is the *music-room* which has a remarkable *ceiling*. In very low relief with gilt enrichment, it has painted round and oval medallions. The design is of a series of concentric circles within a square with fans at the corner. In the middle, a star surrounds the painted roundel (Plate 32). The *walls* follow a similar theme and treatment. All the Adam motifs are used with a high quality of stucco, painting and woodwork craftsmanship. Though small, this is one of the richest Adam rooms in existence.

The little *Etruscan room* next door is charmingly decorated in Pompeian red, black and cream, with round and oval panels in the *ceiling*. The room is square with two straight sides and two slightly curved walls, one for the window and one opposite to it for the two doors. All the members take this shallow curve and there is a wide niche above. The whole room is decorated in the same manner, in very low relief or in painting. The white marble *fireplace* follows suit, with inlaid and painted decoration.

20 St James's Square, S.W.1

Rebuilt for Sir Watkin Williams Wynn, 1772–4.
Present owners: The Distillers' Company.

The Distillers' Company also owns No. 21 next door and, before the Second World War, duplicated the Adam façade so that the two houses form one unit. The two doorways are the same, the ground floor rustication and fenestration stretches across as do the Corinthian pilasters of the giant order. The *doorways*, with their semicircular fanlights and curving ascent steps, are particularly elegant town examples (Fig. 4).

Interior:

No. 20 was severely damaged in the Second World War, both by fire and by high-explosive bombs. The structure remained sound and the rooms have been excellently restored and redecorated. As at Home House in Portman Square, one of the finest features is the *staircase* and hall. The well rises the whole height of the house to an oval, convexly crowned fanlight. The *walls* are simply decorated in restrained, quality stucco, mainly in borders and panels of anthemion, figure compositions, winged lions and arabesques, in white on grounds of two shades of green, yellow and a deep magenta background to the narrower borders. The *staircase hall* is plain, with simple ceiling and ram's head frieze. The dominant feature is the *staircase* itself, ascending in single flights to the first-floor landing. The stairs are stone, the handrail mahogany and the balustrade a beautiful ironwork design (Plate *42*).

On the *first floor* landing is a large semicircular niche with stucco-decorated half-dome. Opposite, on the wall, hung a large picture, a copy of Raphael's 'Transfiguration'. Stored during the war, this was damaged and a new one is being painted. It is the necessary focal centre-piece to the staircase scheme.

At *second-floor* level, the wall is decorated by flat Corinthian order pilasters with arches between. As in the Portman Square house, there are two principal rooms each on ground and first floor.

On the *ground floor*, at the front is the *eating-room* with a shallow, curved recess containing a curved doorway and screened by Composite columns. The *ceiling* is patterned all over with octagons and circles. The white marble *fireplace* has ram's head consoles.

An impressive room but less fine than the larger board-room next door (originally the *music-room*). Symmetrical, it has an apse at each end; a door in the curve of one apse and a window in the other. The whole room is stucco decorated in low relief, using all the Adam motifs. The *ceiling* is especially beautiful. It has a square centre-piece and a fan-filled lunette at each end. Within the main panel are concentric circles broken by circular painted medallions at the four corners. The *walls* are also panelled in low relief stucco, chiefly in arabesque designs. The entablature above has a frieze decorated by portrait roundels. The astylar *doorways* have matching entablatures with the room. The double *doors* are mahogany with ormolu door furniture.

On the *first floor*, at the rear, is the finest room in the house, originally the second withdrawing-room, now the main board-room. The *ceiling* is a segmental barrel vault with a semi-dome at each end. It is one of the finest Adam examples existing. It is panelled with broad bands of low relief decoration. The sections between are then filled with ovals and lunettes of stucco and paintings, all exquisitely done, and the latter ascribed to Angelica Kauffmann. The present colour scheme is in gilt ornament on sombre coloured grounds. It is soon to be redecorated in its original shades of pale yellow, pink and medium green with white stucco ornament and deep caerulean blue grounds for the roundels. The *walls* are hung with figured silk broken only by the doorways, windows, mirrors and fireplace. The ceiling is the *pièce de résistance* of the room, together with its fine proportions.

At the front of the house is the smaller room, now the chairman's office, which has an excellent white marble carved *fireplace*. The frieze, in high relief, depicts Aurora heralding the dawn (Plate *13*).

MIDDLESEX

Osterley Park House

House built 1577 for Sir Thomas Gresham. Altered and decorated mostly by Adam, 1761 onwards, for Mr Child.
Present owner: The National Trust. House managed by the Victoria and Albert Museum. Grounds administered by the Ministry of Works. *House open to the public.*
  Exterior:
House still an Elizabethan block with corner turrets, all in brick with stone facings. Adam altered the fenestration and built the great eastern entrance double portico, possibly partly based on the Temple of the Sun at Palmyra and partly on the Erechtheion in Athens. He set his *piano nobile* above the courtyard level of the old house to provide the entrance steps to the portico (Plate 25). The Ionic portico with its double row of six columns leads directly into the Elizabethan courtyard and then into the eighteenth-century entrance hall. On the opposite elevation Adam designed the classical doorway and curving approach staircase.

Interior:

Entrance Hall. All decorated in stucco, except for the black and white marble floor which echoes the concentric oval design of the *ceiling*. Room is completely symmetrical. A semicircular apse at each end with coffered semi-domes. The apses contain a fireplace and two niches with sculptured figures. *Walls* articulated by pilasters in Adam's non-volute Composite order. Between are *doorways*, with fine mahogany *doors* and ormolu furniture, *windows* and stucco panels of arms and arabesque decoration. The hall is decorated in white on grounds in two shades of blue.

Gallery. A well-proportioned room not altered by Adam. Plain ceiling and early Georgian type of cornice. Adam style gilt mirrors between windows.

Eating-room. A contrast from the cool monumentality of the hall, though the decoration is also all in stucco. *Ceiling* has an oval centre-piece with garlanded leaves wound in and out of it. Within is a decorative oval feature. The colours are white on pink and green grounds. The design is rococo, typical of early Adam schemes. *Walls* are panelled with alternate stucco arabesque designs having small paintings set in them and large paintings of classical ruins. Two of these are by Zucchi. There are *windows* along one side of the room with gilt framed mirrors on the walls between. The colour scheme of the walls is in keeping with the ceiling. The white marble *fireplace* has a simple Doric order. Much of the *furniture* is by Adam, particularly the gold side-tables, lyre-back chairs and pedestal urns.

Library. A lovely room, light, restful, with delicate colours and decoration. Low-relief *ceiling* with circular centre-piece in oyster shades and white. Two white marble *fireplaces*, one at each end of the rectangular room. Wedgwood vases on the mantelpieces. Fine metal grates and fenders. All round the room are *bookcases* carved in wood with Ionic pilasters, all painted white. Above are small, white-framed paintings by Angelica Kauffmann. Finely carved panelled mahogany doors. Instead of the more usual reeded pattern with corner paterae, these panels have key pattern borders with acanthus leaf edging (Glossary).

Tapestry Room. Ceiling design a circle with octagon and four corner fans. Reflects the carpet, made by Moore. *Walls* covered by Boucher-Neilson tapestries: 'Les Amours des Dieux'. *Furniture* upholstery of sofas and chairs by Adam designed to match the Gobelins and echo the warm colours (Plate 26).

Drawing-room. Again, the carpet, made by Moore, echoes the ceiling design. This is an early Adam type, based on octagonal coffers in low relief. There is an oval centre-piece.

Etruscan Room. One of the four Adam examples to survive in reasonable condition. Decoration entirely linear, painted in earth colours of yellows, browns and reds. Many of ceiling and door panels painted on paper by Angelica Kauffmann and other artists.

State Bedroom. Dominated by the large Adam bedstead. A magnificent piece of furniture with a domed interior and elaborate posts and cornice. Covers and counterpane to match the rest of the design.

The stone *staircase* has a simple anthemion Adam metal balustrade with carved mahogany handrail. The staircase well, which extends upwards from ground level (below the hall floor) to the second floor, is fairly narrow. At the first floor is a Corinthian order colonnaded screen and, above, an Ionic one. The ceiling at the top is now plain.

Syon House

Adam redesigned the interior scheme from 1762 for Sir Hugh Smithson, created first Duke of Northumberland 1766.
Present owner: The Duke of Northumberland. *House open to the public.*
Exterior:
Entrance screen and gateway on main road (Fig. 1).
Interior:
Entrance Hall. Floor black and white marble. Rest of apartment in cream and white. Doric order throughout. Coffered apse at one end, screened recess and steps to ante-room at the other. Stucco work by Rose, also the marble statues, including the 'Apollo' in the apse. The replica of the 'Dying Gaul' in front of the Doric screen is in bronze and was cast in Rome.
Ante-room. Floor of scagliola in brilliant shades of blue and dark red, yellow and grey/green. Echoes *ceiling* pattern which is gilt on cream. The Ionic *columns* are of grey/green *verde antico* veneer, with white marble bases and gilded capitals and figures above entablature. Frieze has deep blue ground behind gilt anthemion decoration. Gilded *wall panels* by Rose (Plate *14*). *Fireplace,* white and green marbles. Fine grate and fender. A unique Adam interior with quality materials and rich colour scheme. Furniture of a later date (Plate *12*).
Dining-room. Colour scheme all cream and gold, with white statues and marble fireplace. Fine early Adam *ceiling* in three compartments, with circles and fans, arabesque and anthemion border. Rich entablature below. *Wall* panels by Cipriani in chiaroscuro above niches. Adam *mirrors* between the windows. An *apse* at

each end of the room screened by Corinthian columns carrying a bar entablature and showing gilt decoration of semi-domes above and behind as at Kenwood. Upper part of *chimneypiece* also has flanking Corinthian columns and a pediment. Framed within the columns is a marble panel of high-relief figure sculpture.

Red Drawing-room. Deeply coved *ceiling* decorated all over with medallions painted by Cipriani. Grounds to paintings and paterae in blue, with other grounds of crimson, touches of green and gilded borders throughout. A rich, vivid effect. *Walls* hung with plum-coloured Spitalfields silk with a pattern of flowers and ribbons in grey. Superb *doorways* and *fireplace*. Doorways gilt and cream with ormolu decoration on ivory background in pilasters (Plate *16*). Fireplace of white marble ornamented all over with applied ormolu (Plate *15*). *Carpet* (signed T. Moore) made at Moorfields to Adam's design. Mainly in pinks and yellows. Adam *side-tables*. Much of furniture here is Regency, from Northumberland House.

Gallery. Very low relief stucco decoration to *ceiling* and *walls*. Gilt enrichments. Grounds in greens, mauves and greys, all muted. Stucco motifs Pompeian in character as well as other Adam characteristic designs. Painted roundels and lunettes on ceiling and walls. *Doorways* and *fireplaces* flanked by Corinthian pilasters. Zuccarelli landscapes over the fireplaces. A number of pieces of Adam *furniture* here, especially chairs, tables and sofas.

SOMERSET

Bath

Pulteney Bridge over the River Avon, *c.* 1770.
Adam's classical interpretation of the Ponte Vecchio in Florence. Bridge shortened at the city end later for road widening scheme (Plate *40*).

SURREY

Hatchlands (East Clandon)

Redecorated by Adam for Admiral Boscawen, 1759–62.
Present owner: The National Trust (Tenant: Major Hargreaves). *House open to the public*.

Two rooms on the ground floor are still largely as Adam designed them.

Library (designed as the drawing-room). *Ceiling* most interesting part. One of Adam's earliest designs after his return from Italy, when he was still feeling his way. A circular centre-piece and the rest of the design geometrically divided by radiating ribs. High relief figure sculpture in each section of merfolk, winged maidens, dolphins and young men. A strongly projecting, richly decorated cornice joins ceiling to *walls*, which are fairly plain. *Doorways* of a rococo, earlier style but have beautiful, deeply panelled mahogany doors. Present colour scheme is light, with gilt enrichments on oyster, peach and pale green grounds, with white figure sculpture.

Drawing-room (designed by Adam as the dining-room). A larger, rectangular room with a large semicircular bay on the south side. The *ceiling* is a beautiful early example, more sophisticated than in the library and in lower relief. There is an oval centre with an anthemion bordered eight-sided figure round it. In the corners of the ceiling, outside this border, are large scrolls with centre-pieces of boys, each standing on a shell and holding a dolphin by each hand (Plate 23). This is a similar theme to Adam's stone panels on the Admiralty Screen of the same date. The projecting cornice has a richly ornamented frieze of anthemion and dolphins. In the bay are sea-horses and shells. The *doorcases* here are also further advanced than in the library; simpler and in lower relief. Of particular interest is the *fireplace* with gilt-framed mirror above. A prototype of many others by Adam. The fireplace is of white marble with flanking, draped female figures. The deep frieze has a central panel depicting a two-horse chariot. The sculptor was possibly Rysbrack, as at Hopetoun (Plate 11).

The mirror above has an elegant and typical Adam frame. There is a fine metal grate.

WILTSHIRE

Bowood (near Calne)

Extensions, alterations and interior decoration for the Earl of Shelburne, later Marquess of Lansdowne, 1761–71.
Present owner: the Marquess of Lansdowne.

Diocletian Wing. Now the main house; the remainder demolished 1955. Currently a picture gallery and library with, at one end, the connecting block between the wing and the original main house, at present occupied by Lord Lansdowne. Bell tower a replacement by Sir Charles Barry. Doric order used on façade, except for the central portico, which has Adam's favourite Composite order, with no volutes but a fluted bell with only one row of acanthus leaves (*see* Glossary).

Mausoleum. In the park, well away from the house. Designed 1761 for Lady Shelburne. A domed, square structure with four pedimented faces.

WORCESTERSHIRE

Croome Court (near Pershore)

Interior decoration by Adam for the Earl of Coventry's house, from 1760.
Present owner: St Joseph's Residential Special School.
Exterior:
In the grounds, laid out by Capability Brown, is the Adam circular Garden Room, the Orangery (now partly ruined and largely obscured by trees) and the main entrance gateway from the road, an Ionic archway.
Interior:
Gallery. Best Adam room here. Now used as a dining-room. Long rectangular apartment with coffered octagon ceiling in soft grey. Light green walls, decorated by stucco panels, in white, grey and green. Also some grisaille pictures in Adam frames. *Doorcases* and *window-frames* are simple, *doors* mahogany. In the centre of one long side is a tall bay and, opposite to it, a white marble *fireplace* with flanking female figures.
Tapestry Room. A pleasant Ionic order chimney-piece and typical early Adam ceiling, with concentric circle design, decorated with reeding, swags and arabesques. Tapestries now in the U.S.A.
Library. Retains its finely carved wood bookcases with pediments and decorative pilaster supports.

YORKSHIRE

Harewood House (near Leeds)

Built for Edwin Lascelles, later Lord Harewood, 1759–71, by John Carr of York. Work on the garden façade and all interior decoration by Robert Adam. Extensive alterations by Charles Barry in 1843.
Present owner: the Earl of Harewood. *House open to the public.*
All the extant work is inside the house.
Entrance Hall. One of Adam's finest Doric halls. Entered from the main portico at *piano nobile* level. Deeply panelled *ceiling*, with central circle surrounded by an octagon, then paterae and oval figure panels in remaining area. Borders enriched with key pattern, guilloche and anthemion. Unusual Doric *entablature* with a frieze of

key pattern and paterae alternating with ox skulls. Twelve engaged columns and four corner pilasters round the room. Between are two chief *doorways* and four smaller ones. The *walls* are decorated by stucco panels in arabesque design. There are also the six circular ones containing martial trophies by Rose and two rectangular panels, representing the 'Chariot of Phaeton' and, over the fire-place, the 'Wedding of Neptune and Amphitrite' (Plate 31). There are some elegant Adam chairs placed round the walls.

Gallery. One of the great Adam interiors, mainly unaltered, except for Barry's fireplaces and the removal of the Venetian window columns in favour of brackets.

A remarkable *ceiling*, carried out by Rose, all in low relief panels of different shapes, containing small paintings by Biagio Rebecca (Plate 24). Very richly decorated entablature in gilt and crimson. Harewood House possesses a magnificent collection of Chippendale *furniture* in the Adam style, and much of the best work is in this room. This includes the pier glasses between the windows, with the console tables beneath, the window pelmets, chairs, sofas, side-tables and torchères.

Music-room. A particularly complete Adam room with its delicate *ceiling* design (roundels by Angelica Kauffmann), and the almost matching original *carpet*. Large Zucchi paintings of ruins decorate the *walls*, and there are Adam mirrors and console tables between the windows. The elegant chairs and sofas are Chippendale. A warm colour scheme, the pattern set by the rose pinks, brown and soft green of the carpet and the pink tints in the ceiling. The rose and oyster of the tapestry-covered upholstery of the chairs and sofas blends harmoniously.

Dining-room. Most of the Adam work destroyed by Barry, but the chimneypiece is Adam's and came from the gallery. It is white marble with large flanking figures. The Adam sideboard and urn-topped pedestals were made by Chippendale, as were the chairs. Most of the reception-rooms on the *south front* have been altered, though retaining some of Adam's and Chippendale's work.

Saloon, in the centre, was made into the *library*. The deeply coved Adam ceiling and the apse decoration remain. It is a particularly elegant and typical example, all in light, but not spidery, relief, and using all the Adam motifs.

Staircase. Begins as a central single flight but branches at the first landing into two flights. A finely carved mahogany handrail and wrought-iron balustrade. Attractively decorated stairwell with stucco arabesque panelling.

Newby Hall (near Ripon)

House extended and decorated by Adam for William Weddell, 1765–83.

Present owner: Major E. R. F. Compton. *House open to the public.*

Exterior:

Two wings of the house added by Adam on the east, also the *entrance porch* and the great *stable block*.

Interior:

Entrance Hall. A fine example of an Adam astylar hall, almost unaltered; even the furniture remains. The black and white marble floor echoes the ceiling design in blue, cream and white stucco. The *walls* have the same colour scheme as the ceiling and there are the same motifs, including the panels of arms. The *doors* are mahogany. The whole interior is symmetrical and homogeneous (Plate 29). The *staircase hall* behind is screened by the two Ionic columns, the monolithic shafts of Cippolino marble.

The staircase has a metal balustrade of anthemion pattern, similar to those at Osterley and Kenwood.

Dining-room (now used as the library). This is like the Kenwood library, but the ceiling is flat instead of barrel vaulted. Despite the beautiful treatment, including a central oval painting by Angelica Kauffmann of Bacchus and Ariadne, it appears much lower and less impressive than Kenwood. There is a *screen* of Corinthian columns in front of an apse, at each end of the room, and magnificent panelled mahogany *doors*. The *walls* are decorated with paintings and stucco decorative panels. The *fireplace* is of white marble carved in low relief arabesques. A picture hangs above. The room is softly coloured in peach and green with white and gilt ornament.

Tapestry Room. The *walls* covered by one of the sets of Boucher-Neilson Gobelins tapestries, made there in 1766. François Boucher was the designer and Neilson the workshop manager. The tapestries are signed by both men. The sets differ only in background colour, not in subject. The low-relief *ceiling* design contains roundels painted by Zucchi and representing the seasons. The *carpet* is Savonnerie, made to Adam's design.

Sculpture Gallery. The most important apartment at Newby, designed to display Weddell's sculpture brought from Italy. A Roman scheme with central rotunda and a square room on either side, with vista from end to end. The *rotunda* has diamond-shaped caissons with floral centres. The frieze below has scrolls and anthemion and under this are horizontal stucco panels of putti and arabesques. The niche semi-domes are elegantly decorated with tiny figures and paterae, with a guilloche band below. The pedimented doorways are set in semicircular headed recesses, also stucco decorated. They have beautiful arabesque friezes above a simple architrave and mahogany doors.

Nostell Priory (near Wakefield)

Adam built a new wing and replanned the interior of the house for Sir Rowland Winn, from 1766.
Present owner: The National Trust. Contents still owned by Lord St Oswald. *House open to the public.*
Exterior:
North-east wing and stable block.
Interior:
Hall. A large apartment decorated with stucco ornament throughout. More like a drawing-room than an Adam hall, but the entrance hall is on the floor below. Classical windows along one long side of the room, and opposite is an immense niche containing three doorways, all curved with the wall, though the actual doors are flat. *Ceiling* a fine Adam design, compartmented, in circles, lunettes and rectangles. Two *fireplaces*, one on each shorter wall, opposite to one another. A graceful, pleasant room but not one of Adam's best.
Library. A smaller, square room with bookcases on all four sides with Ionic decorative pilasters. One side contains the fireplace and another the two windows. *Ceiling* a simple, circular design.
Saloon. A very fine room with deeply coved ceiling. The cove is decorated all over with lunettes, and the flat centre-piece with a circle within lunettes. There is a pale green ground and cream and gold decoration. In the centre of the circle is a sculptured figure composition. Between the windows, along one side, are beautiful rectangular Adam-inspired *pier glasses* with marble-topped gilt side-tables beneath. They, like so much of the furniture in the house, were made by Chippendale. Opposite to the *windows* is a large stucco-decorated alcove, flanked by Corinthian pilasters, containing a doorway, with semi-dome above. The two white marble *fireplaces* are most typical of Adam treatment and motifs, especially the capitals and frieze (Plate 30). On the *walls* are large classical landscapes by Zucchi.
Tapestry Room. The *walls* covered by Brussels tapestries dating from 1750, except on the window side which has Adam pier glasses between the windows. The *ceiling* is the finest part of the room, having a star centre-piece and surrounding lunettes. The paintings are by Zucchi, the subject being Cupid and Psyche. All the decoration in the room is delicate, dainty and in low relief. The doorcase and fireplaces are in keeping.

SCOTLAND

AYRSHIRE

Culzean Castle (near Ayr)

Enlarged, altered and decorated by Adam for the Earl of Cassillis from 1776.

Present owner: The National Trust for Scotland. *House open to the public* (except for the top floor of the main part of the house which was put at the disposal of General Eisenhower for his lifetime by Scotland in recognition of his services in the Second World War).

Much of the castellar *exterior* is as designed by Adam, also the terrace garden, forecourt and entrance gateway (Fig. 8).

Interior:

Staircase. The *pièce de résistance* of Culzean. Built on cantilever principle in an oval stairwell with a typical Adam metal balustrade and mahogany handrail. The well has three storeys. There is an oval lantern at the top and stucco decorated walls. The second floor has an Ionic colonnade and the first a Corinthian. The ground-floor hall has Doric pilasters. The decoration, as everywhere in the house, is in beautiful condition, very much in the Adam style of colouring. The stairwell and colonnades are all in pale colours and white with touches of gilt (Plate *41*).

Dining-room. On the ground floor, this has a richly decorated *ceiling* in pale turquoise with cream stucco ornament. The design is panelled into three compartments. The centre one contains concentric circles and outer, smaller, circular, sculptured plaques. The end, rectangular panels are decorated by lunettes. The *windows* are along one side of the room and opposite is a screen of Corinthian columns with twin doorways behind and a sideboard between.

Library. Also on the ground floor, has a typical Adam ceiling with roundels painted by Zucchi.

On the *first floor* is the unusual and beautiful circular saloon, already described on page 176. Set round the oval stairwell at the same level are the two drawing-rooms, ante-rooms and the state bedroom.

The *Long Drawing-room* and the *Green Drawing-room*, in particular, retain some pieces of Adam/Chippendale furniture, good ceilings with Zucchi paintings and Adam *décor* in the form of doorcases, window frames, pelmets and the fireplaces.

Dumfries House (near Cumnock)

Built by Adam in 1754 for the Earl of Dumfries.
Present owner: the Marquess of Bute. House survives almost
unaltered. See description on pages 44–5.

BERWICKSHIRE

Mellerstain (near Gordon)

House completed and decorated by Adam for George Baillie, from
1768.
Present owner: the Earl of Haddington. *House open to the public.*
Exterior:
Unaltered since Adam completed the central part and garden front.
Interior:
Very little altered.

Interesting *bathroom*, on lower ground floor, with dolphin wall
decoration. Bath now filled in.

On the main floor, the *library* is the finest room. The *ceiling* has
three compartments, each with its painted roundel in the middle.
The central panel is surrounded by swags, paterae and decorated
tablets. The ornamentation is in white, on grounds of green, pink
and slate-lilac. The entablature has an anthemion frieze of white on
green. Below the frieze are the Wedgwood-type figure panels. The
figures are white on a deep slate-lilac ground (Plate *38*). *Bookcases*
line much of the room. These are typical Adam: wood, with applied
wood decoration to the lintels and Ionic pilasters. They are painted
white, as are also the *doorcases* and *window shutters*. The *doors* are of
polished wood. The simple, elegant *fireplace* is in white marble
inlaid with blue-grey. There is a burnished steel grate and fender.

Music-room (originally the dining-room). Has one of the most
accomplished Adam ceilings of his classic type. In fairly low relief,
the white stucco decoration is designed with a central octagonal
border, ornamented with arabesques and fan corners. Inside this is a
garlanded circle and, within, a delicate centre-piece of Wedgwood
type plaque. Outside the octagon are lunettes, swags, vases and
paterae. The present colour scheme has grounds of green and blue
with black in the centre-piece (Plate *37*). The finely proportioned
room has good-quality doors, doorcases and furniture.

Drawing-room. Another pleasant room with a more traditional but
fine Adam low relief ceiling and a simple, inlaid fireplace.

Entrance Hall. Most successful. It is plain, decorated throughout
in white and pale stone colour. There is a Doric entablature but no

columns. This entablature is echoed in the doorways. The room is rectangular with a semicircular tribune at each end, containing fireplaces. The *wall* treatment is monumental and simple. There are just wainscot and dado mouldings and niches below the entablature. The *ceiling* design is based on square and circular forms.

Staircase. Less satisfactory, partly due to the intransigence of the client. Upstairs there is a *gallery*. This is a large rectangular room with an Ionic screen at each end. The ceiling is a barrel vault but, again, due to disagreement with the client, was never decorated. Adam's intentions are shown in his design, on display in the room.

EAST LOTHIAN

Gosford House (near Longniddry)

Central block of house built to Adam's designs, largely after his death, for the Earl of Wemyss and March.
Present owner: the Earl of Wemyss and March. The house almost rebuilt in the late nineteenth century. The east façade and central block basically Adam but reclothed. His plans and models and east and west elevations are in the house.

EDINBURGH (Fig. 6)

Charlotte Square

North side built to Adam's designs and largely unaltered (Plate 34).

Queen Street and Castle Street

Doorways.

South Bridge

Construction work only.

St Andrew's Square

Possibly the house next to the Royal Bank of Scotland.

Mausoleum of David Hume

In the Old Calton burial ground in Regent Road. Circular, with Doric entablature. Based on the Mausoleum of Theodoric in Ravenna.

H.M. General Register House

Front façade to Princes Street altered little except for the entrance steps and containing wall. Inside, the dome is as Adam designed it.

The University

The entrance façade to South Bridge is unaltered. It was built to Adam's designs up to the tablet which commemorates him. Only a part of the first court was completed inside the entrance (Fig. 7, Plate 43).

GLASGOW

Of the several buildings designed by Adam here at the end of his life little survives.

The *Trades House*, completed 1794, at 85 Glassford Street, is best preserved. The façade, with its central pediment and Ionic portico, survives, also the Venetian windows, though the central doorway has been altered.

The best Adam building in Glasgow was the *Assembly Rooms*, built 1792–6. This has gone, but its main entrance was re-erected in Charlotte Street in 1893. Now called the McLennan Arch, it makes a well-proportioned, Ionic triumphal entrance to the modern school behind.

WEST LOTHIAN

Hopetoun House, South Queensferry

Built by Sir William Bruce and William Adam for the Earl of Hopetoun. Robert Adam decorated several of the apartments 1753–4.
Present owner: the Marquess of Linlithgow. *House open to the public.*

Yellow Drawing-room. Well proportioned, nearly square room, decorated in Adam's pre-Italy style. Deeply coved *ceiling* of white and gold in rococo design with strongly projecting classical cornice. Yellow *wall hangings* and furniture coverings. Pedimented *doorcases* with consoles and heavy anthemion frieze. Rococo mirrors between the windows and the furniture typical of the early 1750s.

Red Drawing-room. A larger, rectangular room with red silk damask wall hangings and furniture to match. A more deeply coved *ceiling* with rococo decoration all over. A central oval set in a rectangular frame. Ornate cornice and frieze. All in white and gilt, though gilt is sparingly applied. *Windows* on one long side of the room. Opposite is the white marble fireplace with corner caryatid supports (Plate 9). It is interesting to compare this early Adam version (carved by Michael Rysbrack) with his later examples at Hatchlands, Croome or Harewood. The quality of carving on the door and window cases, dado and wainscot is high. The design is more sophisticated than in the yellow drawing-room. It is all in white with gilt enrichments.

Newliston (*near Kirkliston*)

Adam designed a new house here in 1789 for Thomas Hog to replace an older one. Probably completed in 1792 after his death.
Present owner: Major R. T. A. Hog.
   Exterior:
Adam designed a simple, block house with giant Composite order in his individual capitals of only one row of acanthus leaves (Glossary.) A rusticated lower storey.
   David Bryce added wings and a balustraded forecourt in 1845.
   Interior:
Central, spacious *hall* with Doric screen on the principal floor. Nearby are drawing-room and two other apartments.
Ceiling and frieze decoration and fireplace remain; also one or two mirrors and window pelmets.

BIBLIOGRAPHY

THE material from which this book has been compiled has been taken primarily from original sources. These comprise letters and documents written by the Adam family, including Robert himself, friends, colleagues and contemporaries. They include also accounts and documents from Adam houses and other buildings, all of which have been visited personally. Apart from these buildings and Blair Adam itself, the letters and documents consulted are available in H.M. General Register House, Edinburgh. The chief of these include:

The Clerk of Penicuik files, which contain most of the Adam family letters, also accounts of houses built by William Adam and the Scottish firm later administered by John Adam. There are diaries of studies and architectural journeys taken by members of the Clerk and Adam families and documents and letters pertaining to Robert's work in Edinburgh in the 1780s.

The Abercairny documents including the letter by Robert to Lord Kames, studies by James Adam in Rome and designs made by Robert for Scottish houses and castles.

The Dalhousie documents relating to Adam work at Panmure House.

The Buccleuch (Dalkeith) papers with regard to Robert's and John's work at Dalkeith House.

The Seafield letters including descriptions and impressions in Rome of Robert Adam, Piranesi and Angelica Kauffmann, also data on Adam work at Castle Grant. Letters from the Earl of Findlater to his mother, referring to the Adam brothers in Italy, and correspondence with the Earl of Findlater by Robert and James on the Portland Place project.

The majority of original drawings by Robert (nearly nine thousand) of designs for his work are available at the Sir John Soane's Museum in Lincoln's Inn Fields in London.

Valuable background material has been provided by contemporary newspapers, especially Scottish ones, and letters, diaries and journals by personalities of the period, such as Sir Horace Walpole and James Boswell.

The following publications, which have been consulted, may prove useful and interesting to any reader who wishes to make a further study of the works and life of Robert Adam.

Books which include descriptions of Adam and his work

ADDISON, WILLIAM. *Audley End.* J. M. Dent, 1953.
BOLTON, A. T. *The Architecture of Robert and James Adam, 1758–1794.* Country Life, 1922.
    The Architecture and Decoration of Robert Adam and Sir John Soane. Royal Society of Arts, 1920.
    Robert Adam, F.R.S. F.S.A., Bibliographer, Publisher and Designer of Libraries. Blades, East and Blades, 1919.
FITZGERALD, P. *Robert Adam.* T. Fisher Unwin, 1904.
FLEMING, J. *Robert Adam and his Circle.* John Murray, 1962.
HUSSEY, C. *English Country Houses, Mid-Georgian, 1760–1800.* Country Life, 1956.
LEES-MILNE, J. *The Age of Adam.* B. T. Batsford, 1947.
PEVSNER, N. *An Outline of European Architecture*, Jubilee edition. Penguin Books, 1961.
SITWELL, S. *British Architects and Craftsmen.* B. T. Batsford, 1948.
SUMMERSON, SIR J. *Architecture in Britain, 1530–1830*, Pelican History of Art series. Penguin Books, 1953.
SWARBRICK, J. *Robert Adam and his Brothers.* B. T. Batsford, 1915.
YARWOOD, D. *The Architecture of England.* B. T. Batsford, 1963.
WILLIAMS, J. D. *Audley End: the Restoration from 1762 to 1797.* Essex Record Office, 1966.

Eighteenth-century research publications

ADAM, R. *Ruins of the Palace of the Emperor Diocletian at Spalatro in Dalmatia.* London, 1764.
ADAM, R. and J. *The Works in Architecture of Robert and James Adam Esquires*, 3 vols. London, 1773, 1779 and 1822. (Modern excerpt version published in 1959 by Alec Tiranti Ltd, London.)
ADAM, W. *Vitruvius Scoticus.* Edinburgh.
ANON. *Le Pitture Antiche d'Ercolano e contorni.* Naples, 9 vols., 1757.
BLONDEL, F. *Cours d'Architecture.* Paris, 1698.

CAMPBELL, C. *Vitruvius Britannicus*, 2 vols. 1727

CHAMBERS, W. *A Treatise on Civil Architecture*. London, 1759.

CLÉRISSEAU, C. *and* LEGRAND, J. G. *Antiquités de la France*. Paris, 1804.

DESGODETZ, A. *The Ancient Buildings of Rome*, 2 vols. London, 1771.

MAYOR, T. *Les Ruines de Paestum ou de Posidonie dans la Grande Grèce*. London, 1768.

PAOLI, P. A. *Rovine della Città di Pesto detta ancora Posidonia*, 1784. *Antichità di Pozzuoli*, n.d.

SOCIETY OF DILETTANTI, *Ionian Antiquities*. London, 1769.

STUART, J., *and* REVETT, N. *The Antiquities of Athens*, 4 vols. London, 1762.

WOOD, R. *The Ruins of Palmyra*. London, 1753. *The Ruins of Baalbec*. London, 1757.

Background Reading

BOEHN, M. VON. *Modes and Manners*, vol. 4, *the 18th Century*. Harrap, 1935.

BLACKIE, W. B. *Edinburgh at the time of the occupation of Prince Charles*. Constable, 1910.

BOSWELL, J. *Boswell's London Journal, 1762–3*. Heinemann, 1950.

BRACKETT, O. *Thomas Chippendale*. Hodder and Stoughton. *English Furniture Illustrated*. Ernest Benn, 1950.

CARLYLE, A. *The Autobiography of Dr Alexander Carlyle of Inveresk, 1722–1805*. New ed. T. N. Foulis. Edinburgh, 1910.

COWIE, L. W. *Hanoverian England, 1714–1837*. Bell, 1967.

EDWARDS, R., *and* JOURDAIN, M. *Georgian Cabinet Makers, c. 1700–1800*. Country Life, 1955.

HARRIS, E. *The Furniture of Robert Adam*. Alec Tiranti, London, 1963.

MUSGRAVE, C. *Adam and Hepplewhite and other neo-classical Furniture*. Faber and Faber, 1966.

SYMONDS, R. W. *Adam and Chippendale: a myth exploded*. Country Life Annual. 1958.

TREVELYAN, G. M. *History of England*. Longmans, Green, 1948. *Illustrated English Social History*, vol. 3, *the 18th Century*. Longmans, Green, 1952.

YOUNGSON, A. J. *The Making of Classical Edinburgh*. Edinburgh University Press, 1966.

INDEX